1,000 CURIOUS QUESTIONS

AND 1,000 AMAZING ANSWERS

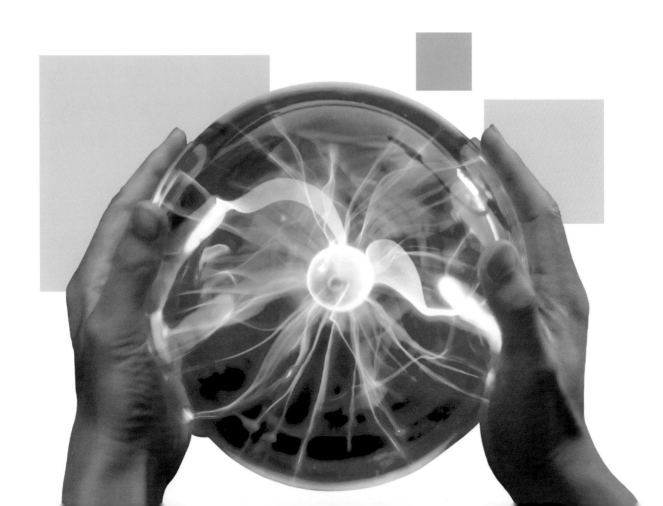

Senior editor Jenny Sich
Senior art editor Rachael Grady
Editors Carron Brown, Michelle Crane,
Binta Jallow, Georgina Palffy,
Vicky Richards, Anna Streiffert Limerick
Senior US editor Kayla Dugger
Executive US editor Lori Cates Hand
Designers Sheila Collins, Mik Gates, Jim Green,
Beth Johnston, Ragini Rawat, Diya Varma
Illustrators Guy Harvey,
Simon Mumford, Simon Tegg
Creative retouching Steve Crozier
Picture research Geetam Biswas
Senior jacket designer Suhita Dharamjit
Jacket designer Rhea Menon
DTP designer Rakesh Kumar
Senior jacket coordinator Priyanka Sharma Saddi
Jacket design development manager
Sophia MTT
Production editor Gillian Reid
Production controller Jack Matts
Managing editor Fran Baines
Managing art editor Philip Letsu

Written by Sophie Allan, Joe Barnes,
Derek Harvey, Simon Holland, Rona Skene,
Anna Streiffert Limerick

Consultants Sophie Allan,
Jonathan Dale, Jacob Field, Derek Harvey,
Penny Johnson, Kristina Routh

First American Edition, 2024
Published in the United States by DK Publishing,
a division of Penguin Random House LLC
1745 Broadway, 20th Floor, New York, NY 10019

Copyright © 2024 Dorling Kindersley Limited
24 25 26 27 10 9 8 7 6 5 4 3 2 1
001–340353–Oct/2024

A catalog record for this book
is available from the Library of Congress.
ISBN 978-0-5938-4380-2

Printed and bound in China

www.dk.com

MIX
Paper | Supporting
responsible forestry
FSC™ C018179

This book was made with Forest
Stewardship Council™ certified
paper—one small step in DK's
commitment to a sustainable future.
Learn more at **www.dk.com/uk/
information/sustainability**

1,000 CURIOUS QUESTIONS
AND 1,000 AMAZING ANSWERS

CONTENTS

SPACE

EARTH

LIFE

SCIENCE

HUMAN BODY

HISTORY

CULTURE

SPACE

BIG BANG: A theory that astronomers use to explain how our Universe began

WHERE DID THE UNIVERSE COME FROM?

About 14 billion years ago, the universe was a small, infinitely hot and dense point that suddenly began to grow outward, stretching at incredible speed. As its expansion slowed down and the universe cooled, energy was transformed into simple matter. Over hundreds of millions of years, the universe as we know it today was formed.

Today, as the universe continues to expand, galaxies are separated by a huge amount of empty space.

100 million years later, dust and gas come together to form the first stars.

3 minutes after, quarks combine to produce the first particles.

A few millionths of a second after the Big Bang, it is cool enough for simple matter, called quarks, to form.

In a single huge explosion, the universe, including space and time, sprang into existence.

The universe grows unimaginably quickly, cooling as it does—this is called inflation.

380,000 years later, the first full atoms form.

300 million years after the Big Bang, gravity pulls stars together into the first galaxies.

HOW LOUD WAS THE BIG BANG?

Scientists think that if the Big Bang made a noise, it was probably a very low-pitched humming sound. However, sound waves cannot travel in the vacuum of space—they need air particles to travel through. So whatever noise it made, no one would have been able to hear it anyway!

IT'S A MYSTERY!

What was there before the Big Bang?

It's impossible to look back in time to before our universe existed. Light, energy, and matter all came into being as a result of the Big Bang. We have no way of knowing what, if anything, existed beforehand.

HOW DO WE KNOW THE BIG BANG REALLY HAPPENED?

When telescopes like the Planck telescope (right) study the night sky, they pick up microwave radiation from all directions. This is the leftover radiation from the Big Bang, cooled to an icy -454°F (-270°C). It is like a fingerprint of the very early universe, showing that it began as a dense point and rapidly expanded.

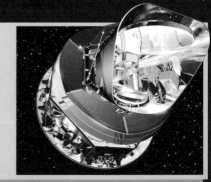

HOW DO WE KNOW THE UNIVERSE IS EXPANDING?

The light from distant galaxies is redder than it should be. Wavelengths of light get stretched if the object they are coming from is moving away. This makes the light look redder, an effect known as redshift. Distant galaxies are moving away from us in all directions, and the only way this is possible is if the universe is expanding.

Moving away

Light from galaxies moving away from us becomes redder (red shift).

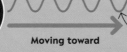

Moving toward

Light from galaxies moving toward us becomes bluer (blue shift).

WHAT IS OUR UNIVERSE MADE OF?

Everything we can see in the universe is made up of matter. But scientists have discovered that most of the universe is not made of normal matter. There is mysterious extra mass, known as dark matter, and an energy that is causing our universe to keep expanding, which is called dark energy.

Normal matter 4.6%

Scientists think most of our Universe is made of dark energy.

Dark matter 24%

Dark energy 71.4%

HOW WILL THE UNIVERSE END?

We used to think that the gravity of the matter in the universe would slow down the expansion and eventually cause it to collapse back in on itself in a big crunch. Evidence today suggests that the universe will keep on expanding forever, getting cooler and darker, and ending in a big freeze.

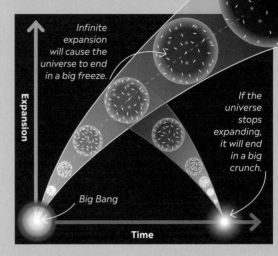

Infinite expansion will cause the universe to end in a big freeze.

If the universe stops expanding, it will end in a big crunch.

Expansion

Big Bang

Time

THE UNIVERSE:

Everything that exists—time, space, energy, and matter

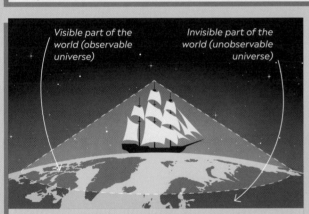

Visible part of the world (observable universe)

Invisible part of the world (unobservable universe)

COULD THERE BE OTHER UNIVERSES?

People have long been fascinated by the idea that there might be other universes out there. One popular theory suggests that the fast expansion our universe experienced could have happened in several places at once, creating bubble universes completely separate from our own. Everything, including the laws of physics, could be very different in these bubbles—but since they are separate, we can never know if they exist!

Each "bubble" represents a different universe, separate from our own.

IS THERE AN EDGE TO THE UNIVERSE?

It is hard to imagine, but scientists do not think that the universe has an edge. However, there is an edge to what we can see. Beyond a certain point, light given out by galaxies will never reach us. Just as sailors can't see beyond the horizon, we can't see beyond this point, known as the cosmic horizon.

IS THE UNIVERSE INFINITE?

To say the universe is infinite means that it goes on forever. We don't know whether this is the case, but we do know that it is enormous and expanding. We could never travel fast enough to catch up to the farthest galaxies, meaning that to us, in terms of exploring it, it goes on forever.

QUICK QUIZ!

HOW OLD IS THE UNIVERSE?

a: 20.5 billion years old

b: 13.8 billion years old

c: 4 billion years old

HOW MANY GALAXIES ARE THERE?

To work out the answer to this question, astronomers used the James Webb Space Telescope, which took this image of a tiny patch of sky. It saw 25,000 points of light, and each one is a galaxy. From this, they estimate that there are 2 trillion galaxies in the universe as a whole.

WHAT IS THE BIGGEST GALAXY?

The biggest galaxy that astronomers have found so far is called Alcyoneus, located 3.5 billion light-years away from Earth. It is a radio galaxy, which means it releases huge amounts of radio energy. At 16 million light-years wide, it is a massive 160 times bigger than our Milky Way Galaxy.

Milky Way Galaxy

Alcyoneus emits radio energy in the form of two huge jets.

IT'S A MYSTERY!

Why are galaxies different shapes?

Astronomers still don't know how galaxies form different shapes. To find out, they replicate the universe using supercomputers, but even the very best ones haven't found the answer yet!

HOW MANY STARS ARE IN OUR GALAXY?

The number of stars in a galaxy can range from around 100 million to over a hundred trillion. Our Milky Way is a fairly large galaxy in terms of number of stars and contains about 200 billion, including the Sun. Astronomers estimate that six or seven new stars form in our galaxy every year.

HOW FAR AWAY IS OUR NEAREST GALAXY?

Our Milky Way Galaxy has a group of small dwarf galaxies orbiting it, and the nearest is the Sagittarius Dwarf Spheroidal Galaxy at 70,000 light-years away from the Sun. However, our nearest full-sized galaxy is a spiral galaxy called Andromeda (pictured below). It is 2.5 million light-years away from us, meaning the fastest spacecraft ever made would take over a billion years to get there!

GALAXIES:

Huge systems of stars, planets, dust, and gas, all held together by gravity

ARE THERE DIFFERENT TYPES OF GALAXIES?

Astronomers group galaxies into three main types, according to their shape. Elliptical galaxies are round or oval-shaped with very little structure. Spiral galaxies, like the Milky Way, are the most common and are disk-shaped. Irregular galaxies have random, unusual, and asymmetrical shapes.

Elliptical galaxies
These are round or oval in shape and contain mainly older stars.

Spiral galaxies
Curved arms and a central bulge are the main features of spiral galaxies.

Irregular galaxies
These oddly shaped galaxies contain a mixture of older and younger stars.

MILKY WAY:

Our home galaxy is a medium-sized spiral galaxy made up of billions of stars

HOW LONG WOULD IT TAKE A ROCKET TO FLY AROUND THE MILKY WAY?

Our galaxy is so huge that it would take a rocket more than 10 billion years to travel around the edge of the Milky Way. Our galaxy is constantly rotating, and our Solar System takes 230 million years to make one full orbit, even at speeds of 450,000 mph (720,000 km/h).

HOW DO WE KNOW WHAT OUR GALAXY LOOKS LIKE WHEN WE ARE INSIDE IT?

There is a lot of dust in our galaxy, and even the most powerful telescopes can't see to the other side. Instead, researchers combine their understanding of gravity and how the stars in the Milky Way move with pictures of other galaxies. This gives them an accurate image of what the Milky Way looks like.

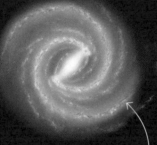

Our Solar System is in one of the Milky Way's spiral arms.

WHAT'S IN THE MIDDLE OF THE MILKY WAY?

Similar to many other large galaxies, a supermassive black hole (see pages 16–17) lies at the center of the Milky Way. Called Sagittarius A*, it is 26,000 light-years from Earth and has a mass 4 million times greater than the Sun. Everything else in our galaxy orbits around this point.

Central bulge contains mainly older stars.

Viewed from the side, the Milky Way looks like a flat disk.

WILL OUR GALAXY LAST FOREVER?

Milky Way

Sadly not! The Milky Way is on a collision course with the Andromeda Galaxy. When this happens, the two will merge to create an even bigger galaxy. However, this will not happen for another 4.5 billion years—about as long as our Solar System has existed!

Andromeda Galaxy

WHEN DID ASTRONOMER GALILEO FIRST SEE THE MILKY WAY?

a: 1435

b: 1550

c: 1610

QUICK QUIZ!

WHY IS OUR GALAXY CALLED THE MILKY WAY?

Before telescopes were invented, early astronomers looking up saw a long, hazy white band across the night sky and thought this was a road to the heavens. The ancient Romans called it *via lactea*, which means "milky road," and it became known as the Milky Way. We now know that this band of light is our view of the stars in our home galaxy from our position inside one of its spiral arms.

WHY DO STARS TWINKLE?

Most stars shine with a steady light. But as the light passes through the Earth's atmosphere, it becomes distorted. This makes it seem as though light from the stars is moving and twinkling.

QUICK QUIZ!

WHICH TYPE OF STAR IS MOST COMMON IN THE UNIVERSE?

a: Supergiant stars

b: Blue giants

c: Red dwarfs

STARS: Giant, luminous balls of extremely hot gas that generate energy in their cores and can shine for billions of years

A star forms in the middle of the disk.

WHERE DO STARS COME FROM?

Stars form in clouds of dust and gas called nebulas (see page 15). Gravity pulls these clouds into clumps, which then form spinning disks. At the center of the disk, a dense ball of gas gets hotter and hotter until it becomes a star. The leftover matter in the disk forms planets.

HOW LONG WOULD IT TAKE TO TRAVEL TO THE NEAREST STAR?

Our nearest star is the Sun. It would take one of our fastest rockets 175 days to reach it. The next nearest star is called Proxima Centauri (pictured). At four light-years away, it would take our fastest rocket more than 140,000 years to get to it!

IS A STAR A BALL OF FIRE?

No, stars are not made of fire. They are made of hydrogen and helium gas that is so hot it forms a state of matter called plasma (see page 110). Plasma is a gas that conducts electricity.

Gases react with electricity in this glass ball, forming streaks of plasma.

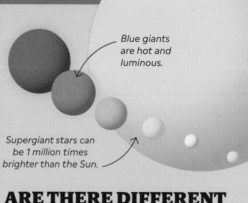

Blue giants are hot and luminous.

Red giants form when a star has run out of fuel.

Supergiant stars can be 1 million times brighter than the Sun.

Our Sun

Red dwarfs are small and dim.

ARE THERE DIFFERENT TYPES OF STARS?

Yes, stars come in different sizes and colors. Hotter stars are blue or white, and cooler stars appear red. Our Sun is an average-sized star—there are some that are smaller and others that are 700 times bigger. This illustration compares the sizes of a few different types of stars.

THE SUN:

A medium yellow star that dominates our Solar System, providing the heat and light needed for life on Earth

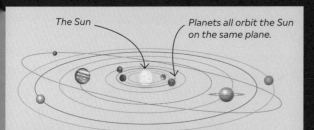

The Sun

Planets all orbit the Sun on the same plane.

WHY DO THE PLANETS ORBIT THE SUN?

The Solar System formed from a cloud of dust and gas around the young Sun. As the cloud collapsed, it began to rotate, spinning out a disk of material from which the planets formed. Today, the planets orbit the Sun in the same direction and on the same plane as the original disk.

WILL THE SUN SHINE FOREVER?

Stars like our Sun burn for around 10 billion years, and our Sun is about halfway through its life. In 5 billion years, the Sun will swell up, becoming a massive red giant. Afterward, it will shrink and end its life as a small, hot star called a white dwarf. Slowly, it will cool down and fade away.

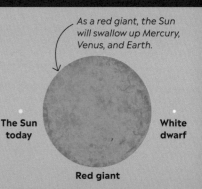

As a red giant, the Sun will swallow up Mercury, Venus, and Earth.

The Sun today

White dwarf

Red giant

WHAT MAKES THE SUN SHINE?

The incredible energy generated by nuclear reactions deep in the Sun's core is what makes it shine so brightly. Hydrogen atoms smash together, forming helium and releasing enormous amounts of energy in the form of light and heat. This process is called nuclear fusion.

A huge explosion on the Sun's surface is called a solar flare.

HOW HOT IS THE SUN?

At its core, the Sun is an incredible 27 million°F (15 million°C). Temperatures are cooler in the regions above—called the convection zone and the radiative zone. However, the surface we see is the coolest part, at about 10,000°F (5,500°C).

Convection zone

Inner core

Radiative zone

Dark sunspots are cooler than the brighter areas on the Sun's surface.

WHY CAN'T WE SEE THE SUN ALL THE TIME?

This is because Earth is spinning around an imaginary line called its axis, making one full rotation every 24 hours. We can only see the Sun when our side of the Earth is facing it, in the daytime. As Earth rotates, our side turns away from the Sun and it is nighttime.

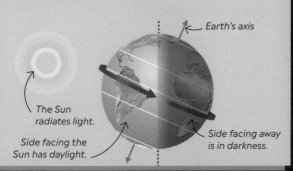

Earth's axis

The Sun radiates light.

Side facing the Sun has daylight.

Side facing away is in darkness.

CAN YOU SEE SUPERNOVAS FROM EARTH?

Yes. To the naked eye, a supernova appears as a bright, new star in the sky. Afterward, the cloud that is left over is called a supernova remnant. The Crab Nebula (right) is the remnant of a supernova seen from Earth in 1054 CE.

QUICK QUIZ!

HOW BIG IS THE CRAB NEBULA?

a: 3 light-years wide

b: 11 light-years wide

c: 58 light-years wide

This image, combining radio waves, X-ray, infrared, and visible light views, reveals the neutron star at the heart of the nebula.

ARE THEY DANGEROUS?

It depends on how far away they are. If a supernova happened within 50 light-years of Earth, the harmful radiation released could destroy our atmosphere and wipe out all life on Earth. Fortunately, the closest star to us that is big enough to go supernova is Spica, at a safe distance of 260 light-years away.

SUPERNOVAS:
Bright and destructive explosions that happen at the end of some stars' lives

DO ALL STARS GO SUPERNOVA?

Stars have different life cycles depending on their size. Only massive stars end their lives in a supernova. Smaller stars gradually fade out instead. After going supernova, the very biggest stars may then become a black hole.

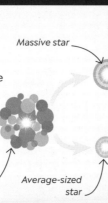
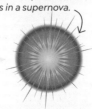

Star forms in a nebula.

Massive star

When fuel runs out, the star forms a supergiant.

Star collapses and explodes in a supernova.

A dense, fast-spinning neutron star remains.

Average-sized star

When fuel runs out, the star forms a red giant.

Star becomes a white dwarf.

Star forms a black dwarf, emitting no light or heat.

Core collapses into a black hole.

HOW DO WE KNOW A STAR WILL GO SUPERNOVA?

Astronomers can predict which stars will go supernova at the end of their lives by calculating their mass. It is thought that Betelgeuse (circled right), a supergiant star in the Orion constellation, will explode as a supernova at any time within the next 100,000 years.

WHY DO STARS GO SUPERNOVA?

A star is in a constant balance between gravity pulling it inward and nuclear fusion in its core creating outward pressure. When a huge star runs out of fuel, gravity takes over and the star collapses in seconds, causing a supernova.

HOW DO STARS FORM?

Stars begin to form when a nebula is disturbed by a trigger event, such as a supernova shockwave, and it collapses. A young star called a protostar forms, and when its core is hot enough, a new star is born.

Nebula
A disturbance causes the nebula to collapse and form clumps.

Protostar
Gravity pulls material in and the core heats up, forming a protostar.

Spinning disk
As the protostar grows, a spinning disk of material forms around it.

New star
The protostar is hot enough for nuclear fusion and becomes a star.

WHAT IS A PLANETARY NEBULA?

A planetary nebula is a collection of hot, bright gas that is left over when a smaller star reaches the end of its life. The star first swells up to become a red giant, then blows off its outer atmosphere, leaving a white dwarf star at its center. The Cat's Eye Nebula (right) ejected its mass in pulses, creating huge shells of dust.

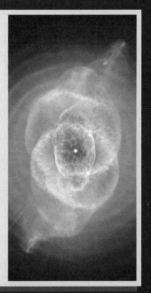

HOW DO WE KNOW WHAT'S INSIDE?

Scientists use space telescopes to observe nebulas in different types of light. This split image shows the Helix Nebula in visible light (on the left), which shows the clouds of dust. On the right is the view in infrared light, which reveals bright stars and strands of cold gas.

WHAT WOULD A NEBULA FEEL LIKE FROM THE INSIDE?

You wouldn't be able to feel anything! Nebulas are visible from very far away, but the gases inside them are far less packed than our own air. It is not much denser than empty space.

WHAT IS A NEBULA?

Nebulas are huge, spectacular clouds of dust and gas in space. Some of the biggest nebulas, such as the Carina Nebula, act as star nurseries—places where new stars are born. At 7,500 light-years away, the Carina Nebula has produced at least 14,000 stars, with more still forming.

This image shows part of the Carina Nebula, called Mystic Mountain.

Blue areas are oxygen and green areas show hydrogen gas—the fuel of stars.

Young stars buried deep inside the nebula release tall jets of gas.

The red areas are sulfur gas and would smell of rotten eggs.

IT'S A MYSTERY!

What are the other objects floating in a nebula?
Within some nebulas, strange Jupiter-sized objects roaming in pairs have been found. Called JuMBOs, scientists have not yet figured out what they are and how they formed.

NEBULAS: Massive clouds made up of dust and gases, most of which are hydrogen and helium

BLACK HOLES:

Areas of space where matter has collapsed in on itself, forming a point so dense that not even light can escape its gravitational pull

HOW DO WE KNOW BLACK HOLES EXIST IF WE CAN'T SEE THEM?

Black holes are not visible, but they are surrounded by an accretion disk—a ring of gas and dust that gives off a huge amount of light. They also bend light around themselves due to their extreme gravity, so this is another sign scientists look for. The biggest black holes can also affect the way stars orbit around them.

HOW MANY ARE THERE?

The more scientists have learned about black holes, the better their estimates have become. They now think that there are at least 40 quintillion black holes in the universe—that's 40 followed by 18 zeros! There may be 100 million black holes in our galaxy alone.

ARE THERE DIFFERENT TYPES OF BLACK HOLES?

Yes, there are two main types. Stellar-mass black holes are formed by dying stars. The other type are supermassive black holes. They are found at the center of galaxies and can be billions of times more massive than our Sun.

WHAT WOULD HAPPEN IF I FELL INTO A BLACK HOLE?

Your body would be "spaghettified." As you are sucked toward the black hole, its strong gravitational pull on your feet would be stronger than the pull on your head. This would stretch you vertically and compress you horizontally, like a noodle!

CAN ANYTHING ESCAPE THE PULL OF A BLACK HOLE?

Anything that passes the event horizon, the boundary that marks the outer edge of a black hole, cannot escape being sucked in. Because black holes have such a powerful gravitational pull, even matter in the accretion disk will slowly work its way toward this outer edge and then get pulled in. However, if an object is far away enough, it will not fall into the black hole!

A halo of light appears around the black hole because its gravity bends the light from the accretion disk.

The event horizon marks the point of no return, where not even light can escape.

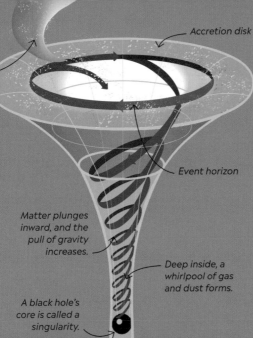

Gradually, matter is sucked into the swirling accretion disk.

Accretion disk

Event horizon

Matter plunges inward, and the pull of gravity increases.

Deep inside, a whirlpool of gas and dust forms.

A black hole's core is called a singularity.

WHERE DOES THE MATTER IN A BLACK HOLE GO?

If material is pulled into a black hole, it gets squashed into an incredibly small point. Scientists are not quite sure what happens next. It is thought that the singularity in the center could form a wormhole—a portal to another point in space—or the material inside could collapse in on itself, causing the black hole to explode!

DO BLACK HOLES EAT STARS?

Some do, but not all in one bite! A star that gets too close to a black hole will first go into orbit around it. Then, as the star gets closer, the black hole begins to suck material from it, pulling the star apart. This phenomenon is called a "tidal disruption event."

HOW CLOSE IS EARTH'S NEAREST BLACK HOLE?

The closest is a stellar-mass black hole called Gaia BH1, 10 times bigger than the Sun. It is an average-sized stellar-mass black hole, as they only reach up to 20 times more massive than the Sun. At 1,560 light-years away, it would take our fastest spacecraft over 2.5 million years to reach Gaia BH1.

Within the event horizon, at the heart of the black hole is a singularity, where matter has been squished to an infinitely dense point.

A cloud of dust and gas called the accretion disk swirls around the black hole.

Matter at the outer part of the disk moves inward, where it falls into the event horizon.

IT'S A MYSTERY!

How do supermassive black holes form?

Many galaxies, including the Milky Way, contain one of these huge black holes at their center, millions of times more massive than a stellar-mass black hole. No one knows how they form.

PLANETS:
Large, spherical objects that orbit a star, and whose gravity is enough to have cleared other objects out of their path

Jupiter's outer layer is made of whirling clouds of gas.

Deep inside, gases become superheated and start behaving like a liquid metal.

Jupiter

Metallic inner core is mostly made of iron.

Mercury

Thin, hard surface layer is called the crust.

The mantle, a thick layer of hot, solid rock, lies between the crust and the core.

WHAT ARE PLANETS MADE OF?

Our Solar System has two types of planets. Rocky planets like Mercury are made of rock and metal. Gas planets, such as Jupiter, are made mostly of hydrogen and helium, with a small rocky core at the center. The two planets are not shown to scale here—Jupiter is almost 30 times bigger than Mercury!

WHY IS PLUTO NOT A PLANET?

Pluto is round and orbits the Sun, but it shares its orbit with other objects. At only two-thirds the diameter of Earth's moon, Pluto isn't big enough to clear these other objects from its path. Instead, astronomers label Pluto as a smaller "dwarf planet."

Earth's moon   **Pluto**

WHY ARE PLANETS ROUND?

Planets form when material orbiting a star clumps together under gravity. If enough material is pulled together, it heats up, becoming a ball of rock and metal that contains so much mass that gravity pulls it into a sphere.

HOW MANY PLANETS ARE THERE?

It is likely that most stars have planets orbiting around them, so in the universe as a whole, there are probably billions of planets. Scientists use space telescopes like Kepler (left) to hunt for planets outside our Solar System. So far, they have found more than 5,500, although they can only see the biggest ones.

WHICH PLANET IS THE FARTHEST FROM THE SUN?

Our Solar System has eight planets. The four closest to the Sun are smaller rocky planets and the outer four are larger gas planets. Neptune is the farthest away at a distance of about 2.8 billion miles (4.5 billion km). This image shows the planets in order, but not their distances from each other. Neptune is 30 times farther away from the Sun than Earth is!

Mercury   Venus   Earth   Mars   Jupiter   Saturn   Uranus   Neptune

WHY IS MARS RED?

This is because rocks and soil found on Mars have a large amount of iron in them. When iron comes into contact with oxygen, it oxidizes and rusts, turning a reddish-brown color. At some point in Mars' past, the iron in the Martian rocks gradually rusted, making its surface and atmosphere appear red.

IS THERE WATER ON MARS?

Scientists think there are underground lakes of water beneath Mars' south pole, but there is no liquid water on the surface. There is lots of ice at Mars' poles though, and some is even found in craters. Korolev crater (right) is 50 miles (82 km) wide and filled with ice.

FAST FACTS

- **Temperatures** on Mars can reach **-225°F (-142°C)**.

- A year on Mars is **twice as long** as a year on Earth.

- You could **jump about three times higher** on Mars than you can on Earth due to the planet's weaker gravity.

COULD HUMANS LIVE ON MARS ONE DAY?

Not very easily! Mars is cold, has no liquid water, and has a very thin carbon dioxide atmosphere, making it an inhospitable planet. If humans were to live on Mars, we would need to wear spacesuits all the time and build bases with everything needed for survival.

HOW LONG DOES IT TAKE TO GET TO MARS?

Journeying at speeds of 24,600 mph (39,600 km/h), it takes spacecraft about seven months to travel 300 million miles (480 million km) and reach Mars. NASA's Mars 2020 mission delivered a rover called Perseverance to the surface of Mars (see page 30) to collect soil and rock samples.

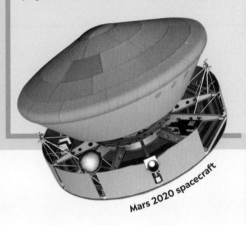

Mars 2020 spacecraft

MARS: The rocky red planet that is one of Earth's closest neighbors in space

WHAT IS IT LIKE ON THE SURFACE?

Mars' surface is very dry and rocky and covered with craters. The sandy soil is sometimes picked up in huge dust storms. It can be a tricky place for rovers to navigate, and their paths are carefully planned.

A camera acts as the eyes of the rover.

NASA's Curiosity Mars rover

Robotic arm can hold tools and take samples.

Wheels have cleats to help with grip when climbing over rocks.

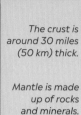

The crust is around 30 miles (50 km) thick.

Mantle is made up of rocks and minerals.

Solid iron core

WHAT IS THE MOON MADE OF?

Much like Earth, the Moon is made up of rock and metal. It has a metallic core at its center, surrounded by a rocky material very similar to rocks found on Earth. The Moon's crust is covered in high mountains and deep valleys, as well as impact craters from asteroids, meteoroids, and comets striking its surface.

WILL PEOPLE LIVE ON THE MOON ONE DAY?

Potentially. Plans to send astronauts back to the Moon within the next few years are well underway. NASA is also planning to construct a fixed base camp on the Moon for astronauts to live and work in. It will likely be built near the lunar south pole, where there may be access to ice, and will house up to four crew members for a month-long visit.

FAST FACTS

● Only **12 people** have ever **walked** on the **Moon.**

● The Moon **moves** 1.5 in (3.8 cm) **away from Earth** each year.

● **Earthquakes** on the Moon can last for up to **half an hour.**

WHAT IS IT LIKE TO WALK ON THE MOON?

The Moon's gravity is one-sixth that of Earth, so if you were to walk on the Moon, you would be able to jump a lot higher! The Apollo astronauts who went to the Moon in the 1960s and '70s wore bulky spacesuits. This meant they had to skip-shuffle across the regolith—the rocky dust that covers the Moon's surface. Due to the lack of an atmosphere, the sky would be pitch-black during the day and night.

This image shows Buzz Aldrin on the Apollo 11 mission to the Moon in 1969.

Neil Armstrong is visible in the visor, taking the picture.

THE MOON:
Earth's only natural satellite, and the brightest object in our night sky

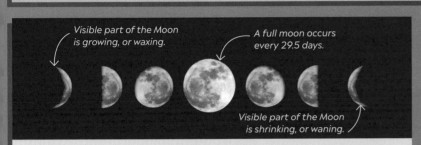

Visible part of the Moon is growing, or waxing.

A full moon occurs every 29.5 days.

Visible part of the Moon is shrinking, or waning.

WHY DOES THE MOON CHANGE SHAPE?

As the Moon orbits Earth, different areas of it are lit up by the Sun. These shapes are called phases. A new moon (when the Moon is not visible at all) occurs when the Moon is between Earth and the Sun, with the shadowed side facing us. Gradually, the Moon moves until the side facing us is fully illuminated by the Sun, creating a full moon.

ARE ALL MOONS LIKE OUR MOON?

Potato-shaped Hyperion has a spongy texture.

Moons come in different shapes and sizes. Most are roughly spherical like Earth's moon, but others have very irregular shapes, such as Hyperion (a moon of Saturn). Their surfaces can be very different, too. Io (a moon of Jupiter) is volcanic, spewing out melted rock. Other moons have surfaces covered in ice.

WHAT ARE THE DARK PATCHES?

The bright areas of the Moon's crust are known as the highlands. The dark areas are called maria (Latin for "seas"). These are impact craters that were filled with lava when the Moon was volcanically active. It then solidified into dark basalt rock between 3 and 3.8 billion years ago.

Tycho Crater is one of the most noticeable craters on the Moon.

A large object collides with our planet.

Debris from the collision will form the Moon.

Young Earth

HOW MANY OTHER MOONS ARE THERE?

There are more than 290 moons in our Solar System, but this number constantly changes as astronomers find new ones. The biggest is Ganymede, a moon of Jupiter, which is slightly smaller than planet Mars. The image below shows the eight biggest moons to scale.

Ganymede (Jupiter)

Titan (Saturn)

Callisto (Jupiter)

Io (Jupiter)

Moon (Earth)

Europa (Jupiter)

Triton (Neptune)

Titania (Uranus)

WHERE DID THE MOON COME FROM?

About 4.5 billion years ago, when Earth was a young, melted ball of rock and metal, it collided with a Mars-sized space object. The impact created a cloud of debris, which clumped together in an orbit around Earth, forming the Moon.

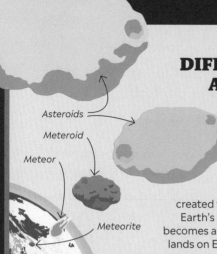

WHAT'S THE DIFFERENCE BETWEEN AN ASTEROID AND A METEOROID?

An asteroid is rocky object that is much smaller than a planet, orbiting the Sun. Most have irregular shapes and are covered in craters. A meteoroid is a small fragment of an asteroid and is often created from a collision. If a meteoroid enters Earth's atmosphere and begins to burn up, it becomes a meteor. If it survives this journey and lands on Earth's surface, it is called a meteorite.

Asteroids
Meteroid
Meteor
Meteorite

IS IT SAFE TO FLY THROUGH THE ASTEROID BELT?

The Asteroid Belt is a region between Mars and Jupiter where most asteroids are found. Pictures often show the asteroids very close together, but in reality, they are quite spaced out, making it safe to fly through. No spacecraft has ever been damaged while flying through it!

ASTEROIDS: Small chunks of rock left over from the formation of the Solar System, orbiting the Sun

IS IT POSSIBLE TO LAND ON AN ASTEROID?

Yes! In 2001, NASA's NEAR spacecraft became the first to land on an asteroid. Since then, several missions have visited asteroids. OSIRIS-REx (pictured) collected material from asteroid Bennu and brought it back to Earth to be studied.

HOW OFTEN DO ASTEROIDS STRIKE EARTH?

Impacts from big asteroids only happen roughly every 500,000 years. However, Earth is hit by smaller meteorites every day! Most fall to Earth's surface as tiny dust-sized particles.

WHAT'S THE BIGGEST ASTEROID?

The biggest known asteroid is called Ceres. At about a quarter of the size of our Moon, it is the largest space object in the Asteroid Belt. It is spherical in shape and also considered a dwarf planet. The image below shows the five biggest known asteroids in our Solar System compared to the size of Earth.

Ceres is 584 miles (940 km) wide.

Vesta is 326 miles (525 km) wide.

Pallas is 316 miles (510 km) wide.

Hygiea is 254 miles (410 km) wide.

Interamnia is 196 miles (317 km) wide.

WHY DO COMETS HAVE TAILS?

Comets only grow tails when they approach the Sun. The icy nucleus heats up, forming a cloud of dust and gas that bursts out of the comet. This is called a coma. Energy from the Sun pushes this cloud into a long, glowing tail that points away from the Sun.

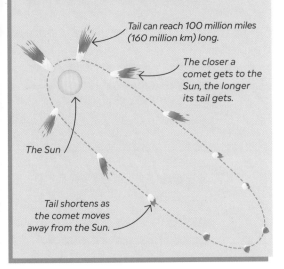

Tail can reach 100 million miles (160 million km) long.

The closer a comet gets to the Sun, the longer its tail gets.

The Sun

Tail shortens as the comet moves away from the Sun.

WHAT ARE COMETS MADE FROM?

Comets are made of a mixture of dust and ice, which is why they are nicknamed "dirty snowballs." The center of the comet is called the nucleus, which is typically between 0.6 to 6 miles (1 and 10 km) wide. As the comet approaches the Sun, jets of gas and dust start to erupt from the surface.

A thin soot-black coat of dust covers most of the nucleus.

Frozen core consists of lumps of ice, dust, and rock.

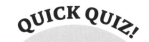
COMETS: Often called "dirty snowballs," these cold objects orbit the Sun from beyond the outer edge of the Solar System

WHERE DO COMETS COME FROM?

Comets are found in two regions of space. Those that take decades to orbit the Sun come from the Kuiper Belt, just beyond Neptune's orbit. Comets with longer orbits come from the Oort Cloud, a spherical cloud made up of icy objects that surrounds our Solar System. This illustration shows the Kuiper Belt within the Oort Cloud.

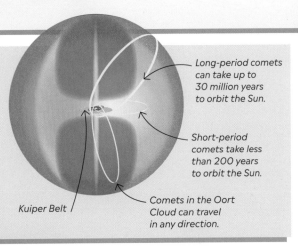

Long-period comets can take up to 30 million years to orbit the Sun.

Short-period comets take less than 200 years to orbit the Sun.

Comets in the Oort Cloud can travel in any direction.

Kuiper Belt

WHAT ARE METEOR SHOWERS?

Meteor showers occur when Earth passes through the dust tail left behind by a comet. When this happens, dust particles burn up in Earth's atmosphere and produce an impressive show of shooting stars. The fastest and largest meteors tend to glow the longest. While small meteors are visible for about a second, larger meteors can glow for up to several minutes.

WHAT WAS THE BRIGHTEST COMET EVER?

Many consider comet McNaught (pictured) to be one of the brightest comets seen in recent times. Its long, dazzling tail was visible in broad daylight in 2007. The Great September Comet of 1882 is thought to be the brightest comet ever recorded, but the historical photos are not clear enough to be certain.

TELESCOPES:

Tools used by astronomers to make distant objects appear bigger

HOW DO SIMPLE TELESCOPES WORK?

Optical telescopes use a lens or mirror to collect light from distant objects and bring it to a focus, magnifying the image. There are two main types of telescopes—refractors for seeing objects farther away and reflectors for viewing nearby objects.

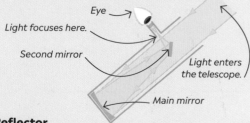

Eye

Light focuses here.

Second mirror

Light enters the telescope.

Main mirror

Reflector

A curved mirror gathers light and reflects it onto a smaller second mirror, which directs the light to a focus. The image is then seen using an eyepiece.

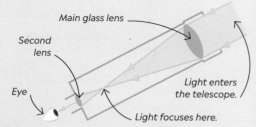

Main glass lens

Second lens

Eye

Light enters the telescope.

Light focuses here.

Refractor

A glass lens gathers light and focuses it into an image. A smaller second lens magnifies the image, which is then seen using an eyepiece.

WHY ARE OBSERVATORIES SO HIGH UP?

Light from the stars has to travel through the atmosphere to reach us. This light gets bounced around by the air, making our images appear fuzzy. Many large telescopes are housed inside observatories that are located in high places because the higher up you go, the less air there is for the light to travel through, giving clearer images.

DO I NEED A TELESCOPE TO LOOK AT THE STARS?

On a clear night, you can make out groups of stars in the sky with your eyes. However, to see distant star clusters or spot craters on the Moon, you will need to magnify what you are looking at. You can use a pair of binoculars, which are made up of two telescopes, one for each eye.

IT'S A MYSTERY!

Who invented the telescope?

Historians are not absolutely certain who invented the telescope. Dutch eyeglass maker Hans Lipperhey applied for the first patent in 1608, but telescopes may have existed before this.

WHAT IS THE BIGGEST TELESCOPE ON EARTH?

The largest type of telescope is a radio telescope, used to detect and study radio waves from space. The world's biggest one is the FAST telescope in China's Guizhou Province. Located in a natural basin, it took five years to construct, and its dish is a massive 1,600 ft (500 m) wide.

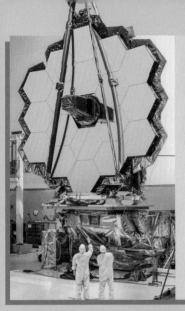

WHAT IS THE BIGGEST TELESCOPE EVER SENT TO SPACE?

The biggest is an infrared telescope called the James Webb Space Telescope. To see infrared light, it has a large mirror that is covered in a very thin layer of gold. It is as tall as a three-story building and as wide as a tennis court!

WHAT HAVE WE SEEN WITH A SPACE TELESCOPE?

Astronomers have used space telescopes to discover many things in our universe, from planets that orbit other stars, to huge clouds of dust and gas like the Butterfly Nebula (right). This image was taken by the Hubble Space Telescope, which has made over 1.6 million observations since 1990.

WHY DO WE NEED TO PUT TELESCOPES IN SPACE?

The air of our planet distorts the light from objects in space. Telescopes such as TESS (right) are useful because they go above the atmosphere, giving astronomers the clearest possible view of distant stars. A space telescope also allows them to see types of light that can't get through our atmosphere, such as infrared.

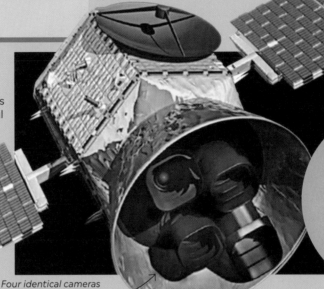

Two solar array wings power the TESS telescope.

Four identical cameras collect light from distant stars.

QUICK QUIZ!

HOW MUCH DID THE JAMES WEBB SPACE TELESCOPE COST TO BUILD?

a: $10 billion

b: $22 billion

c: $37 billion

SPACE TELESCOPES:
Telescopes that orbit Earth or travel farther into space to observe the universe

WHAT HAPPENS TO OLD SPACE TELESCOPES?

Most space telescopes that reach the end of their lives are programmed to slow down so they fall out of orbit and burn up in Earth's atmosphere. Others are sent even farther away into what scientists call a "graveyard orbit" so they won't get in the way of other missions.

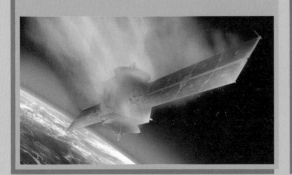

Space Shuttle's robotic arm grabs onto the Hubble Telescope while astronauts repair it.

CAN WE FIX A SPACE TELESCOPE IF IT BREAKS?

Yes, but only if the space telescope is in Earth's orbit. During a servicing mission in 1999, the Hubble Space Telescope (right) was repaired by two astronauts and the Space Shuttle's long robotic arm. If a space telescope is farther out in space, such as the James Webb Space Telescope orbiting the Sun, it is too far away to be reached and cannot be repaired.

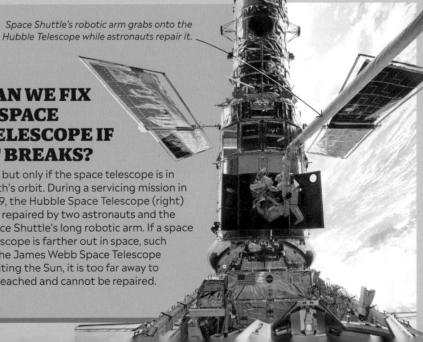

SPACE STATION:

Humankind's base in space, this giant orbiting laboratory is the largest space structure ever built

WHERE IS THE SPACE STATION?

The International Space Station (ISS) is in orbit 254 miles (410 km) above Earth. It completes a full lap of Earth once every 90 minutes. Earth is rotating at the same time, so the ISS passes over a different part of the globe with each orbit. The picture below shows the path of the ISS over the course of four days.

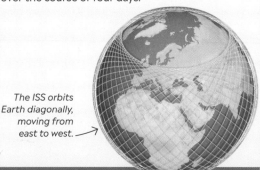

The ISS orbits Earth diagonally, moving from east to west.

HOW FAST DOES IT TRAVEL?

Very fast! The ISS travels at a speed of 4.7 miles per second (7.6 km per second). In a single day, it covers 435,000 miles (700,000 km)—that's the same distance as going to the Moon and back. It can travel so fast because there is hardly any drag (the resistance force formed when an object pushes through air) from the atmosphere at that height.

CAN YOU SEE THE ISS FROM EARTH?

At dawn or dusk, it can appear as a bright white pinpoint moving across the sky, similar to an airplane. It is usually visible for a few minutes but can't always be seen—the angle between you, the Sun, and the station has to be just right.

HOW BIG IS THE ISS?

This ISS consists of eight solar arrays and 16 living and working areas, called modules, which are attached to a central frame called the truss. Including the solar arrays, the ISS is 354 ft (108 m) long, which is roughly the same size as a soccer field. The living and working space in the station is larger than a six-bedroom house!

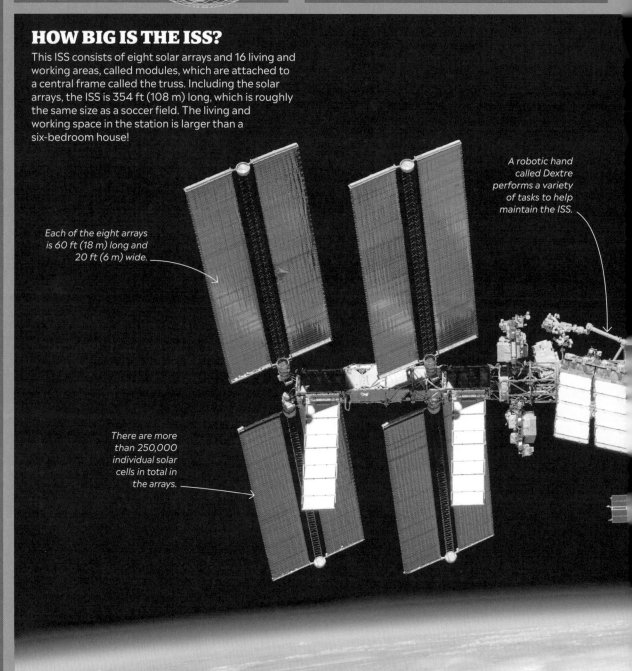

Each of the eight arrays is 60 ft (18 m) long and 20 ft (6 m) wide.

A robotic hand called Dextre performs a variety of tasks to help maintain the ISS.

There are more than 250,000 individual solar cells in total in the arrays.

WHAT'S INSIDE?

The ISS is a huge science laboratory with 16 pressurized modules where astronauts live and work. It has everything needed for survival, including six sleeping quarters, two bathrooms, a gym, and even a system to produce oxygen from water. The Zvezda module (right) was launched by Russia in 2000.

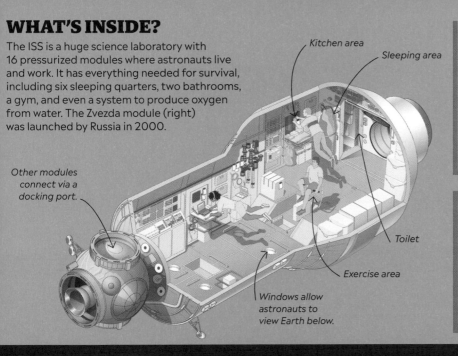

Kitchen area

Sleeping area

Other modules connect via a docking port.

Toilet

Exercise area

Windows allow astronauts to view Earth below.

WHAT DO ASTRONAUTS DO ON THE ISS?

The main purpose of the ISS is as a science laboratory, so astronauts spend a lot of time doing science experiments, such as growing plants and food in space. In their free time, they read books, listen to music, and enjoy amazing views of Earth.

IS THE ISS THE ONLY SPACE STATION?

There is currently one other space station: China's Tiangong station. There are also plans to build a new station orbiting the Moon. Space agencies from the US, Europe, Japan, United Arab Emirates, and Canada will work in collaboration to create it.

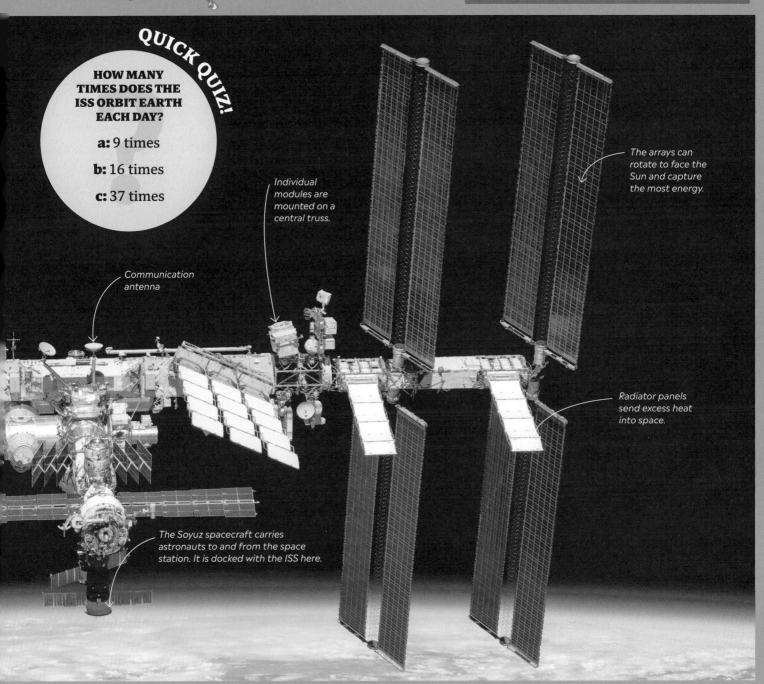

QUICK QUIZ!

HOW MANY TIMES DOES THE ISS ORBIT EARTH EACH DAY?

a: 9 times

b: 16 times

c: 37 times

Individual modules are mounted on a central truss.

The arrays can rotate to face the Sun and capture the most energy.

Communication antenna

Radiator panels send excess heat into space.

The Soyuz spacecraft carries astronauts to and from the space station. It is docked with the ISS here.

WHAT DOES WEIGHTLESSNESS FEEL LIKE?

Astronauts experience weightlessness while they are in orbit, and it feels like they are floating freely. They can twist and turn their body around but not move easily from place to place unless there is something solid to push against. At times, astronauts can feel nauseous as their sense of up and down gets confused!

This astronaut is pictured outside the ISS during a spacewalk.

QUICK QUIZ!

WHO WAS THE FIRST HUMAN IN SPACE?

a: Yuri Gagarin

b: Neil Armstrong

c: Buzz Aldrin

ASTRONAUTS:

People who are trained to travel into space to live and work

HOW MANY PEOPLE HAVE BEEN INTO SPACE?

Since humans first lifted off in the 1960s, fewer than 700 people have gone into space. Most of these space travelers have come from the US or Russia. The number continues to increase, especially as people go into space for tourism.

Backpack contains oxygen and removes carbon dioxide.

Gloves are flexible and provide protection.

Helmet ventilation system provides oxygen.

Visor protects astronaut's eyes from the bright sunlight.

Thruster jets help astronauts fly back to safety in an emergency.

Undergarment keeps astronauts cool during spacewalks.

A spacesuit can have up to 16 layers.

HOW DO ASTRONAUTS TRAIN?

Astronauts train in everything, from how to put on their pressurized spacesuits to how to dock new modules to the ISS. They sit in giant spinning arms to prepare for launch acceleration, and practice their spacewalks in swimming pools (pictured above) to replicate the feeling of weightlessness.

CAN TOURISTS TRAVEL TO SPACE?

Yes. It is expensive, but more companies are creating space travel options for the public. In 2008, British-American game developer Richard Garriott paid $30 million to spend 12 days as a tourist on the ISS. He is pictured here on the ISS.

HOW LONG COULD YOU SURVIVE IN SPACE WITHOUT A SUIT?

A spacesuit provides oxygen and maintains air pressure to keep bodily fluids in a liquid state. Without one, you would suffocate and the water in your body would boil. You could not survive more than 90 seconds!

WHAT ARE UFOS?

Unidentified flying objects are anything seen in the sky that scientists cannot immediately identify. Often, sightings that are interpreted as spacecraft can be due to weather effects, like unusual lightning high in the atmosphere (right).

DO ALIENS EXIST?

Scientists are not sure yet. They search the skies for signals, but space is huge, and it takes a long time for communications signals to reach us. No evidence has been found yet, but some scientists are convinced that the sheer size of the universe means there is a chance that other life is out there!

ALIENS: Life forms from somewhere in the universe other than planet Earth

HAVE WE EVER SENT A MESSAGE INTO OUTER SPACE?

Yes! In 1977, two Voyager spacecraft each carried a disk with a variety of information about life on Earth. Called the "Golden Record," they included photos, greetings in 55 languages, and 90 minutes of music.

Instructions help decode the data on the disks.

Small iron core is surrounded by a large layer of rock.

Europa's frozen surface is 10 to 15 miles (15 to 25 km) thick.

A salty ocean with twice as much water as all of Earth's oceans lies beneath an icy shell.

Europa

WHERE IN THE SOLAR SYSTEM MIGHT LIFE EXIST?

When scientists search for life on other planets, they begin by looking for liquid water—a key ingredient for life as we know it. This means the most likely places are ice moons such as Europa, which orbits Jupiter. Under its icy surface there is thought to be a liquid water ocean.

IT'S A MYSTERY!

Where did the Wow! signal come from?

In 1977, an unusual radio signal, known as the Wow! signal, was received from space. Some think it was caused by a comet, while others believe it is a sign of alien life. Its origin has never been explained.

Each VLA dish is 82 ft (25 m) wide and can be moved individually.

IS THERE ANYONE OUT THERE?

If there is, telescope systems like the Very Large Array in New Mexico may be able to find out. Its 27 dishes work together as one enormous telescope to detect radio waves from space that could be communications from alien civilizations.

SPACECRAFT:

Vehicles that travel in space to explore places beyond our own planet

WHAT'S THE FARTHEST A SPACECRAFT HAS TRAVELED?

Launched in 1977, the Voyager 1 and 2 spacecraft have traveled farther than any other human-made object. Traveling at a speed of 11 miles per second (17 km per second), they are about 20 billion miles (32 billion km) away from Earth. It will still take them about 300 years to enter the start of Oort Cloud, the region of icy bodies that surrounds our Solar System.

Voyager 1 has swept past Jupiter, Saturn, Uranus, and Neptune and is heading toward the start of the Oort Cloud.

FAST FACTS

As of 2024, the **fastest** spacecraft was the Parker Solar Probe – so fast, it would get from **New York to Tokyo** in one minute!

In 2015, New Horizons became the **first spacecraft** to orbit and explore the dwarf planet, **Pluto**.

SpaceShipTwo, designed for **space tourism**, made its first flight to space carrying four paying passengers in July 2021.

HOW FAR CAN WE GO IN SPACE?

This is limited by how much fuel a spacecraft can carry. A spacecraft can keep going without fuel, as space has no air resistance to slow it down, but it can't change direction. To travel beyond our Solar System in a controlled way, we need new technology. Solar sails (above) use sunlight bouncing off a shiny surface, just as the wind powers a ship's sail on Earth.

At around 7 miles (11 km) above the surface, a parachute is deployed to slow down the spacecraft.

Spacecraft enters the Martian atmosphere traveling at a speed of 12,500 mph (20,000 km/h).

A heat shield protects the spacecraft from the heat and friction of entry into the atmosphere.

HOW DOES A ROVER LAND SAFELY ON MARS?

The rovers that travel across Mars, exploring the planet's surface, make the long journey from Earth on board a small spacecraft. When it reaches Mars's atmosphere, a parachute opens to slow the craft down very quickly. The craft itself does not land on the surface—it delivers the rover using long cables and then flies away.

About 5 miles (8 km) above the surface, the heat shield falls away.

The craft separates from the casing and parachute.

Rocket-powered thrusters slow the craft down to walking speed.

The craft flies off after releasing the rover.

The rover is lowered to the ground on strong cables.

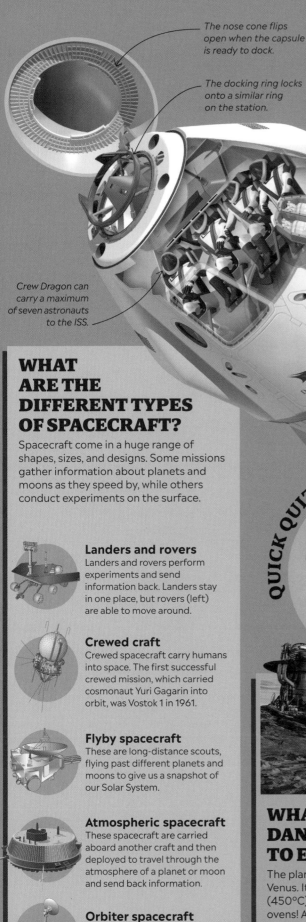

The nose cone flips open when the capsule is ready to dock.

The docking ring locks onto a similar ring on the station.

Crew Dragon can carry a maximum of seven astronauts to the ISS.

HOW DO CREW TRAVEL TO THE INTERNATIONAL SPACE STATION?

The main spacecraft used to transport astronauts to the ISS is SpaceX's Crew Dragon, which can be reused up to 15 times. This futuristic spacecraft launches on top of a Falcon 9 rocket. The rocket is made up of two parts called stages that fall away as the fuel inside them is used up (see page 115). The Crew Dragon capsule then uses power from its own thrusters to match the speed of the ISS, carefully creeping up alongside it to dock.

The Crew Dragon capsule sits at the top of the huge rocket.

Second stage

Falcon 9 rocket

The trunk can carry additional cargo.

The first stage of the rocket returns to Earth to be reused.

The fins are needed to give the rocket stability when it launches.

WHAT ARE THE DIFFERENT TYPES OF SPACECRAFT?

Spacecraft come in a huge range of shapes, sizes, and designs. Some missions gather information about planets and moons as they speed by, while others conduct experiments on the surface.

Landers and rovers
Landers and rovers perform experiments and send information back. Landers stay in one place, but rovers (left) are able to move around.

Crewed craft
Crewed spacecraft carry humans into space. The first successful crewed mission, which carried cosmonaut Yuri Gagarin into orbit, was Vostok 1 in 1961.

Flyby spacecraft
These are long-distance scouts, flying past different planets and moons to give us a snapshot of our Solar System.

Atmospheric spacecraft
These spacecraft are carried aboard another craft and then deployed to travel through the atmosphere of a planet or moon and send back information.

Orbiter spacecraft
Some missions journey to a planet or moon and then slow down and enter its orbit, studying it from above.

QUICK QUIZ!

WHICH SPACECRAFT BECAME THE FIRST SUCCESSFUL MISSION TO ANOTHER PLANET?

a: New Horizons

b: Marina 2

c: Galileo

WHAT'S THE MOST DANGEROUS PLANET TO EXPLORE?

The planet with the harshest conditions is Venus. Its surface temperature is over 842°F (450°C)—more than twice as hot as most ovens! Add to that the crushing air pressure, and a spacecraft will compress and melt at the same time. Venera 13 (above) landed in 1981 and survived just over two hours!

WHAT'S THE WEIRDEST THING WE HAVE SENT INTO SPACE?

In 2018, SpaceX sent an electric Tesla car into space as a stunt to publicize the test of its Falcon heavy rocket. Other strange objects have been sent up to the ISS, including dinosaur bones and toys such as Shaun the Sheep and Buzz Lightyear.

The Tesla launched with a dummy in the driver's seat.

EARTH

WHAT IS INSIDE EARTH?

Earth is made up of several layers. At the center is the solid inner core made of hot metal, surrounded by a liquid outer core. The biggest section inside Earth is the semisolid mantle, which is more than 1,800 miles (2,900 km) thick. A thin crust sits on top of all these layers.

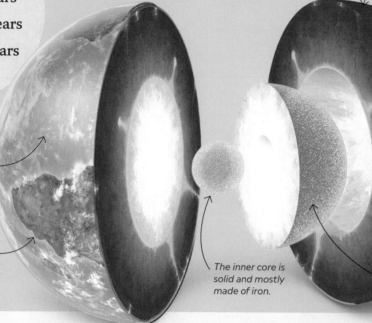

The mantle is mainly solid and made of rock that is very hot and dense.

A thick atmosphere surrounds Earth.

The crust beneath the oceans is up to 3 miles (5 km) thick and made of dense rock.

The crust that forms the continents is thicker and less dense.

The inner core is solid and mostly made of iron.

The outer core is a layer of liquid iron and nickel.

PLANET EARTH:

The giant spinning ball of rock that we all live on

WHY CAN'T I FEEL EARTH SPINNING?

You can't feel Earth spin because you are moving with Earth at the same speed. Earth spins on its axis and completes one full rotation every 23 hours and 56 minutes, which gives us the length of one day.

HOW LONG WOULD IT TAKE TO FALL TO THE CENTER OF THE EARTH?

The center of Earth is about 4,000 miles (6,400 km) beneath your feet. If there was a hole all the way down, it would probably only take you 20 minutes to fall all that way because Earth's gravity would cause you to accelerate to incredible speeds—making you fall at thousands of miles per hour.

HOW HOT IS IT INSIDE EARTH?

When molten rock from inside Earth erupts to the surface, it can be up to 2,190°F (1,200°C). But deep down in the core, it is much hotter—ranging from 7,232°F (4,000°C) to 10,800°F (6,000°C), making it potentially 10 times hotter than the surface of the Sun!

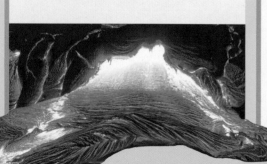

If all Earth's water was scooped up, it would make a ball 860 miles (1,384 km) wide.

HOW MUCH OF EARTH'S SURFACE IS COVERED BY WATER?

Around 71 percent of Earth's surface is covered by water, with most of this found in the vast oceans. Because the oceans take up so much of Earth's surface, it is often called the Blue Planet.

If it was possible to drill, the hole would be almost as deep as the Amazon River is long.

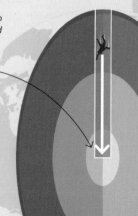

TECTONIC PLATES:
Pieces of Earth's crust that fit together to cover the whole planet

WHAT ARE TECTONIC PLATES?

Earth's outer layer—the crust fused together with the upper part of the mantle—is not one solid shell, but is divided into pieces called tectonic plates. There are seven large plates and six smaller ones. Lots of Earth's volcanic and geological events happen at the boundaries where plates meet.

Volcanic eruptions are shown as red dots.

South America and Africa begin to move away from each other.

Past Earth
100 million years ago

Africa today is completely separate from South America.

Present-day Earth
Earth today has seven continents.

HOW FAST DO TECTONIC PLATES MOVE?

Earth's tectonic plates are constantly moving, but at a very slow speed of 0.5 in (1.5 cm) per year. As they move, so do the continents in a process called continental drift. This means the continents we know today look very different to those in the past, having moved over millions of years!

Tectonic plates move at the same speed that fingernails grow.

WHAT WILL EARTH LOOK LIKE IN THE FUTURE?

Around 300 million years ago, all the land on Earth existed as one big supercontinent called Pangea. As the tectonic plates moved over time, Pangea gradually broke up and formed the continents we know today. In the future, scientists think a new supercontinent might form.

Future Earth
In 250 million years, a supercontinent called Novopangea could form.

Magma rises from the mantle to form new crust.

Plates move away from each other.

HOW OLD IS EARTH'S CRUST?

Parts of Earth's crust can be billions or millions of years old, but new crust is continually being made as tectonic plates move. At boundaries where two plates are pulling apart from each other, magma rises up to fill the gap, which then hardens into new crust.

WHAT'S THE DEEPEST HOLE EVER DRILLED?

The deepest hole ever drilled is the Kola Superdeep Borehole in Russia, created between 1970 and 1994. It eventually reached a depth of 7.6 miles (12.26 km)—deeper than Mount Everest is tall. However, Earth's crust averages around 22 miles (35 km) thick, meaning the hole only made it around a third of the way through the total crust depth.

The Kola Borehole is 9 in (23 cm) wide and took 20 years to drill.

The Mariana Trench—the deepest point in the ocean—is less deep than the hole.

35

WHERE DOES LAVA COME FROM?

Lava starts out as magma—molten rock that is found beneath Earth's crust. When magma erupts onto Earth's surface, it is called lava, and it can take many different forms. Some lava is thin and runny. It flows fast and when it cools it forms a light, holey rock. Thicker lava flows slowly and can harden to form a dome over the volcano.

IT'S A MYSTERY!

How do we know if a volcano is going to erupt? Scientists measure many things to try to predict eruptions, including earthquake activity, swelling of the surface of the volcano, and changes in gases. However, eruptions can only be reliably predicted just a few days in advance.

VOLCANOES: Openings in Earth's surface through which lava, ash, and gases can erupt

WHAT MAKES A VOLCANO ERUPT?

Eruptions happen when magma rises from deep within Earth and collects in a magma chamber below the surface. As more builds up, it eventually forces its way through weak spots in the crust. The magma can also trap gases as it rises, making the eruption very explosive!

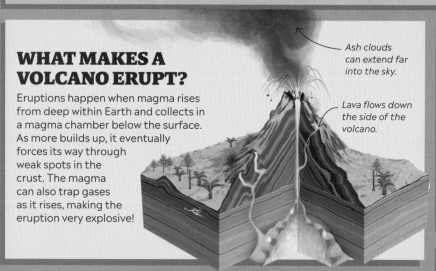

Ash clouds can extend far into the sky.

Lava flows down the side of the volcano.

WHAT HAPPENED IN POMPEII?

When Mount Vesuvius in Italy erupted in 79 CE, a cloud of hot ash, rock, and gas surged down the volcano's slopes at around 180 mph (290 km/h). People in the city of Pompeii below did not have time to escape. Their bodies were trapped in the ash, later leaving voids that were then filled with plaster to make casts.

HOW DANGEROUS ARE VOLCANOES?

It is hard to measure the worst eruption, but many have killed or injured thousands. Eruptions today continue to have massive impacts—wiping out homes and essential infrastructure, such as this 2024 eruption in Grindavík, Iceland.

WHY DO VOLCANOES GO DORMANT?

A volcano's magma supply can be cut off if Earth's tectonic plates shift and move it away from the rising magma. These volcanoes, such as the Calderón Hondo volcano (left) in Fuerteventura, Canary Islands, are called dormant.

EARTHQUAKES: Shaking of the ground caused by movement of tectonic plates

HOW DO WE CLASSIFY EARTHQUAKES?

There are different levels of earthquakes. To calculate their power, we can measure the vibrations that travel through the ground.

Minor
Some shaking. Not always felt, but recorded.

Moderate
Slight damage to buildings and other structures.

Major
Serious damage spreading across a wide area.

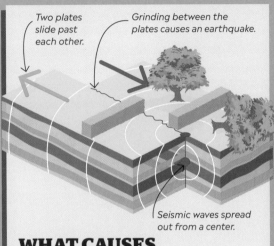

Two plates slide past each other.

Grinding between the plates causes an earthquake.

Seismic waves spread out from a center.

WHAT CAUSES EARTHQUAKES?

Earthquakes happen along fault lines, where tectonic plates meet and move past or against each other. When there is sudden movement along a fault line, it generates waves of energy, called seismic waves, that can make the ground shake.

CAN WE PROTECT OURSELVES FROM EARTHQUAKES?

Although we can't predict earthquakes, scientists have devised early warning systems that detect the first waves and advise people when to take cover. Buildings in earthquake-prone areas are often built with flexible foundations and other devices to reduce the impact of vibrations.

The Tokyo Skytree has a central concrete tube that can sway in earthquakes, reducing the impact to the building.

HOW DEEP CAN THE EARTH CRACK DURING AN EARTHQUAKE?

During an earthquake, the ground doesn't actually open up, even though damage can often make it look as though it has. Fault lines can extend to great depths, destroying roads such as this highway in the Philippines, which was torn apart by a 2012 earthquake.

The powerful earthquake caused huge landslides.

HOW HIGH ARE TSUNAMI WAVES?

When earthquakes begin under the ocean, the shaking of the seabed causes huge waves to form, spreading out and growing into tsunamis like the one (right) that struck Miyako, Japan, in 2011. Their waves can reach 100 ft (30 m) tall.

ROCKS:
Solid materials made from minerals, which form the surface of Earth, and are constantly changing

Granite (igneous rock)

Limestone (sedimentary rock)

Gneiss (metamorphic rock)

WHAT TYPES OF ROCKS ARE THERE?

There are three main types of rocks. Igneous rocks, such as granite, form when molten rock solidifies. Sedimentary rocks, such as limestone, are formed from minerals and organic particles, and metamorphic rocks form from other rocks when exposed to high temperatures and pressures deep within Earth.

WHAT IS A MINERAL?

Minerals are the building blocks of rocks. They are naturally occurring substances, each with their own unique structure and properties. Some, such as quartz (right), have colorful crystals. Rocks are usually made up of two or more minerals and are formed in the rock cycle.

IS SAND MADE OF ROCKS?

Yes! If you look at sand under a microscope, you'll see that it is made up of lots of tiny pieces, which are rock fragments. Over millions and millions of years, big rocks are slowly broken down into smaller and smaller pieces—for example, by wind, rain, and changing temperatures—eventually forming sand.

WHY DO ROCKS HAVE LAYERS?

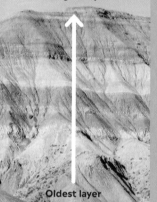

Youngest layer

Oldest layer

Sedimentary rocks build up over long periods of time. Layers formed at different times often have varying colors and different properties. By examining rock layers—from the youngest at the top to the oldest at the very bottom—geologists can learn about the history of Earth. Some layers may even contain ancient fossils!

HOW DO ROCKS FORM?

The rocks on Earth are constantly changing forms in a cycle. Under the ground, heat and pressure can turn softer sedimentary rock into metamorphic rock. When this melts, it erupts as magma, cooling to form igneous rock (some of which also forms below the surface). This can be eroded by the weather into smaller pieces that eventually form back into sedimentary rock.

Sedimentary rock forms over many years as layers of sediment cement together.

Exposed rock is worn down by weathering (see page 42) and broken into small pieces.

(see page 42)

Rivers transport bits of weathered rock into the seas and oceans.

Lava erupting from volcanoes forms igneous rock.

Sedimentary rock buckles into mountains and becomes metamorphic.

Intense heat causes metamorphic rock to melt into magma.

Heat turns some sedimentary rock into metamorphic rock.

WHY ARE GEMSTONES DIFFERENT COLORS?

A gemstone's color is caused by the way light is reflected through it and the trace substances it contains. For example, turquoise gets its blue-green color from the presence of copper, and a ruby is red because it contains chromium.

HOW HARD ARE GEMS?

The strength of gems varies and is measured on the Mohs Hardness Scale, which tests how resistant a gem is to scratching. The top-ranking gem is diamond—scoring 10! Diamonds are so strong, they are used in the blades of saws and the tips of drills (above) to cut into other tough objects.

GEMS: Precious stones that are prized for their beauty and shaped and polished to make jewelry

Amethyst is the most popular type of purple gemstone.

Emerald is made from a mineral called beryl.

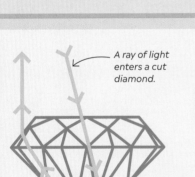

A ray of light enters a cut diamond.

The light bounces off the facets of the cut gem.

WHY DO GEMS SPARKLE?

Cut gems have many tiny sides, which are called facets. The more facets there are, the more surfaces there are to reflect light. A beam of light bounces off lots of facets inside the gem, causing it to sparkle! Gems are also highly polished, and more light reflects off shiny surfaces than dull ones.

WHAT IS THE MOST EXPENSIVE GEMSTONE?

Rare blue diamonds are often the priciest, such as the Hope Diamond (left). Diamonds are measured by the carat, and the record price paid for a diamond per carat was also for a blue diamond—the Blue Moon of Josephine, which sold for $48,468,158 in 2015.

 Round **Oval**

 Cushion **Pear**

 Emerald **Princess**

HOW DO JEWELERS SHAPE GEMS?

Raw gemstones can be oddly shaped and not very shiny, so jewelers use saws to cut them into shapes. They then grind, sand, and polish them so they are highly reflective. Common jeweler's cuts have standard names (left).

IT'S A MYSTERY!

Are there different gems on other planets?

Scientists suspect there are many different gems across the planets in our Solar System. They predict it could be raining diamonds on Neptune and Uranus, but so far no spacecraft has got close enough to find out!

FOSSILS:

Preserved remains, impressions, or traces of a living organism, usually found in rock and often only discovered millions of years later

WHAT IS A FOSSIL?

There are two main types of fossils: body fossils and trace fossils. A body fossil is the preserved remains of a living thing, usually the hard parts, such as bones, teeth, or shells. Occasionally, a complete skeleton is found! A trace fossil is evidence of an animal's activity, such as a footprint, a burrow, or even a coprolite (fossilized poop).

DO ONLY ANIMALS BECOME FOSSILS?

In the right conditions, any organism can become a fossil. Impressions of ancient plants are preserved in rock, and whole fossilized forests have been found that are 390 million years old. You can also find tiny microfossils that are the remains of bacteria and pollen and can only be seen under a microscope!

WHERE ARE FOSSILS FOUND?

Fossils are mostly found in sedimentary rocks and are often exposed near the sea on rocky cliffs and beaches, which have been weathered by the waves. When scientists find an embedded fossil, they carefully reveal it and extract it from the rock using tools such as brushes and chisels.

IS AMBER A FOSSIL?

To be preserved as a fossil, an organism usually needs to be rapidly covered by sediment. But some creatures, such as insects, can also be trapped and preserved in sticky tree resin. This hardens into amber, forming a see-through cast around it. Scientists have found more than 1,000 species preserved in amber and even discovered intact dinosaur feathers!

From the tip of its tail to its head, the animal was around 24 in (60 cm) long.

HOW IS A FOSSIL FORMED?

Fossils form when an organism dies and its remains are covered with sediment. Soft remains are dissolved by water, leaving the shape of the organism in the rock. Hard remains, such as bones, are then replaced by minerals, turning into rock in the shape of the creature—a fossil.

Sediment falls on top of the creature.

Ammonite dies
An ancient marine creature dies and sinks into the sediment. Layers build on top of it.

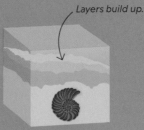

Layers build up.

Decomposition
The soft parts of the body decompose and leave behind the hard parts.

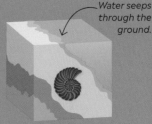

Water seeps through the ground.

Fossilization
Water dissolves the hard remains, and minerals in the water harden to replace these.

The fossil becomes exposed.

Reveal!
Rock is gradually worn away by weathering, exposing the hard fossil.

WHAT IS THE MOST COMMON FOSSIL?

The most common fossils are of ancient marine life, such as ammonites—small, sea-dwelling creatures that first appeared 450 million years ago. The fossil remains of their spiral shells are found in large numbers all over the world. Fossilized sharks' teeth are also common because sharks have 50–300 teeth and old ones often become buried on the sea floor.

WHAT IS THE OLDEST FOSSIL EVER FOUND?

The oldest fossils on record were found in Western Australia and are around 3.5 billion years old! They are called stromatolites and are layered rock formations produced by a type of bacteria called cyanobacteria.

Seymouria baylorensis had a deep skull like many present-day amphibians.

Each of the distinct arm and finger bones has been preserved.

WHY DON'T WE HAVE FOSSILS OF EVERY ANCIENT CREATURE?

Fossilization is rare because it needs very specific conditions to happen. Fossils are more likely to form in water, where they will quickly be covered in sediment. In dry areas, animals decay quickly, can be scavenged by predators, and are unlikely to be buried. This fossil (left) is of *Seymouria baylorensis*—a creature called a tetrapod that lived 250 million years ago. Despite its lizardlike appearance, scientists now think it was an amphibian that lived in watery environments, which may be why its fossil has survived to this day.

IT'S A MYSTERY!

How many creatures become fossils?
It is thought that less than one-tenth of a percent of living things become fossils and that only one bone in a billion gets fossilized. But we have no way of truly knowing!

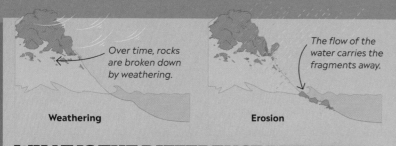

Over time, rocks are broken down by weathering.

Weathering

The flow of the water carries the fragments away.

Erosion

WHAT IS THE DIFFERENCE BETWEEN EROSION AND WEATHERING?

You might notice that some rocks have holes in them or are crumbling into small pieces. This is the effect of weathering, which wears away rocks and can be caused by wind, rain, waves, changes in temperature, or even plants and animals. Erosion is the process where the weathered fragments are transported away, often causing massive changes to the surrounding landscape, carving valleys and cliffs.

CAN EROSION BE PREVENTED?

Erosion by the sea can destroy coastal settlements and infrastructure, such as this road in Skipsea, UK. To prevent this, some countries have built huge sea walls and rock armor to protect the coastline from the pounding waves. Smaller defenses can also be put on beaches.

EROSION: A natural process where rocks and other materials are worn away and moved across the landscape

Headlands of harder rock stick out from the coast.

Softer rock

WHY ARE PEBBLES SMOOTH?

When rock fragments fall into a moving stream, the flow of water causes them to collide and rub against each other. All this scraping together is called abrasion and produces a pebble's rounded shape and smooth surface. Pebbles can also be formed from concrete, brick, and glass.

HOW DOES THE SEA SHAPE THE LAND?

Waves, tides, and currents all wear away the coastline. Softer material is eroded much more easily, creating bays that sit between headlands of harder rock. Waves also crash against weak points in the exposed rock, causing caves to form as well as shapes such as columns or arches.

Waves curve around to strike the cliffs, gradually wearing their rock down.

Arches and pillars of rock called stacks are some of the coastal formations formed by the sea.

QUICK QUIZ!

HOW OLD IS THE GRAND CANYON?

a: 20 million years

b: 70 million years

c: 2 billion years

WHAT CAUSES EROSION?

Erosion is usually caused by wind, water, or ice—most often as it moves through the land slowly in a glacier. Over millions of years, the effects of erosion can be seen on landscapes, often carving patterns into the rocks, such as in this sandstone rock formation in Arizona called "The Wave."

HOW DO CAVES FORM?

Rain mixes with carbon dioxide from the air as it falls, which turns it into a weak acid. As the acidic rainwater travels through the soil, it slowly dissolves certain rock such as limestone, gypsum, or dolomite to form a cave system.

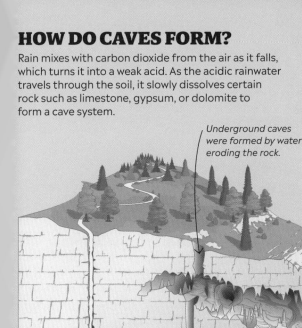

Underground caves were formed by water eroding the rock.

Some chambers are dry caves.

Water flows through the rock to form underground streams.

WHY DO BATS LIVE IN CAVES?

Dark and shady, caves make ideal shelters for animals seeking to avoid predators. Bats are nocturnal and go out to hunt at night, so caves provide a safe space for them to sleep during the day. They are also home to many other creatures, such as unique species of fish and reptiles.

IT'S A MYSTERY!

Why do humans make their own caves?
Discovered in 1992, the Longyou Caves in Zhejiang, China, are 24 hand-built caverns thought to be 2,000 years old. But historians do not know why they were built!

CAVES: Natural openings in the ground that are large enough to explore

Stalactites form at the top of a cave.

DID HUMANS USED TO LIVE IN CAVES?

Yes! In the Stone Age, humans would shelter in the mouths of caves, cook in them, and even paint on the walls. Some of the prints in the Cave of the Hands (above) in Santa Cruz, Argentina, are more than 13,000 years old!

WHAT'S THE BIGGEST CAVE?

The largest cave chamber in the world is Hang Son Doong in Vietnam. It is more than 5.8 miles (9.4 km) long, and in places even rises to a height of 660 ft (200 m)—so big that you could fit a New York City block with 40-story skyscrapers in.

WHAT'S THE DIFFERENCE BETWEEN A STALAGMITE AND A STALACTITE?

Many unique rock formations are found in caves, known as speleothems. Stalactites hang down from the cave ceiling, whereas stalagmites grow up from the cave floor. These icicle shapes are formed as water deposits minerals as it drips.

As water drips from above, it forms columns.

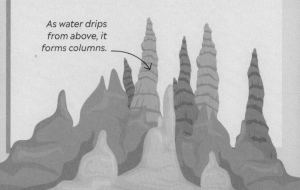

HOW MANY MOUNTAINS ARE THERE?

It is impossible to count them all, but mountains cover around 25 percent of Earth's surface. Some mountain ranges are so long, they stretch across continents—such the Andes (above) in South America, which passes through seven different countries.

MOUNTAINS:

Landforms with steep sides that rise high above the surrounding area

As rock shifts upward, it forms into peaks.

WHERE IS THE LONGEST MOUNTAIN RANGE?

It is not where you might expect—hidden deep under the ocean! A massive continuous chain of mountains called the mid-ocean ridge wraps around the globe for a staggering 40,390 miles (65,000 km), and more than 90 percent of it is underwater.

Mid-ocean ridge marked in red

Fold mountain

HOW DO MOUNTAINS FORM?

Mountains form over millions of years—due to the slow movement of tectonic plates—and in different ways. The most common are fold mountains, formed when two plates collide, crumple, and push the ground upward. Volcanoes are another type of mountain, growing with each layer of erupted lava.

HOW HIGH UP CAN ANIMALS LIVE?

A yellow-rumped leaf-eared mouse holds the record for the animal spotted at the highest altitude—22,100 ft (6,736 m) up Llullaillaco volcano, bordering Argentina and Chile. But many animals have adaptations that allow them to make their home in snowy peaks. Takins living in the Himalayas have thick coats and big nostrils that warm up the cold air as they inhale.

HOW MANY PEOPLE HAVE CLIMBED EVEREST?

Mount Everest was first climbed by mountaineers Edmund Hillary and Tenzing Norgay in 1953. Since then, more than 6,000 people have reached the summit. So many people now attempt the climb that local authorities ask people to pick up their poop and take it with them in order not to pollute the mountain!

FORESTS: Large areas of land that are mostly covered with trees

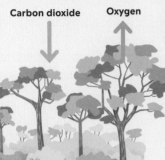

Carbon dioxide   Oxygen

DO FORESTS HELP US BREATHE?

Rainforests are often called the lungs of the planet. This is because they absorb large amounts of carbon dioxide and release oxygen back into the atmosphere. It has been estimated that the world's forests produce up to 40 percent of the oxygen that we breathe!

Scarlet macaws are one of many colorful rainforest birds.

ARE FORESTS IMPORTANT ANIMAL HABITATS?

Yes! Around 80 percent of land-based animals, plants, and insects can be found in forests. More than 30 million species inhabit the world's forests, and there are thought to be many more that scientists have not yet discovered! Deforestation is putting these important animal habitats under threat.

HOW MANY TYPES OF FORESTS ARE THERE?

There are three main types. Tropical forests are warm and wet and are found near the equator, whereas temperate forests grow where it is neither too hot or too cold. The driest and coldest parts of the world are home to boreal forests, filled with snow-covered trees with thin, tough leaves.

IT'S A MYSTERY!

Have we discovered all the forests on Earth?

Maybe not! In 2018, scientists began exploring a hidden forest in the crater of ancient volcano Mount Lico in Mozambique. They only realized the forest was there from pictures by Google Earth!

The emergent layer has trees up to 200 ft (60 m) tall.

The canopy is where most animals live, with thick, sturdy trees that get dappled sunlight.

Leafy bushes and trees make up the understory layer, which is darker and more humid than those above.

HOW MANY TREES HAVE BEEN CUT DOWN?

Over the last 10,000 years, the world has lost more than one-third of its forests, with billions of trees lost every year. In the Amazon rainforest alone, an area the same size as a soccer field is cut down every minute.

HOW MANY TREES DOES THE AMAZON HAVE?

There are nearly 400 billion trees in the Amazon rainforest—making it the biggest rainforest in the world. In the hot, humid environment, trees grow at different heights, some stretching tall to catch the bright sunlight and others flourishing in shady patches below. A rainforest has four main layers: the emergent layer, the canopy, the understory, and the forest floor.

At the bottom is the forest floor, covered in fallen leaves and bark.

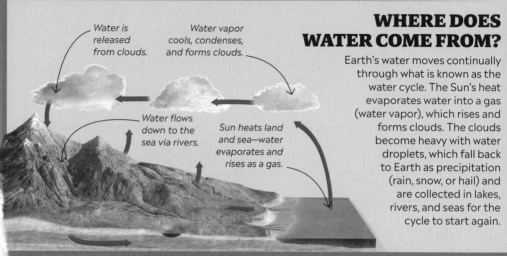

WHERE DOES WATER COME FROM?

Earth's water moves continually through what is known as the water cycle. The Sun's heat evaporates water into a gas (water vapor), which rises and forms clouds. The clouds become heavy with water droplets, which fall back to Earth as precipitation (rain, snow, or hail) and are collected in lakes, rivers, and seas for the cycle to start again.

Water is released from clouds.

Water vapor cools, condenses, and forms clouds.

Water flows down to the sea via rivers.

Sun heats land and sea—water evaporates and rises as a gas.

HOW DO YOU FIND WATER IN THE DESERT?

Animals need water to live, so following them could lead to a potential source. Some, like this donkey in central Asia, dig to reach underground water, which is less likely to evaporate. Plants are also a sign that water is nearby.

WHAT IS THE LONGEST RIVER IN THE WORLD?

The longest river is the Nile, which stretches 4,132 miles (6,650 km) from Lake Victoria in east central Africa, through 11 countries to the Mediterranean Sea in northern Egypt. The Amazon (below) in South America is the second-longest river, but it carries a larger volume of water, making it the biggest river.

WHY IS WATER PRECIOUS WHEN THERE'S SO MUCH OF IT?

Two-thirds of our planet is covered in water, but only a tiny amount of it is water we can drink. About 97 percent is salty ocean water. On top of that, most of the freshwater is locked up in ice caps or glaciers or held in rocks underground. Only 0.3 percent of Earth's freshwater is found at the surface in lakes, rivers, swamps, and waterfalls.

IS WATER BLUE?

Yes, water is blue. Small amounts can look colorless, but in seas, the blue is more obvious. Water can take on other colors, too, depending on what it contains. Rivers can be brown because of sand or soil. Tiny, floating life forms called algae can turn water green—or sometimes even pink, as in Australia's Hutt Lagoon (above).

WATER: A liquid made from hydrogen and oxygen that falls from clouds as rain, hail, or snow and forms lakes, rivers, and seas

OCEANS: Massive bodies of salty water on Earth's surface

The top 656 ft (200 m) is the sunlight zone. Most sea life lives here.

WHAT'S THE BIGGEST OCEAN?

The ocean is divided into five main regions: the Pacific, Atlantic, Indian, Southern, and Arctic oceans. The Pacific is the largest, spanning an area of more than 60 million sq miles (155 million sq km). Covering more than 30 percent of the globe, it is so big that from one side, Earth looks entirely blue!

PACIFIC OCEAN

Fewer animals live in the twilight zone between 656–3,280 ft (200–1,000 m).

Only deep-sea animals survive under 3,280 ft (1,000 m).

WHY IS THE SEA SALTY?

The salt comes mainly from rain eroding rocks on land. The runoff carries salts and minerals into rivers that flow into lakes and seas. The Dead Sea, a landlocked lake in West Asia, has some of the saltiest water. It has so much salt that it makes floating in it even easier.

HOW DEEP IS THE OCEAN?

The ocean isn't the same depth all around the world. Close to land, it is shallower, and home to the most creatures. As it gets deeper, it splits into different zones, each with less life in them. The deepest, darkest parts are long, narrow valleys called trenches.

Not much is known about life below 9,840 ft (3,000 m).

IT'S A MYSTERY!

How many animals live in the ocean?
No one knows. More than four-fifths of the ocean are unexplored. Scientists estimate that 91 percent of all ocean species are yet to be found.

Very few humans have explored the trenches. They have to use special craft called submersibles.

WHAT CAUSES WAVES?

Waves are mainly caused by wind. When the force of the wind blows across the surface of the ocean or a lake, it transports energy, causing water molecules to travel in a circular motion. This up-and-down motion creates a wave that travels in the direction of the wind.

HOW DEEP HAVE HUMANS EXPLORED?

In 2019, US explorer Victor Vescovo reached a depth of 35,872 ft (10,934 m) in Challenger Deep, the deepest known point in the ocean, in the Mariana Trench. It took around 3.5 hours to reach the bottom.

WHEN WAS THE ICE AGE?

There have been many! During an ice age, global temperatures fall and ice sheets cover large areas of land. Scientists also think there was a period around 700 million years ago where Earth was completely covered by ice—a theory known as Snowball Earth. The first ice age began over 2 billion years ago and lasted around 300 million years, but since then, there have been four more major ice ages. We are still technically in an ice age today, but in its warmer interglacial period!

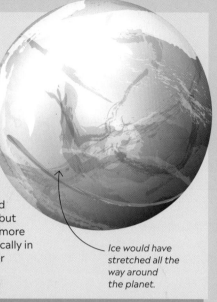

Ice would have stretched all the way around the planet.

WHAT IS A GLACIER?

Glaciers are masses of slowly moving ice. They form on land over hundreds of years and are made from built-up snow that has been compressed into ice. Sometimes, when glaciers reach the sea, huge chunks break off—this is known as calving.

IS EARTH'S ICE MELTING?

A huge amount of water is stored in the ice sheets at each pole, and rising global temperatures are causing these to melt. Antarctica loses around 150 billion tons (136 billion tonnes) of ice per year, and Greenland loses 270 billion tons (245 billion tonnes). This is a fivefold increase since the 1990s.

HOW BIG IS AN ICEBERG?

For a floating chunk of ice to be classified as an iceberg, it must be at least 16 ft (5 m) tall above sea level and 98–164 ft (30–50 m) wide. Around 90 percent of an iceberg will be underwater. Smaller chunks of ice are called "growlers" or "bergy bits."

ICE: The frozen form of water, which makes up Earth's huge glaciers and ice sheets, especially in high mountains and polar regions

DO ALL SNOWFLAKES REALLY LOOK DIFFERENT?

If you look at a bunch of snowflakes under a microscope, they will each appear unique. Snowflakes usually form when raindrops freeze around a dust or pollen particle. Although they are all hexagonal in shape, they look different due to changes in temperature and how much water is in the air as they fall.

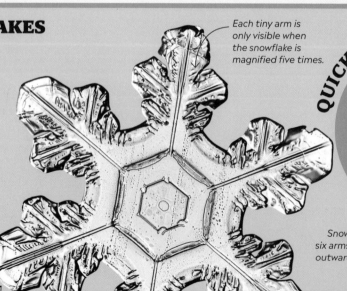

Each tiny arm is only visible when the snowflake is magnified five times.

Snowflakes have unique patterns but are always symmetrical.

Snowflakes with six arms branching outward are called dendrites.

QUICK QUIZ!

HOW MUCH OF EARTH'S FRESH WATER IS ICE?

a: 44%

b: 56%

c: 68%

POLES: The northernmost and southernmost points on Earth

North Pole in winter

North Pole in summer

HOW MUCH ICE IS AT THE POLES?

In winter, the combined Arctic and Antarctic sea ice covers an area of around 13 million square miles (34 million square km). In the south, vast ice sheets also cover the landmass of Antarctica. The amount of ice changes with the seasons, as shown on the maps above.

In summer, the average North Pole temperature is 32°F (0°C).

Temperatures below zero are shown on the scale as negative numbers.

HOW COLD ARE THE POLES?

The South Pole is colder than the North Pole, partly because its ice sits on land and is higher above sea level. In winter, the temperatures drop to -76°F (-60°C) at the South Pole and -40°F (-40°C) at the North Pole. The coldest temperature ever recorded was -128.6°F (-89.2°C) in Antarctica on July 21, 1983.

CAN PEOPLE LIVE AT THE POLES?

No one lives at the poles because they are too cold and remote. However, in Antarctica, there are monitoring stations where scientists stay to carry out research. German research station Neumayer 3 (above) is built on adjustable stilts, so it can be raised if the ice or snow below thickens.

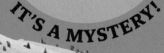

IS IT ALWAYS DARK AT THE NORTH POLE?

In winter it is! In early October, the Sun sets and doesn't rise again until the end of March. But in summer, daylight lasts for a full 24 hours. The opposite effect happens at the South Pole—daylight in winter and darkness in summer.

In an Arctic summer, the position of the Sun changes every hour, but it does not set below the horizon.

DO POLAR BEARS EAT PENGUINS?

No! They would never have the chance to, because polar bears are only found in the Arctic regions, and penguins are mainly found in the southern hemisphere, as far south as Antarctica. But penguins do need to keep an eye out for hungry leopard seals and killer whales!

Vast emperor penguin colonies in the Antarctic can contain more than 5,000 penguins.

What lives beneath Antarctic ice sheets?

Scientists used to think not much could live in such conditions due to the cold and lack of sunlight, but they have recently found creatures such as sponges down there. Who knows what else might thrive below the ice!

IT'S A MYSTERY!

Exosphere
This layer contains very few gas molecules. It fades into space with no clear boundary.

Above 400 miles (600 km)

Many satellites orbit Earth in the exosphere.

Thermosphere
This is the hottest layer, with heat increasing to 3,630°F (2,000°C) at the top of the thermosphere.

50–400 miles (80–600 km)

The International Space Station is in the upper thermosphere.

The aurora borealis can be seen in the lower thermosphere.

Mesosphere
The coldest part of the atmosphere is at the top of the mesosphere, with an average temperature of -120°F (-85°C).

30–50 miles (50–80 km)

Most meteors burn up in the mesosphere.

Stratosphere
The stratosphere contains the ozone layer. Life on Earth is possible because the ozone layer absorbs most of the harmful ultraviolet (UV) radiation from the Sun.

10–30 miles (16–50 km)

Weather balloon

Troposphere
This lowest layer contains the air that we breathe and almost all of the planet's weather.

0–10 miles (0–16 km)

QUICK QUIZ!

WHICH GAS IN AIR IS NEEDED FOR LIFE?

a: Nitrogen

b: Oxygen

c: Argon

HOW HIGH UP ARE CLOUDS?
Most clouds form in the troposphere, the layer of atmosphere closest to Earth's surface. The lowest clouds are about 1.2 miles (2 km) above the ground. The atmosphere itself stretches up more than 6,000 miles (10,000 km)!

WILL EARTH'S OXYGEN RUN OUT?
Yes, but not for a billion years. Oxygen is produced by plants and algae during photosynthesis (see page 68), and we have more than we need. In a billion years, though, our planet will be too warm for plants and algae to survive. As they die, Earth's oxygen will eventually run out.

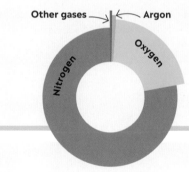

WHAT IS THE ATMOSPHERE MADE OF?
The atmosphere is made of different gases: 78 percent is nitrogen, 21 percent is oxygen, and 0.9 percent is argon. The remaining 0.1 percent is made up of small amounts of other gases, including carbon dioxide, methane, water vapor, and neon.

Other gases — Argon

Nitrogen

Oxygen

ATMOSPHERE:
The layers of gases that surround Earth and protect us from the Sun's rays

WHERE DOES SPACE START?
There's no clear boundary where Earth's atmosphere stops and space begins. The two merge as the atmosphere gets thinner and thinner. In fact, space is often said to begin in the thermosphere, about 62 miles (100 km) above Earth's surface. This is the point where there is not enough air to provide lift for an airplane to fly.

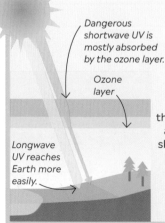

Dangerous shortwave UV is mostly absorbed by the ozone layer.

Ozone layer

Longwave UV reaches Earth more easily.

HOW DOES THE ATMOSPHERE PROTECT US?
Ozone is a thin layer of gas within the stratosphere that absorbs almost all harmful shortwave UV radiation from the Sun. This UV can damage the DNA of all living things, leading to sunburn and skin cancer in humans. Longwave UV can also cause sunburn, but it also helps us make vitamin D for strong bones.

WEATHER:

The conditions of the atmosphere—including temperature, wind, and humidity—at a certain place and time

HOW HEAVY IS A CLOUD?

Clouds come in all shapes and sizes, but scientists have worked out that an average cloud weighs around 550 tons (500 tonnes). Each cloud is made up of many water droplets—the cloud floats in the air because the droplets are less dense than the dry air around them.

WHY DO RAINBOWS HAPPEN?

Sunlight is made from seven colors all mixed together. A rainbow appears when sunlight hits raindrops in the air and the light is scattered into its seven colors. As many raindrops are hit at once by sunlight, an arc of the seven colors—a rainbow—forms in the sky facing the Sun.

WHAT IS WIND?

Wind is the movement of air. The Sun heats Earth's surface, which warms the air above it. This warm air rises, flows sideways, then cools and falls, moving heat around the world. The whole time, Earth is spinning, which swirls the wind to either side of the equator.

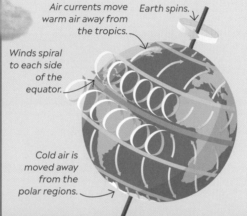

Air currents move warm air away from the tropics.

Earth spins.

Winds spiral to each side of the equator.

Cold air is moved away from the polar regions.

HOW DO WE KNOW WHEN IT WILL RAIN?

Weather forecasters rely on different instruments, such as weather balloons in the stratosphere and weather stations on Earth's surface, to gather data about weather patterns. By comparing this data with past patterns, they can predict weather conditions in the immediate and near future.

WHAT CAUSES EXTREME WEATHER?

There have always been extreme weather events, but climate change (see page 54-55) has made these events both more frequent and more severe. An increase of heat-trapping gases caused by human activities, such as burning fossil fuels, warms land and sea and introduces more energy into the atmosphere. This helps make extreme weather, such as heat waves, droughts, floods, and powerful storms.

What is ball lightning?
People have reported seeing floating orbs of light named ball lightning, ranging from tiny to a yard wide, during thunderstorms. Ball lightning remains unexplained and very rare and cannot be predicted.

IT'S A MYSTERY!

Fire tornadoes can form when wildfires create their own wind.

Wildfires can start when heat waves dry the ground.

STORMS:

Extreme weather conditions with heavy winds that can range from rain showers to severe hurricanes

WHAT HAPPENS WHEN LIGHTNING REACHES THE GROUND?

When a bolt of lightning strikes, electric current spreads out through the ground. In sand or sandy soil, the heat can fuse this material together to create a glassy tubelike mineral called fulgurite, often called fossilized lightning.

DO STORMS RAGE ON OTHER PLANETS?

Some planets have only a thin atmosphere, so they don't have winds or storms. But any planet with a substantial atmosphere can produce high winds. The Great Red Spot on Jupiter is the largest storm in the Solar System and is thought to have been raging for hundreds of years. It is 10,160 miles (16,350 km) wide—bigger than the width of Earth!

HOW MUCH RAIN CAN A STORM PRODUCE?

Tropical storms have the potential to produce huge amounts of rain. In 2022, Hurricane Ian hit southwest Florida, with some areas seeing 12 in (30 cm) of rainfall in just one day. Climate change is thought to be increasing the average amount of rain produced by storms.

QUICK QUIZ!

HOW FAST CAN STORM WINDS GET?

a: 137 mph (220 km/h)

b: 222 mph (357 km/h)

c: 253 mph (407 km/h)

HOW BIG CAN STORMS GET?

The biggest storm ever recorded was Typhoon Tip, a tropical cyclone that formed in the Pacific in 1979. At its peak, the eye of the storm measured 9.3 miles (15 km) wide. Around 22 cyclones are thought to form over the Atlantic and Pacific Oceans each year, such as cyclone Florence (below), which struck the east coast of the United States in 2018.

HOW DO CYCLONES FORM?

Tropical cyclones are a type of storm that forms over the ocean. Warm air above the surface of the water rises quickly in a spiral, drawing in more moist air and creating strong winds. The rising air eventually cools, and the water vapor in it condenses to form bands of cloud. As more warm, moist air is drawn in, the storm gets stronger.

WHAT MAKES THUNDER SO LOUD?

The loud shocks we hear as thunder are actually produced by lightning. A lightning bolt rapidly heats a narrow column of air, which expands outward into the cooler surrounding air. This creates a shock wave that we hear as a clap of thunder. The closer you are to the lightning, the louder the thunder will be.

WHAT IS A BLIZZARD?

A blizzard is a severe snowstorm where strong winds and heavy snowfall combine to form a dangerous combination as large clumps of snow whirl through the air. To be classified as a blizzard, the snowstorm needs to have wind speeds of more than 35 mph (56 km/h) and visibility of less than 1,300 ft (400 m) in front of you!

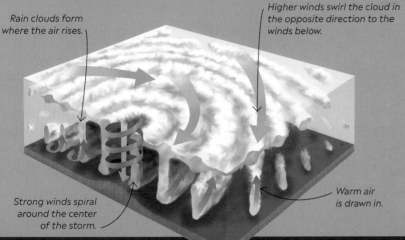

Rain clouds form where the air rises.

Higher winds swirl the cloud in the opposite direction to the winds below.

Strong winds spiral around the center of the storm.

Warm air is drawn in.

The eye of a storm is relatively calm, with the strongest winds and heaviest rains in the eye wall that surrounds it.

The International Space Station captured pictures of this storm as it orbited Earth.

WHAT CAUSES CLIMATE CHANGE?

Although Earth has had periods of natural climate change, since the 1800s, the main cause of climate change has been human activities. Actions such as burning increasing amounts of fossil fuels and cutting down forests have released more of the greenhouse gas carbon dioxide into the atmosphere, warming Earth and leading to other climatic changes.

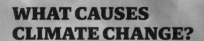

QUICK QUIZ!

HOW MUCH ARCTIC SEA ICE IS BEING LOST EVERY 10 YEARS?

a: 6%

b: 12%

c: 16%

CLIMATE CHANGE:

Long term shifts in temperatures and weather patterns, driven by human activities

FAST FACTS

🌡 Up to **20%** of greenhouse gas emissions come from **deforestation**.

🌡 An estimated **3.6 billion** people live in areas that are **vulnerable** to the effects of climate change.

🌡 The **10 warmest years** on record all occurred within the last decade.

HOW HOT IS THE WORLD GOING TO GET?

Scientists predict that without any action to prevent it, global average temperatures could rise by up to 7.2°F (4°C) by 2100. This might not sound like much, but it has a big impact. Warmer, drier conditions make extreme weather events—such as drought and floods—more common, water more scarce, and some foods harder to grow. Targets have been set to reduce the amount of warming, but we are not yet on track to meet these.

HOW DO WE KNOW HUMAN ACTIONS ARE TO BLAME?

By studying natural features, such as ice cores (left), scientists can find out the amount of greenhouse gases in the atmosphere and how this has changed over the decades. Their data has shown a huge increase in temperatures since the 1800s, when the Industrial Revolution (see pages 208–209) began.

WHY CAN'T WE JUST VACUUM UP GREENHOUSE GASES?

Sucking gases out of the air is not as simple as it sounds! They would have to be carefully filtered out by complicated technology. Some products exist that can extract carbon dioxide and store it underground. But they are a new technology that requires a lot of energy, is very expensive, and is hard to operate on a large scale.

Carbon dioxide makes up only 0.04 percent of the air, so it is hard to extract.

WHAT WILL HAPPEN IF SEA LEVELS CONTINUE TO RISE?

The global average sea level has risen by 8–9 in (21–24 cm) since 1880 and is continuing to rise. Many areas are currently at risk of coastal flooding over the next decades, especially low-lying island nations, and many people could be forced to leave their homes. Scientists predict that up to a third of Indonesia's capital city Jakarta (left) could be entirely submerged by 2050.

DOES CLIMATE CHANGE AFFECT THE OCEANS?

Yes! It is thought that the ocean has absorbed 90 percent of the excess heat trapped in the atmosphere. Warmer ocean temperatures have affected wildlife, with species struggling to adapt to changing temperatures. Important habitats such as coral reefs are also under threat due to an effect called coral bleaching.

Before
Coral reefs are usually brightly colored due to microscopic algae that live in the coral, helping them make food.

After
If ocean water is too warm, coral can expel the algae. Then the corals' color fades and they begin to starve.

WHAT CAN WE DO TO COMBAT CLIMATE CHANGE?

The simplest way we can help combat climate change is to reduce the energy we use so that fewer gases are emitted into the atmosphere. Small actions that cut our consumption or switch it to sustainable sources can make a difference, as well as lobbying governments and companies to cut down their emissions.

Use less energy
Turning off devices that have been left on standby and that you're not using saves energy.

Reduce, reuse
Cutting down what we buy and recycling products so they can be used again saves energy.

Transportation
Walking or cycling do not emit carbon dioxide, unlike traveling by car and other vehicles.

Food
Reducing food waste and cutting down on meats such as beef can reduce emissions.

WHAT ARE GREENHOUSE GASES?

Gases in the atmosphere, known as greenhouse gases, trap heat that is reflected off the Earth's surface, keeping our planet at the right temperature for life to exist. Burning fossil fuels produces more greenhouse gases, so more heat is being trapped. This increase in average temperatures is called global warming.

Heat from the Sun warms Earth.

Around 30 percent of the Sun's heat is reflected off Earth's surface.

Some heat is reflected off the atmosphere back into space.

Greenhouse gases stop some heat from escaping into space, warming up the Earth.

Earth's atmosphere traps some gases.

LIFE

LIFE: The quality that animals, plants, fungi, and other organisms have but rocks, air, water, and dead things do not

CAN ANYTHING LIVE FOREVER?

Living things die because their bodies wear out as they reach old age. For ancient trees, which grow slowly, this can take thousands of years, while many small animals, such as insects, last just days. But a few creatures, including the immortal jellyfish (right), have life cycles that renew their cells—effectively making them live forever.

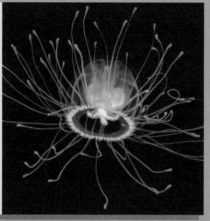

WHAT ARE LIVING THINGS MADE OF?

All living things are made up of one or more cells. These are the basic building blocks of life, which carry out all of life's functions. Cells are made up of water, minerals, and carbon-containing substances, including sugar and protein.

Cell walls can be seen in this magnified image of a moss leaf.

HOW DO WE KNOW SOMETHING IS ALIVE?

Plants, fungi, animals, and all other living things share certain traits to stay alive and produce more of their own kind. They make or consume food that acts like fuel to give them energy and the materials to grow. They also expel waste, move, and respond to their surroundings and reproduce when old enough.

Wings help hummingbird move by flying.

Hummingbird gets nectar for food from flower.

Flower grows on plant so it can reproduce.

CAN LIFE EXIST WITHOUT WATER?

Water is essential for all life. This is because life's vital processes, such as digesting food and releasing energy, involve substances that must be dissolved or mixed in water to react together. Microscopic tardigrades are unusual in being able to survive as "tuns" for up to 30 years without water.

Tardigrade
These tiny creatures are super-resilient and can tolerate extreme temperatures and even the vacuum of space.

Tardigrade tun
They shrivel up into dry bundles called tuns to survive, losing more than 90 percent of their water.

HOW MANY KINDS OF LIFE ARE THERE?

A family tree for life on Earth would show at least seven main branches of living things. Most—including archaea, bacteria, algae, and protozoans—are mainly single-celled organisms. Fungi, plants, and animals usually have bigger, multicelled bodies.

Archaea

Bacteria

Algae

Protozoans　　**Fungi**　　**Plants**

Animals

Plant can sense light, touch, and even sound.

Green leaves enable plant to make food from sunlight.

IT'S A MYSTERY!

How did life begin?
All living things are descended from one kind of single cell that lived nearly 4 billion years ago. Scientists have theories but are not sure how this first organism developed from nonliving materials.

ARE ALL MICROBES ALIVE?

Most microbes are cells that need food and live just like animals and plants. But viruses are different: they are little more than specks of nonliving material such as DNA and protein that infect real living cells to replicate their own kind. Some viruses, called bacteriophages, infect bacteria (below).

WHAT IS A MICROBE?

Although all microbes are too small to see without a microscope, they are more diverse in structure and how they live than plants and animals. Many, but not all, are made of just one cell. Here are some common types, shown from smallest to biggest (not to scale).

Arms engulf prey.

Bacteria

Virus

Tail-like flagellum is used to propel E. coli bacterium.

Water-dwelling diatoms have silica shells.

Virus
The smallest of all, most viruses are parcels of genetic material wrapped in protein.

Bacteria
These are the tiniest of cells, and they lack internal structures such as a nucleus.

Yeast
Used to make beer or raise bread, yeast cells are a kind of microscopic fungus.

Diatom
Algae, such as diatoms, are fueled by sunlight—just like plants.

Amoeba
Some big microbes, such as this amoeba, prey on smaller microbes.

MICROBES: Living things so small that they cannot be seen with the naked eye

HOW SMALL ARE MICROBES?

It can be hard to imagine how small microbes are. If you were shrunk to the size of a bacterium, a grain of rice would be like a mountain and a hair as wide as a river. A virus—the smallest of microbes—would fit in your pocket!

This mountain represents a grain of rice.

Human shown is the size of a bacterium.

Their mobile phone is the size of a virus.

ARE MICROBES EVERYWHERE?

Microbes can survive wherever there is water—but that includes some extreme places. Tough microbes called archaea even thrive in hot volcanic springs, where no other living thing can grow, such as Grand Prismatic Spring in Yellowstone National Park (above). They take over these strange habitats and their large colonies swell into colorful patches.

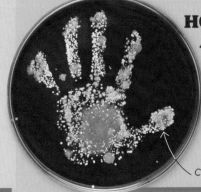

HOW MANY MICROBES ARE ON ME?

A human body is a good place for bacteria and fungi to grow, feeding on oils and other nutrients on warm, damp skin. This photo shows microbes growing in a lab from a handprint. Each tiny spot is a colony containing thousands of cells. That adds up to 40 trillion on the entire body. Most microbes are harmless, and some even help keep the skin healthy.

Clusters of bacteria and microscopic fungi

WHAT IS EVOLUTION?

Evolution is when the characteristics of a group of organisms change over generations. This happens because offspring are not identical to their parents. Over millions of years, these differences build up—so animals today look very different from prehistoric ones. For example, modern elephants are quite different from their prehistoric relatives.

Palaeomastodon

30 million years ago, this small elephant had a short trunk and tusks.

Gomphotherium

15 million years ago, this long-trunked elephant was about the size of an Asian elephant.

Primelephas

5 million years ago, this elephant was unusual in having four tusks.

HOW DOES EVOLUTION HAPPEN?

Every baby resembles its parents because it inherits DNA from its mother and father. But the offspring may also be different because of mutations (changes in the DNA) that alter organisms between generations. Mutations may help or hinder an organism's chances of survival.

This fur seal has a mutation that makes its coat white.

WHY DO LIVING THINGS FIT THEIR SURROUNDINGS?

Individuals that fit their surroundings are more likely to survive. This is known as adaptation. Because their chances of survival are better, these individuals are more likely to pass on their characteristics to the next generation. This is called natural selection. Peppered moths adapted to be hidden from predatory birds on soot-covered city trees (left)—but today's cleaner trees are better for light-colored moths, so they are now more common.

EVOLUTION: The process by which living things change over many generations and millions of years

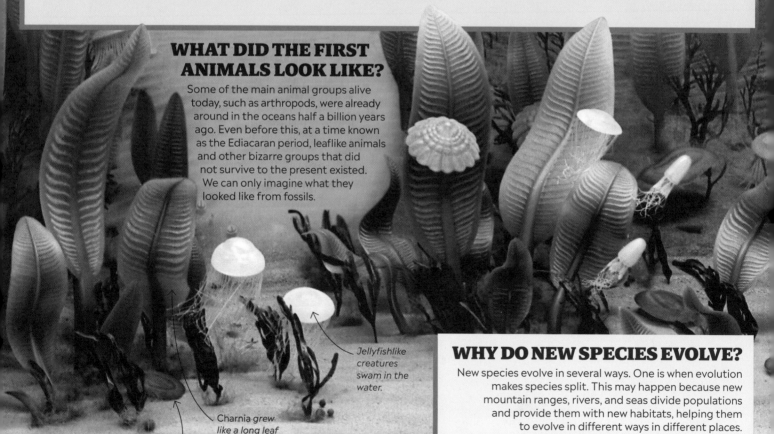

WHAT DID THE FIRST ANIMALS LOOK LIKE?

Some of the main animal groups alive today, such as arthropods, were already around in the oceans half a billion years ago. Even before this, at a time known as the Ediacaran period, leaflike animals and other bizarre groups that did not survive to the present existed. We can only imagine what they looked like from fossils.

Jellyfishlike creatures swam in the water.

Charnia grew like a long leaf attached to the ocean floor.

Bottom-dwelling Dickinsonia was unlike any animal alive today.

WHY DO NEW SPECIES EVOLVE?

New species evolve in several ways. One is when evolution makes species split. This may happen because new mountain ranges, rivers, and seas divide populations and provide them with new habitats, helping them to evolve in different ways in different places.

EXTINCTION:

When the very last individual of a kind dies and a species disappears forever

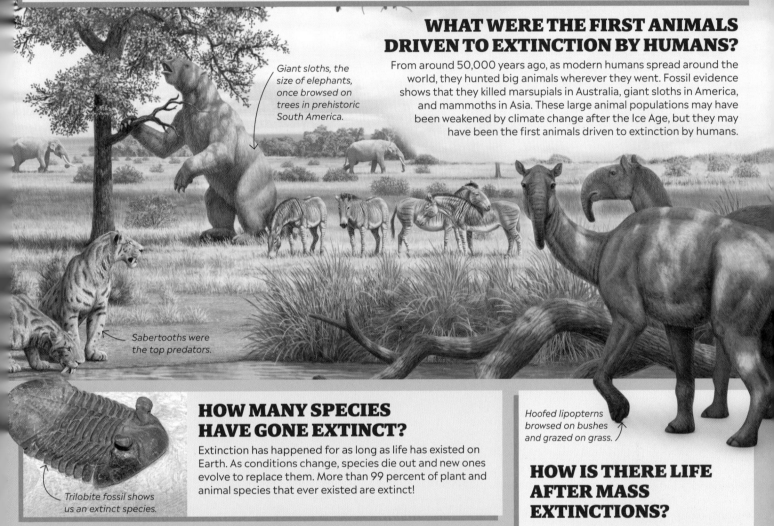

Giant sloths, the size of elephants, once browsed on trees in prehistoric South America.

Sabertooths were the top predators.

Hoofed lipopterns browsed on bushes and grazed on grass.

WHAT WERE THE FIRST ANIMALS DRIVEN TO EXTINCTION BY HUMANS?

From around 50,000 years ago, as modern humans spread around the world, they hunted big animals wherever they went. Fossil evidence shows that they killed marsupials in Australia, giant sloths in America, and mammoths in Asia. These large animal populations may have been weakened by climate change after the Ice Age, but they may have been the first animals driven to extinction by humans.

HOW MANY SPECIES HAVE GONE EXTINCT?

Extinction has happened for as long as life has existed on Earth. As conditions change, species die out and new ones evolve to replace them. More than 99 percent of plant and animal species that ever existed are extinct!

Trilobite fossil shows us an extinct species.

HOW IS THERE LIFE AFTER MASS EXTINCTIONS?

Because plants and animals are adapted to their surroundings in different ways, some will do worse than others when catastrophe hits. An asteroid killed large dinosaurs since they were vulnerable to the long winter it caused. But small, furry mammals survived, and for a time shade-loving ferns flourished.

WHY DO SPECIES GO EXTINCT?

If conditions change, a species can go extinct. Earth has suffered some catastrophic changes, known as mass extinctions, that wiped out many species at once. Some 250 million years ago, the Permian extinction ended almost all life. Theories about what caused it include volcanic eruptions in Siberia (below).

ARE HUMANS MAKING ANOTHER MASS EXTINCTION HAPPEN?

For the last few thousand years, humans have changed the world by hunting animals, clearing natural habitats for farming and industry, and polluting the environment. This has made so many species disappear so quickly that scientists think we should call it a mass extinction.

Present-day fern

Present-day mouse opossum

DINOSAURS:

Reptiles that dominated Earth from around 240 million years ago

Barosaurus
Like other sauropods, this dinosaur probably grazed on tall vegetation.

WHY DID DINOSAURS GROW SO BIG?

The biggest dinosaurs were the long-necked, plant-eating sauropods. *Argentinosaurus* was one of the biggest of these, weighing more than 66 tons (60 tonnes). Giant bodies may have provided better protection from predators, and the ability to survive for longer without food or water.

Argentinosaurus   Six fire engines

HOW MANY SPECIES OF DINOSAURS WERE THERE?

More than 1,000 species of dinosaurs have been identified from fossils on all the major continents. But because the chances of being fossilized are so slim, there would have been many more than this that lived in prehistoric times. This line-up shows species from a few of the main groups that lived at different periods.

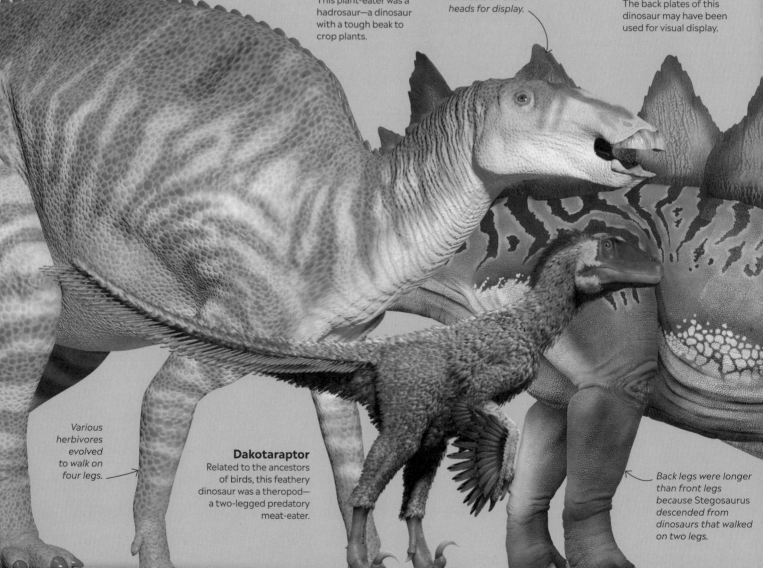

Edmontosaurus
This plant-eater was a hadrosaur—a dinosaur with a tough beak to crop plants.

Many hadrosaurs had crests on their heads for display.

Stegosaurus
The back plates of this dinosaur may have been used for visual display.

Various herbivores evolved to walk on four legs.

Dakotaraptor
Related to the ancestors of birds, this feathery dinosaur was a theropod—a two-legged predatory meat-eater.

Back legs were longer than front legs because Stegosaurus descended from dinosaurs that walked on two legs.

DID ANY DINOSAURS LIVE UNDERWATER?

There were big reptiles that lived in prehistoric seas, such as dolphin-shaped ichthyosaurs, long-necked plesiosaurs, and toothy nothosaurs (below). But these do not share all the traits of dinosaurs and belong to different groups. Many land-living dinosaurs could probably swim, but none lived underwater.

Archaeopteryx

Archaeopteryx had teeth, unlike modern birds.

ARE CHICKENS REALLY DINOSAURS?

Birds belong to a group of two-legged dinosaurs called theropods that included *T. rex*, so they are part of the dinosaur family tree. This means today's birds are really feathered dinosaurs that survived the extinction event that killed off the rest of their family.

Chicken has hinged ankle joints, like its ancestors.

Chicken

COULD WE EVER BRING DINOSAURS BACK TO LIFE?

Specimens of extinct animals can contain DNA or tissues that could be copied and grown to make living clones. But dinosaur fossils are too old, and no material like this is left intact. The oldest preserved DNA scientists have ever found was 2 million years old. Dinosaur fossils are more than 60 million years older than that!

Fossil skull no longer contains any DNA.

IF AN ASTEROID WIPED OUT MOST DINOSAURS, HOW COME OTHER ANIMALS SURVIVED?

Sixty-six million years ago, there was a catastrophe when an asteroid from space collided with Earth, darkening the skies with dust and plunging the world into a cold winter that lasted several years. Large animals, like nonbird dinosaurs, were all wiped out. Small mammals and birds survived because they could hide in holes or feed on tough foods such as seeds.

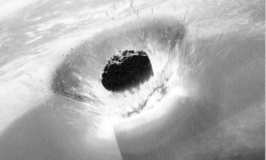

IT'S A MYSTERY!

Did dinosaurs roar?
No one is sure what sound dinosaurs made. However, it is more likely that they cooed like a dove or growled like a crocodile than roared like a lion.

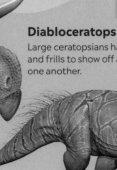

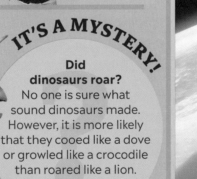

Diabloceratops
Large ceratopsians had horns and frills to show off and fight one another.

Psittacosaurus
This small ceratopsian lacked the horns of larger relatives but shared their parrotlike beak.

Archaeopteryx
Called the oldest bird, it had feathered wings that helped it to fly.

TYRANNOSAURUS REX:

A massive, meat-eating dinosaur that was one of the most powerful predators ever

DID T. REX LIVE IN PACKS?

While fossils of *Tyrannosaurus rex*, also known as *T. rex*, are usually found in isolation, the fossils of several related tyrannosaurs have been found together in the same rocks. This suggests that they spent at least some time together, although it is not clear whether they hunted as a group.

DID ANYTHING EAT T. REX?

T. rex was the top predator of its time. Other meat-eaters were longer or taller, but bulkier *T. rex* probably had the strongest bite. Fossils of *T. rex* with bite marks made by their own kind even suggest that they preyed on one another. Bigger *T. rex* probably routinely ate smaller ones!

HOW TALL WERE THEY?

Models and pictures of *T. rex* from decades ago show an animal standing vertically upright. Scientists now know that its posture was more horizontal, with head and tail pointing front and back. This means its highest point was over the hips—but it was still more than twice as high as an adult human.

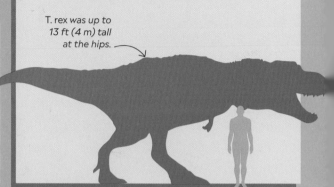

T. rex *was up to 13 ft (4 m) tall at the hips.*

HOW MANY BONES DID T. REX HAVE?

No one has yet found a fossilized skeleton of a *T. rex* that is entirely complete, but by studying other dinosaurs, scientists know that the living animal probably had about 380 bones. The most complete skeleton found so far—a specimen named Sue—had 250 bones, but most of the missing ones are tiny.

The largest T. rex *skull found so far is 5 ft (1.54 m) long.*

Long tail counterbalanced the huge body.

Tiny arms had two small digits.

Each foot had four toes, three massively clawed.

IT'S A MYSTERY!

Why did T. rex have such tiny arms?
T. rex's tiny clawed arms probably had little use as weapons. So what did it use these miniature appendages for? We may never know for sure!

COULD T. REX RUN FAST?

Dinosaur speed can be estimated from fossilized footprints, but top speed is difficult to work out. Modern studies of *T. rex* suggest it could not have managed more than about 12 mph (20 km/h). At faster speeds, the leg bones would have shattered under its weight.

WHERE IN THE WORLD DID T. REX LIVE?

All *T. rex* fossils come from what is now western North America. When *T. rex* was alive 70–66 million years ago, the continent was split in two by a huge, shallow sea, making it impossible for *T. rex* to cross to the east.

DID THEY HAVE FEATHERS?

Fossils show that smaller relatives of *T. rex* might have been covered in feathers, possibly to help keep them warm. Patches of *T. rex* skin impressions show the typical scales of dinosaurs. However, it is possible that feathers did not fossilize well or were present on patches that have not been found yet.

Large, air-filled spaces in various skull bones helped reduce its weight.

Fossil impressions show T. rex had scaly skin.

Eyes faced forward, which could have helped T. rex judge distance when chasing prey.

WAS T. REX A HUNTER OR A SCAVENGER?

T. rex had all the hallmarks of a hunter: forward-facing eyes that track distant prey and a powerful killing bite. But, like most meat-eaters, it would happily scavenge on the carcasses of already dead animals when it found them, too.

The largest teeth were 12 in (30 cm) long, including the root. The crown is about half that length.

Jaws could open more than 60 degrees wide to deliver a formidable bite.

Hips and hind legs had the biggest bones of the body—helping support a weight of more than 8.8 tons (8 tonnes).

ARE FUNGI PLANTS?

Many fungi grow from the ground like plants, but they belong to a different group of living things. Whereas plants are powered by light to make their food, fungi extract their food from material around them, such as dead, fallen leaves. There are three main groups.

Yeasts
These microscopic, single-celled fungi feed on sugar and are used in baking and wine-making.

Molds
Many molds grow as woolly tufts on rotten food, but some are used to help flavor cheese.

Mushrooms
The capped stalks of mushrooms and toadstools sprout from fungi that grow underground.

FAST FACTS

2,000 new species of **fungi** are discovered **each year**.

155,000 species have been described **so far**.

A total of **2.5 million** species are thought to **exist**.

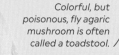

Colorful, but poisonous, fly agaric mushroom is often called a toadstool.

A veil of a thin membrane that once covered the growing mushroom

DO FUNGI HAVE SEEDS?

No. When fungi reproduce, they release spores into the air—sometimes in clouds, like this puffball. Each spore can germinate into a new individual. Unlike plant seeds, which are bigger, tiny spores are just one cell big and float like dust in the air.

WHAT IS A MUSHROOM?

Most fungi produce their spores in stalked caps. Some of the biggest of these are what we call mushrooms. They are sometimes known as "fruiting bodies" of the fungus.

The root threads of fungi are called hyphae. The network of hyphae is known as the mycelium.

QUICK QUIZ!

HOW BIG IS THE BIGGEST FUNGUS ON EARTH?

a: 1.5 sq in (10 sq cm)

b: 108 sq ft (10 sq m)

c: 3.9 sq miles (10 sq km)

FUNGI: Nature's recyclers, including mushrooms, toadstools, molds, and yeasts

WHY ARE FUNGI IMPORTANT?

By feeding on dead waste material, fungi help release nutrients back into the ground, making them available to plants. We also use some fungi to make food and even medicines, such as antibiotics.

HOW DO FUNGI GROW?

The main part of a fungus grows as an underground network of threads that absorbs food from dead and waste material around it. This then occasionally produces a reproductive fruiting body above ground.

Fruiting body grows from stalk.

Mature mushroom releases spores from under its cap.

Threads bunch together to form a stalk.

Spore (magnified) grows a new thread.

Mycelium releases chemicals to digest food.

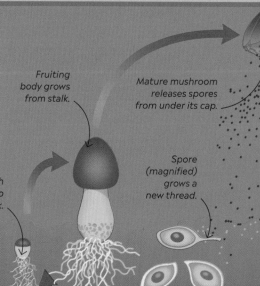

TREES:
Vital to life, these woody giants are some of the biggest and longest-lived organisms on the planet

WHY DO LEAVES CHANGE COLOR?

In cold, dark winters and tropical dry seasons, some trees lose their leaves because photosynthesis is hard. Before the leaves drop, the light-absorbing green pigment chlorophyll breaks down into red and yellow pigments.

WHY DO TREES GROW SO TALL?

Like other plants, trees need light energy to make their food. They grow tall to escape the shade from other vegetation around them. To reach the greatest height, they grow strong, woody trunks to support their weight.

Heartwood in the trunk's center is dead.

Living sapwood carries water up the tree.

Protective outer bark

Spongy layer carries sugars from leaves.

Thin layer forms new sapwood.

Massive coast redwoods can be over 330 ft (100 m) tall.

CAN TREES REALLY TALK TO EACH OTHER?

Trees cannot talk, but they do communicate with each other—with the help of fungi. The underground threads of fungi attach to tree roots to exchange nutrients. Fungi also link trees in a "wood-wide web." Trees use this to send warning signals—stimulating one another, for example, to produce insect-repelling chemicals.

QUICK QUIZ

HOW MANY TREES ARE THERE FOR EACH PERSON ON EARTH?

a: 37

b: 375

c: 3,750

WHY DO TREES HAVE LEAVES?

The leaves of plants work like solar panels to capture energy from sunlight. Plants use this to make sugar in a process called photosynthesis. Thousands of leaves on a single tree add up to a very big area. Trees have different kinds of leaves depending on the type and where they grow.

Trees that produce flowers generally have broad leaves to trap more solar energy.

Cone-producing trees have needlelike leaves to resist cold and wet weather.

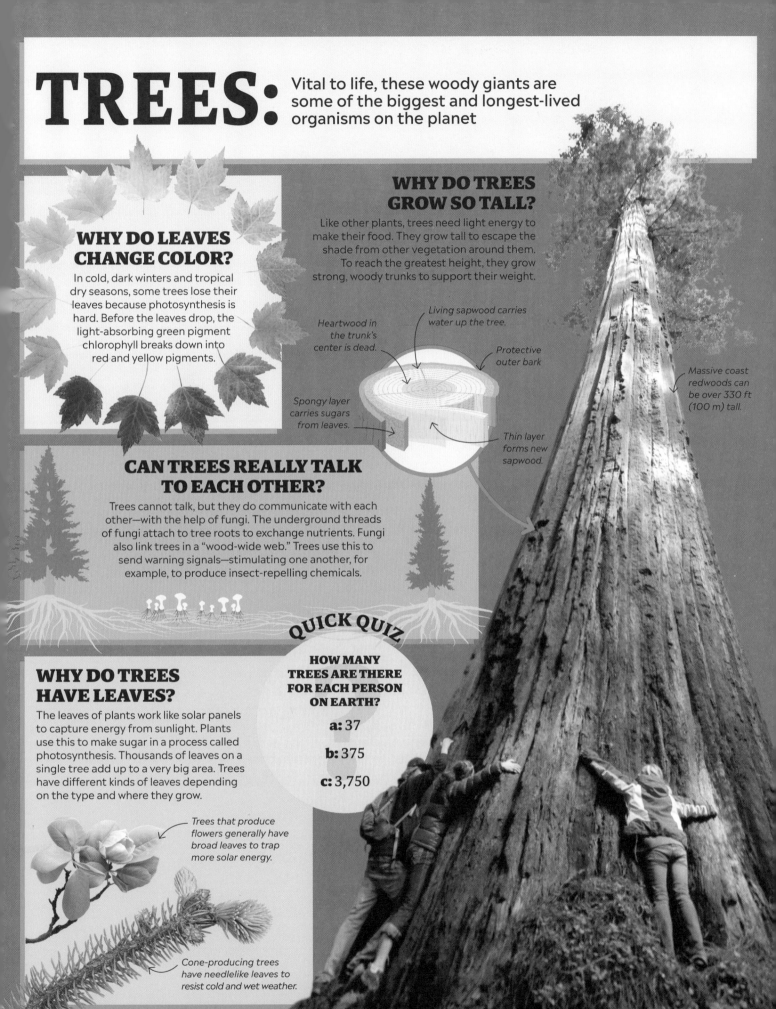

PLANTS: Multicelled living things that make food using sunlight and are essential to animal life

WHY ARE MOST PLANTS GREEN?

Plants make their own food by a process called photosynthesis. The plant captures energy from the Sun to convert carbon dioxide and water into sugar and oxygen. It's a green pigment called chlorophyll in leaves that absorbs the energy needed for this reaction. This is why most plants have green leaves.

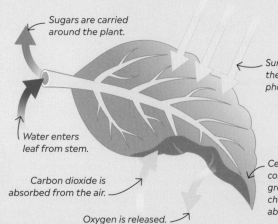

Sugars are carried around the plant.

Sunlight provides the energy for photosynthesis.

Water enters leaf from stem.

Carbon dioxide is absorbed from the air.

Oxygen is released.

Cells in leaves contain the green pigment chlorophyll, which absorbs sunlight.

HOW MANY TYPES OF PLANTS ARE THERE?

There are around 425,000 known species of land plants, from spore-producing liverworts, mosses, and ferns to seed-producing conifers and flowering plants. Liverworts and mosses lack the complex roots and water-transport tubes of other plants and cannot grow as tall. Flowering plants form 96 percent of all plant species.

Liverworts
Simple plants that usually grow as ribbons.

Mosses
Typically grow upward as short, leafy tufts.

Club mosses
Have taller, stiffer stems than true mosses.

Ferns
Mostly have spreading, finely divided leaves.

Conifers
Woody trees with seed-bearing cones.

Flowering plants
Range from tiny tufts to giant trees.

Only the wings, legs, and external skeleton will survive the plant's digestive juices.

Flytrap snaps shut in less than a second when prey is detected.

Sharp spines interlock and stop prey from escaping.

WHY DO SOME PLANTS EAT ANIMALS?

Although plants make their own food, some grow in soil that lacks vital nutrients such as nitrogen. To make up for this, carnivorous plants trap and digest insects. The Venus flytrap can snare a fly in seconds between its spiny leaves. Digestive juices then take about a week to break down the fly's body.

DO PLANTS FEEL PAIN?

Plants cannot feel pain because they lack the pain receptors, nervous system, and brain that are found in animals. However, they can react to physical triggers such as touch.

Cutting a leaf does not hurt it.

DO PLANTS MOVE?

Although most plants are rooted in the ground, their parts can move to reach light and water. Leaves will turn to face the Sun, some flowers close up at night, and climbing plants with touch-sensitive tendrils reach out for objects to coil around.

Curly tendrils grow at the end of stems.

Sweet pea stems can grip onto supports, coiling around them to climb toward the light.

IF ALL PLANTS DIED, COULD ANIMALS SURVIVE?

Plants are vital to life on Earth; without them, animals would die out. This is because, unlike plants, animals cannot make their own food and have to feed on other life forms for survival. Plants are the ultimate food source for all animals, even those that eat other animals.

Bird of prey feeds on small bird.

Small bird feeds on caterpillars.

Caterpillars feed on plants.

Plants produce their own food.

WHY DO SHOOTS GROW UP AND ROOTS GROW DOWN?

Shoots grow upward toward the sunlight, while roots grow downward to find water and minerals in the soil. A plant knows which way to grow because it contains chemicals that work like hormones and make the parts respond to light and gravity.

Shoots grow up toward light and away from the direction of gravity.

Roots grow down, away from the light and in response to the direction of gravity.

IS SEAWEED A PLANT?

Seaweeds are big types of algae that have leafy fronds and grow in the ocean. Like other algae, they do not have the proper roots, stems, and leaves that are found in true plants, so scientists classify them in groups that are separate from the plant kingdom.

IT'S A MYSTERY!

Why do some clovers have four leaves?

Most clovers have three leaves, but some people believe finding a four-leaf clover brings luck. Scientists are not sure if the four-leaf clover is caused by a genetic mutation or the soil it grows in.

WHAT IS THE MOST EXTREME PLACE A PLANT CAN GROW?

Astronauts have grown salad leaves in space, but plants grow in extreme places on Earth, too. Aloes have adapted to survive in some of the planet's harshest deserts, such as in the extremely dry Canary Islands. Their thick, waxy leaves contain a gel that stores water, which helps them thrive in dry periods.

Pollen is produced in anthers at the top of each filament; together, these make up the stamen.

Colorful petals attract insect pollinators, leading them to nectar at the petal's base.

IT'S A MYSTERY!

What color was the first flower?
The earliest fossilized flowers date back to the dinosaur age. Flies and beetles, which are drawn to yellow, were around at that time, but there are no fossil traces to indicate what color the flowers were.

A sticky stigma sits on top of the style and collects pollen; together, these make up the carpel.

A capsule contains ovules; each ovule contains an egg that can be fertilized by pollen and develop into a seed.

WHAT IS THE BIGGEST FLOWER?

The world's biggest single flower also produces the biggest stink! A _Rafflesia_ flower can be wider than a car wheel, but the rest of it lives as a parasite inside a tropical vine—so it has no leaves, stems, or roots. The flower releases the scent of rotting meat to attract pollinating flies.

A single flower can be 3 ft (1 m) across.

WHAT ARE FLOWERS FOR?

Flowers carry the sex organs of a plant. The female organs (carpels) contain eggs, while the male ones (stamens) release pollen. To help pollen reach flowers on separate plants, pollen may be released on the wind. But many plants have colorful flowers to attract pollinators such as bees to carry the pollen for them.

Stem

FLOWERS: The reproductive structures of plants that produce and grow from seeds

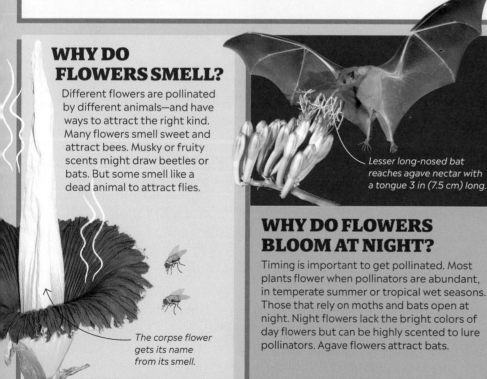

WHY DO FLOWERS SMELL?

Different flowers are pollinated by different animals—and have ways to attract the right kind. Many flowers smell sweet and attract bees. Musky or fruity scents might draw beetles or bats. But some smell like a dead animal to attract flies.

Lesser long-nosed bat reaches agave nectar with a tongue 3 in (7.5 cm) long.

WHY DO FLOWERS BLOOM AT NIGHT?

Timing is important to get pollinated. Most plants flower when pollinators are abundant, in temperate summer or tropical wet seasons. Those that rely on moths and bats open at night. Night flowers lack the bright colors of day flowers but can be highly scented to lure pollinators. Agave flowers attract bats.

The corpse flower gets its name from its smell.

WHY ARE FLOWERS DIFFERENT COLORS?

Different-colored flowers attract different pollinators. Bees are drawn to blue, and birds to red. The pollinators must have good color vision, and sometimes they can even see things that we can't. Many insects and birds see colors and patterns of ultraviolet (UV) light reflected from flowers.

Flower in UV light, as an insect sees it.

Flower in daylight, as we see it.

FRUIT: The seed-bearing part of a flowering plant that develops when the flower is pollinated

HOW DO SEEDS GROW INTO NEW PLANTS?

The seeds inside a fruit contain the makings of a whole new plant. Like other kinds of seeds, beans released from podlike fruits germinate on moist, sunlit ground. The seeds contain a food store to help nourish their early growth.

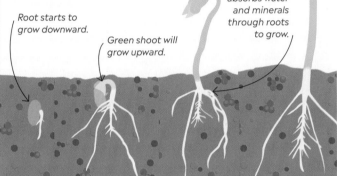

Seedling grows leaves.

Seedling absorbs water and minerals through roots to grow.

Root starts to grow downward.

Green shoot will grow upward.

WHAT'S THE SMELLIEST FRUIT?

Fruits of the durian tree smell like onions, sweaty socks, and honey, but orangutans—and some people—love them! However, the fruit is banned on Singapore's buses because of its pungent aroma.

IF I SWALLOW AN APPLE SEED, WILL A TREE GROW INSIDE ME?

Seeds need the right conditions to grow, including moisture, nutrients, and sunlight. This means they cannot grow inside your stomach. But the seeds of some plants can pass right through an animal's digestive system and germinate after emerging in poop.

DO ALL PLANTS HAVE FRUIT?

Only flowering plants produce true fruit. After a flower is pollinated, a fruit forms around the developing seeds at the base of the female part of the bloom. Nonflowering plants have other ways to disperse their next generation: ferns scatter spores on the wind, while pines scatter seeds from cones.

Fern spores
Ferns scatter tiny spores on the wind from under their fronds.

Conifer seeds
Conifers such as pine trees and fir trees grow seeds in cones, not fruit.

Fruit seeds
The fruit of many flowering plants contain seeds in juicy flesh to help their dispersal.

Stalk where fruit was joined to tree branch.

ARE TOMATOES A FRUIT?

Stores arrange tomatoes with vegetables, but they are really fruit—you can see their seeds if you cut into them. Many fruits are juicy and delicious so that animals will help disperse seeds away from parent plants by eating the fruit and discarding the seeds.

Each seed is joined to the pod by a short stalk.

Seed is inside the hard stone.

Seeds are surrounded by juicy pulp.

Pea
The fruit is a pod containing the seeds.

Hazelnut
The shell is a hard, dry fruit; the kernel inside is a seed.

Peach
The fruit's juicy flesh surrounds an inner shell and stone.

Tomato
The soft and juicy fruit contains numerous seeds.

Pear
Seeds are contained in the fruit's core.

Raspberry
Lots of little fruits are joined together, with a seed in each.

HOW MANY TYPES OF INVERTEBRATES ARE THERE?

More than 95 percent of animal species are invertebrates. Scientists have described about 1,300,000 so far, but millions more may remain to be discovered. These are some of the main groups.

Arthropods
The largest group, these animals with jointed legs include insects, spiders, millipedes, and crustaceans.

Mollusks
Some soft-bodied mollusks, such as snails and clams, have shells. Others, including squid, do not.

Worms
A wormlike shape is good for burrowing, but many worms live as parasites in other animals' bodies.

Echinoderms
These ocean animals have round, long, or star-shaped bodies and include starfish and urchins.

Cnidarians
Aquatic animals with tentacles, they either swim like jellyfish or are fixed to the seabed likes anemones.

FAST FACTS

⭐ The lion's mane **jellyfish** can have **tentacles** that are more than **88 ft** (27 m) long.

⭐ 15,000-year-old **glass sponges** may be the longest-lived animals.

⭐ Microscopic **worms** called **nematodes** may be Earth's most **abundant** animals.

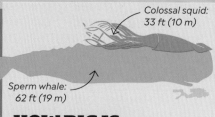
Colossal squid: 33 ft (10 m)

Sperm whale: 62 ft (19 m)

HOW BIG IS THE BIGGEST INVERTEBRATE?

The coconut crab weighs more than a human baby and is the biggest land invertebrate, but ocean invertebrates grow much bigger. Deep-sea colossal squid hold the record—they can grow almost as long as a sperm whale.

ARE CORALS REALLY ANIMALS?

Rocky corals might not look alive, but up close, they have tiny rings of moving tentacles that catch prey. They produce rocky skeletons to protect their colonies.

CAN A WORM GROW BACK IF IT IS CUT IN TWO?

If cut in two, some kinds of tiny worms regenerate easily from either the front or back ends. In earthworms, both parts can die—but if enough of the head end is intact, it may grow a new tail.

Earthworm's front end contains vital organs, such as brain and hearts.

"Saddle" produces egg sac.

INVERTEBRATES:
Animals that do not have a backbone

WHAT DO INVERTEBRATES HAVE INSTEAD OF A SKELETON?

The bodies of most vertebrates are supported by a bony skeleton on the inside. Some invertebrates, including arthropods such as bugs or crabs, have an outer skeleton that works more like a suit of armor. But soft-bodied invertebrates such as this sea slug rely on the pressure of their body fluids to hold their shape.

Sensory tentacles are used for smelling and tasting.

Fingerlike projections contain stinging cells.

Sea slug crawls along on a muscular foot.

OCTOPUSES: Clever invertebrates with eight arms

WHY DO OCTOPUSES MAKE INK?

Most octopuses, as well as related squid and cuttlefishes, have an ink sac in their body that contains a dark pigment called melanin. By squeezing the sac, octopuses squirt the ink into the face of attackers, helping them to escape behind the dark cloud.

Holding on
Rows of suckers along each arm are used for gripping prey and for movement.

WHY DO OCTOPUSES HAVE EIGHT ARMS?

Octopuses have eight arms that they use to walk and swim and to catch and eat food. To control their arms, they have nine brains. Each arm has its own mini-brain, which means it can move independently to react rapidly to stimuli, but a main brain in the octopus's head takes overall charge.

IS IT TRUE THAT OCTOPUSES ARE SUPER-SMART?

An octopus's main brain is shaped like a donut and encircles its food pipe. As a proportion of total body size, no other invertebrate has a bigger brain than octopuses. This helps them find creative ways to solve problems in order to find food or escape from danger.

Small spaces
Being soft-bodied means an octopus can squeeze into tiny hiding places, such as coconut shells or bottles.

Tentacle weapons
Blanket octopuses rip off tentacles from the venomous Portuguese man o' war to use as weapons.

Shell armor
Octopuses make use of objects on the seafloor—even building shelters and body armor from shells.

WHERE ARE BABY OCTOPUSES BORN?

All octopuses hatch from eggs tended by a caring mother, usually in a nursery den on the seafloor. Up to 500,000 eggs are laid in grapelike clusters. Once they hatch, the mother dies and tiny babies float in the ocean plankton before sinking back to the bottom as they grow older.

Hatching octopus

WHY DO OCTOPUSES CHANGE COLOR?

Octopuses have tiny bags of pigment in their skin that shrink or swell to change body color. For some, like the venomous blue-ringed octopus (right), color is a warning. But changing color can also make an octopus blend into its surroundings to hide.

DO ALL INSECTS HAVE SIX LEGS?

All adult insects have six legs and a three-part body. The head carries the brain and main sense organs, the thorax is where the legs and wings are attached, and the abdomen contains the digestive system and reproductive organs. Not all insects have wings—silverfish are among those that do not.

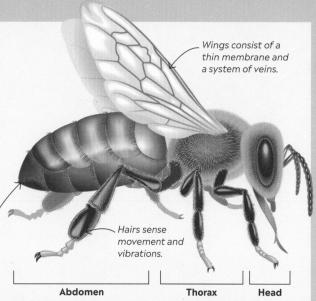

Wings consist of a thin membrane and a system of veins.

Striped abdomen of honey bee acts as a warning to predators.

Hairs sense movement and vibrations.

Abdomen   Thorax   Head

HOW MANY TYPES OF INSECTS ARE THERE?

Scientists classify insects into around 25 different groups. Most species belong to one of the five main types below.

Beetles
Recognizable by their shiny exoskeleton, beetles make up a quarter of all animal species.

Moths and butterflies
This group of insects has big, colorful wings that are covered in tiny scales.

Wasps, bees, and ants
Many of these membrane-winged insects are social and have stings.

True flies
Flies have one pair of wings, a movable head, and large, compound eyes.

Bugs
These insects are known for their sharp mouthparts, used to pierce food.

WHAT IS THE BIGGEST INSECT?

One of the largest and heaviest insects is the giant wētā, found in New Zealand. They can reach 4 in (10 cm) long, and pregnant females can weigh as much as 2.4 oz (70 g)—heavier than a sparrow!

QUICK QUIZ!

HOW MANY TIMES DO A BEE'S WINGS BEAT PER SECOND?

a: 55

b: 110

c: 190

INSECTS: Invertebrates with jointed legs, supported by an external skeleton, and usually having wings

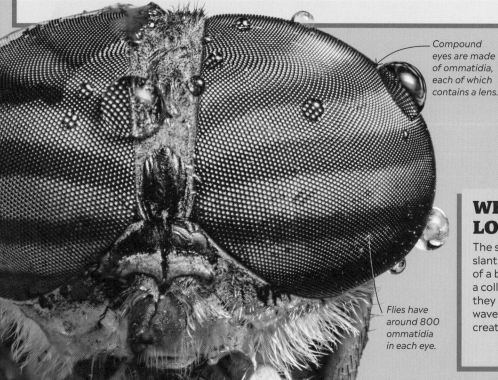

Compound eyes are made of ommatidia, each of which contains a lens.

Flies have around 800 ommatidia in each eye.

HOW MANY EYES DOES A FLY HAVE?

Flies have two eyes, but they are compound eyes. This means that each one is made up of many microscopic lenses. Compound eyes see less detail than a human eye, but they are quicker at spotting movement. Think about how difficult it is to swat a fly!

WHY DO SOME BEETLES LOOK METALLIC?

The shine is caused by tiny, slanting ridges on the surface of a beetle. Similar to a collection of lenses, they reflect different wavelengths of light to create a metallic effect.

74

ANTS:

Highly social and organized insects that live and work together in a structured nest community

WHAT'S INSIDE AN ANT HILL?

Ants are social insects that live together in ant hills. Inside, there is a large, egg-laying queen and many female "worker" ants who protect her, look after the nest, and gather food. The ants work together as a team to ensure the community survives.

Ant eggs become worm-shaped larvae after 3 to 4 weeks.

Larvae develop into pupae before becoming adult ants.

Antennae detect signals and smells.

Ants touch their antennae together to communicate.

DO ANTS TALK TO EACH OTHER?

Yes, they do. Ants communicate by releasing pheromones (chemical signals) to exchange information, such as where food might be. Other ants detect these signals using their antennae, which contain their smell and touch organs.

WHICH INSECT HAS THE MOST PAINFUL STING?

The bullet ant is known for having the world's most painful insect sting. This ant species uses venom that targets nerve cells to inflict pain that is 30 times worse than a bee sting. Lasting for up to 12 hours, it is described as a deep, drilling pain felt in the bones.

DO ANTS HAVE TOES?

Not quite! Like many other insects, ants have two tarsal claws at the end of each of their six legs. This magnified image shows two pairs of these hooked claws. They are used for walking as well as climbing and gripping different types of surfaces.

HOW MUCH CAN AN ANT CARRY?

Ants can carry up to 50 times their body weight, and they even work together to lift heavier objects. Columns of leafcutter ants in Central and South America may be made up of hundreds or even thousands of foraging ants.

Leaf is several times larger than the ant.

Leaf wedges are carved out using an ant's sharp mandibles.

Leaf fragment is gripped in the ant's jaws.

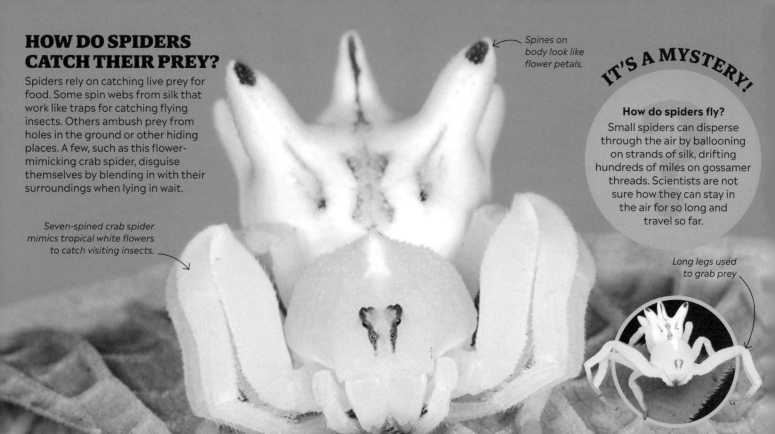

HOW DO SPIDERS CATCH THEIR PREY?

Spiders rely on catching live prey for food. Some spin webs from silk that work like traps for catching flying insects. Others ambush prey from holes in the ground or other hiding places. A few, such as this flower-mimicking crab spider, disguise themselves by blending in with their surroundings when lying in wait.

Spines on body look like flower petals.

Seven-spined crab spider mimics tropical white flowers to catch visiting insects.

IT'S A MYSTERY!

How do spiders fly?
Small spiders can disperse through the air by ballooning on strands of silk, drifting hundreds of miles on gossamer threads. Scientists are not sure how they can stay in the air for so long and travel so far.

Long legs used to grab prey

SPIDERS: Predatory, eight-legged invertebrates that belong to a group called arachnids

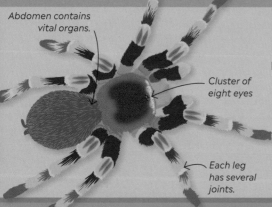

Abdomen contains vital organs.

Cluster of eight eyes

Each leg has several joints.

IS A SPIDER AN INSECT?

Like insects, spiders are jointed-leg animals called arthropods. But whereas insects have six legs and usually have wings, spiders are eight-legged, wingless arachnids.

WHY DON'T SPIDERS GET CAUGHT IN THEIR WEBS?

Only some strands of a spider's web are sticky—and a spider typically avoids walking over these. But the clawed feet of a spider also have special nonstick surfaces that protect the web-maker from getting caught in its own trap.

DO ALL SPIDERS HAVE VENOM?

Almost all spiders, like this large huntsman, kill prey by injecting it with venom from fangs. The exception is hackled orbweavers—the only spiders without venom glands, they wrap prey tightly in silk to subdue it.

DO SPIDERS ALL MAKE SILK?

Yes. Silk can be strong enough to cocoon eggs or delicate enough to carry the vibrations of struggling prey in a web. It all starts as a liquid in glands, turning to solid threads as the spider teases it out of its rear end with its legs.

CRABS:
Invertebrates with a hard, shell-like external skeleton that belong to a group of animals called crustaceans

WHY DO CRABS DRESS UP?

For many crabs, nipping claws are a good defense, but some—especially small ones—use camouflage, too. Decorator crabs attach objects to their shell using bits of seaweed and even sometimes sea urchins (above) so they can blend into the seabed and escape the attention of predators.

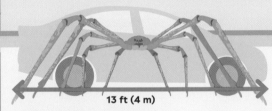

13 ft (4 m)

WHICH CRAB IS THE BIGGEST?

The Japanese spider crab lives in the deep waters of the Northwest Pacific, where it grows legs longer than an adult human. It relies on the water to support its 44-lb (20-kg) weight.

DO ALL CRABS LIVE IN THE SEA?

Most crabs live in freshwaters or the sea, where they breathe underwater using gills like fish. However, some can breathe on land and spend their lives there. These include the world's biggest land invertebrate—the coconut crab. This 10-lb (4.5-kg) giant even climbs trees in its tropical island home.

Body of coconut crab contains lunglike organs for breathing air.

QUICK QUIZ!

WHERE DOES THE YETI CRAB LIVE?

a: In cold Siberian lakes

b: In Himalayan snow

c: Near hot, deep-sea volcanic vents

WHY DO FIDDLER CRABS HAVE ONE BIG CLAW?

Most crabs have 10 legs, but the front two legs are used as grasping claws to grab food or for defense. In some crabs, one claw is bigger than the other. Fiddler crabs wave the big claw to signal to mates and competitors.

In some crabs, such as this one, the left claw is biggest; in others, it is the right.

Large claw works like a signal or as a strong pincer for defense.

Small claw is used to pick up bits of food.

Crab's head, thorax, and abdomen are fused into one boxlike body.

Fiddler crabs stand tall on their strong legs and can run fast.

CAN CRABS ONLY WALK SIDEWAYS?

Most crabs find it easier to walk sideways than straight ahead. This is because their bodies have legs splayed out from the sides and their joints bend this way, too. As the legs flex and stretch, they pull the body to the left or right.

FISH:

Animals that live in water, and have gills for breathing and fins for swimming

Water flows into the open mouth.

Water passes over gills and oxygen is taken in.

HOW DO FISH BREATHE UNDERWATER?

Fish get the oxygen they need from the water around them. Water flows in through the mouth and out through feathery gills. The gills take oxygen from the water, which then passes into the bloodstream.

DO ALL FISH LAY EGGS?

Most fish lay eggs, but a few give birth to live young. Some scatter their eggs and leave them, but others are better parents. Male seahorses incubate eggs in a pouch and give birth to the hatchlings.

WHAT TYPES OF FISH ARE THERE?

More than 90 percent of fish species have bony skeletons. The rest are mainly sharks and rays (with skeletons of rubbery cartilage) and jawless fish.

Bony fish
These fish live in both saltwater and freshwater.

Cartilaginous fish
Most sharks and rays live in saltwater in the oceans.

Jawless fish
Lampreys and hagfishes have suckerlike mouths.

WHAT'S THE FASTEST FISH?

The fastest fish in the open ocean have torpedo-shaped bodies to cut through water. The sailfish can reach more than 68 mph (110 km/h). To swim forward, most fish rely on muscles that swing their body from side to side. Fins keep the body steady.

DO FISH DRINK?

Freshwater fish absorb so much water through their bodies that they rarely drink. In the ocean, salt draws out water from the body, so saltwater fish have to drink seawater, excreting excess salt, to live.

QUICK QUIZ!

OCEAN SUNFISH LAY MORE EGGS THAN ANY OTHER FISH. HOW MANY?

a: 300,000

b: 3,000,000

c: 300,000,000

HOW MANY FISH ARE THERE IN THE SEA?

No one knows how many fish there are. Freshwater rivers and lakes have as many species as saltwater seas, but the oceans have much bigger numbers and shoals of one kind. Deep-sea lightfishes could be the most abundant of all—numbering thousands of trillions.

Queen angelfish lives in subtropical seas.

Long toes and strong legs help the frog jump.

Legs extend to propel frog forward.

Five-toed feet are webbed for swimming.

Jellylike eggs (frogspawn) are laid in water.

Swimming tadpoles have gills.

Tadpole grows legs before tail starts to be absorbed.

Frog grows bigger and legs grow stronger.

Air-breathing froglet moves onto land.

DO ALL FROGS START LIFE AS TADPOLES?

Many frog species follow the life cycle of the common frog (left), but many develop differently. Some lay eggs that hatch directly into tiny froglets, and a few even give birth to live young.

Frogs live near water to keep their skin wet.

A third eyelid protects the eyes and frog can see underwater.

CAN AXOLOTLS REALLY GROW NEW LEGS?

Many animals have special tissues that can rebuild major body parts, such as limbs. Most of these regenerating creatures are invertebrates. Axolotls and other salamanders are unusual among vertebrates because they can regrow limbs lost through injury.

Axolotol

DO FROGS HOLD THEIR BREATH WHEN THEY DIVE?

Air-breathing animals hold their breath when submerged, but this is no problem for frogs. Tadpoles have gills, while adult frogs breathe using lungs like us, but oxygen seeps through their moist skin, too—both on land and in water.

AMPHIBIANS: Moist-skinned animals that live both on land and in water

WHAT ARE THE MAIN KINDS OF AMPHIBIANS?

Over 90 percent of amphibian species are frogs and toads. Here are the main groups:

Frogs and toads
Most frogs have short bodies with longer hind legs; those with drier, warty skin are called toads.

Newts and salamanders
Some of these tailed amphibians live in water, while others live in caves, burrows, or shady forests.

Caecilians
Most of these worm-shaped amphibians burrow through leaf litter and soil.

IT'S A MYSTERY!

Why does the olm live so long?
The olm is a pale salamander with feathery gills that lives in dark underground caves in southern Europe. It can live for 100 years—but no one knows why.

WHAT IS THE MOST POISONOUS FROG?

Many amphibians rely on poisons for defense. The slimy skin of a yellow poison frog from the Amazon rainforest could kill 10 adult humans if they touched it.

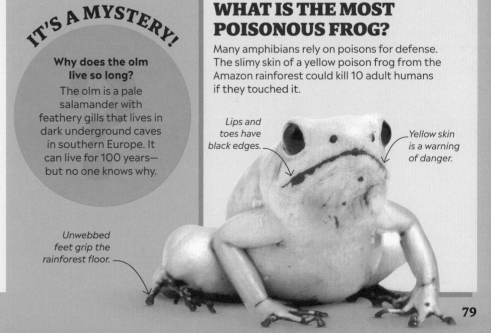

Lips and toes have black edges.

Yellow skin is a warning of danger.

Unwebbed feet grip the rainforest floor.

SHARKS:

Fishes with rough, sandpaperlike skin and skeletons made of rubbery cartilage instead of bone

WHAT IS THE BIGGEST SHARK?

The biggest shark alive today is also the world's biggest fish. A whale shark grows as long as a bus—120 times bigger than the smallest shark species.

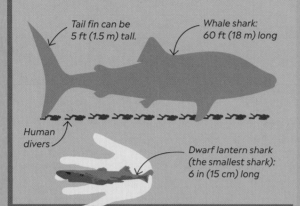

Tail fin can be 5 ft (1.5 m) tall.

Whale shark: 60 ft (18 m) long

Human divers

Dwarf lantern shark (the smallest shark): 6 in (15 cm) long

HOW MANY TEETH DO SHARKS HAVE?

Sharks have many more teeth than humans, and the amount varies between different species. Teeth grow constantly and are replaced. Great whites have about 300 teeth at one time but can go through thousands in their lifetime.

DO SHARKS EAT PEOPLE?

Only a few species of sharks have been known to attack people. Great white sharks hunt seals and occasionally mistake a swimming human for their usual prey. Bull sharks swim up rivers, so they come close to humans and might attack. However, most sharks are harmless—more sharks are killed by people each year than people by sharks.

HOW MANY TYPES OF SHARKS ARE THERE?

There are more than 600 species of sharks. Some are smaller than an otter, while others grow larger than a dolphin. Most sharks, such as these lemon sharks, live in coastal waters, but some species hunt in the open ocean far from land or deep in the darkest depths.

Pointed teeth lack the serrated edges found on teeth of many other sharks.

HOW DO SHARKS FIND THEIR PREY?

Sharks have excellent senses to help them locate prey in the ocean. They can smell blood and flesh from miles (kilometers) away and—as they swim closer—can detect slight movements in the water and even electrical signals coming from the movement of their target.

Tail thrust can give a quick burst of speed.

Eye allows 360° vision.

Tiny, jelly-filled pores detect electrical fields generated by fish moving in water.

Widely spaced nostrils can locate the source of the scent of blood.

Sensory cells in the hammer-shaped head of this species pick up smells.

Hammerhead shark

ARE ALL SHARKS HUNTERS?

Most sharks have knifelike teeth and a taste for meat, which makes them top predators in the ocean. But some have specialized diets. Bullhead sharks have flatter teeth for crunching shellfish. Whale sharks and basking sharks are filter feeders, gulping seawater to strain, then eat tiny plankton.

DO SHARKS LAY EGGS?

Some sharks, such as catsharks, lay egg capsules that sink to the seafloor. But for most, the young grow inside them in a womb, connected by an umbilical cord, like a mammal. These sharks give birth to live young. In tiger sharks, the strongest babies eat the weaker ones while still in the womb.

Two triangular dorsal (back) fins steady the body and often stick out of the water.

Brownish-yellow color gives lemon shark its name.

Lemon sharks gather in groups of up to 20 individuals.

Remora fish cling to sharks, eat parasites, and hitch a free journey.

Small eyes are typical of shark species that hunt in shallow, brightly lit waters.

IT'S A MYSTERY!

Where do sharks give birth?

Many sharks, such as blacktip reef sharks, give birth in shark nurseries along coastlines, where the water is warm and predator-free and food plentiful. But no one knows if great white sharks give birth in nurseries—or where these might be.

HOW DOES A CHAMELEON CHANGE ITS COLOR?

Chameleons have a unique way of changing color—their skin has microscopic crystals that bunch together or scatter apart to reflect light of different colors, all controlled by their brain. This is different from other animals, such as octopuses, which change color with tiny sacs of pigment in their skin that shrink and swell.

WHY DO REPTILES HAVE SCALES?

Hard scales help prevent reptiles from drying out and can protect them. Many reptiles have colorful scales, too, to attract mates or warn others they are venomous. There are different types of scales.

Radiated tortoise
Big scales grow on bony plates that make up the protective shell.

Nile crocodile
Crocodile scales have bony supports, too—but more like a flexible suit of armor.

Boa constrictor
Overlapping back scales allow flexible motion, while wide belly scales provide grip.

Colors get brighter when chameleon is excited.

Small, transparent scales cover color-reflecting crystals.

Panther chameleon

REPTILES:
Air-breathing animals with a backbone and scaly skin

DO ALL REPTILES LAY EGGS?

Turtles, crocodiles, and most lizards and snakes lay hard-shelled eggs. Unlike birds, which sit on their eggs, reptiles rely on the warmth of the surroundings to incubate theirs. A few kinds of lizards and snakes are live-bearing—this means they give birth to their babies.

Tokay gecko hatchling emerges from egg.

Draco lizard extends arms with skin flaps to glide.

CAN ANY REPTILES FLY?

Apart from birds, which are really feathered reptiles, the only reptiles capable of powered flight with flapping wings were extinct pterosaurs—and they included the biggest flying animals ever. Today, there are lizards and even snakes that occasionally glide through the air—such as the draco lizard, which glides from tree to tree on leathery skin flaps.

HOW MANY TYPES OF REPTILES ARE THERE?

More than 12,100 species of reptiles are known. Lizards and snakes together make up over 95 percent of them.

Turtles
There are around 365 species of turtles and tortoises.

Crocodilians
Crocodiles, alligators, and gharials make up 27 species.

Lizards and snakes
More than 7,400 lizards and 4,100 snake species are known.

Tuatara
A single species survives from this prehistoric group.

TURTLES:

Reptile group that includes both aquatic turtles and land-living tortoises, which have a body encased in a bony shell

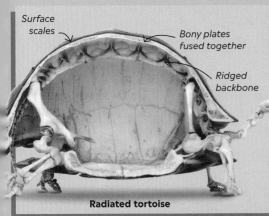

Surface scales

Bony plates fused together

Ridged backbone

Radiated tortoise

WHAT IS UNDER A TURTLE'S SHELL?

A turtle or tortoise's shell is made from interconnected bony plates and covered by horny scales. Beneath that are muscles and vital organs. The upper plates are attached to the backbone and ribs, making the body rigid. But the shell has openings so the legs, head, and tail can move. Many species can pull their limbs in for protection.

WHAT DO TURTLES EAT?

Most aquatic turtles eat invertebrates, such as shellfish. Many marine species—such as green sea turtles (above)—eat jellyfish. The largest, leatherbacks, feast exclusively on jellyfish; their scaly skin protects them from the sting. Land-living tortoises are mainly vegetarian.

HOW DO TURTLES BREATHE IN WATER?

Turtles, which have lungs and breathe air, must come to the surface to take a breath. But some freshwater turtles can stay under water for long periods, absorbing oxygen through their skin or even bottoms!

Webbed feet for swimming

Bottom opening (cloaca)

Oxygen is absorbed from air chambers.

QUICK QUIZ!

WHAT GIVES THE GREEN SEA TURTLE ITS NAME?

a: Green body fat

b: A green shell

c: Green skin

Hatchlings use their forelimbs to pull themselves toward the sea.

Short, spoon-shaped hind limbs

HOW LONG CAN A TORTOISE LIVE FOR?

Giant tortoises can live for over a century, but it is hard to confirm when old-timers hatched. A Seychelles giant tortoise is thought to have turned 191 in 2024.

Galápagos tortoise

HOW DO BABY TURTLES SWIM?

Baby ocean turtles like this green sea turtle hatch at night from eggs buried on a sandy beach. They instinctively make for starlight reflected on water, dashing across the sand to avoid predators. Born knowing how to swim—by paddling with their flippers—they head rapidly for the open sea, where they ride on ocean currents.

Long, paddle-shaped forelimbs for pushing through water

SNAKES:

Reptiles with long, slender bodies that lack legs, expert at hunting other animals

DO ALL SNAKES LIVE ON LAND?

No—many kinds of snakes can swim. True sea snakes spend their lives in water, even giving birth there—they only need to surface to breathe. Other aquatic snakes, such as sea kraits (above), must come ashore to lay eggs on land.

HOW DO SNAKES KILL AND EAT THEIR PREY?

Apart from egg-eating snakes, all snakes kill moving prey for food. Some constrict prey until it is dead, while others kill with venom. All have flexible jaws that can open wide enough to swallow prey whole without chewing.

HOW DO SNAKES MOVE WITHOUT LEGS?

A snake has lots of muscles running along the side of its body that enable it to bend in different places and twist and turn. These curves catch against the ground and surrounding objects to help push the body forward. Legless lizards such as slow worms move in similar ways.

Gaboon viper fangs are up to 2 in (5 cm) long.

WHAT IS THE DEADLIEST SNAKE?

The Gaboon viper has the biggest fangs of any snake but is a shy forest dweller that rarely bites people, so it is seldom deadly. Australia's inland taipan has the most potent venom, but it meets few people in the outback. By contrast, tiny saw-scaled vipers are common in villages across Africa and Asia, so the bite risk is greater—and they probably kill more people than any other snake.

Why are there no snakes in Ireland and New Zealand?

Some places have no snakes. Maybe snakes never reached these islands or ice age climates made it impossible for them to survive there. No one knows for sure.

IT'S A MYSTERY!

Slit pupils may help vipers focus. Snake vision is better than their hearing.

Pit contains sensors for detecting body heat of prey.

Nostril

Two tongue tips pick up scents coming from different directions.

IS IT TRUE THAT SNAKES HAVE EXTRA SENSES?

The flickering tongue of a snake can "smell" the air, helping detect food and danger. The forked tip collects the scent and delivers it to a special sense organ on the roof of their mouth. Snakes such as vipers that target warm-blooded prey also have heat-sensing pits on their head to pick up the trail of a meal.

ARE CROCODILES SMART?

Crocodilians are among the smartest of reptiles. Recent studies suggest that they even use tools to hunt. They have been spotted using sticks to lure birds looking for nest material, then grabbing the birds when they are close enough. They also make good parents, caring for newly hatched babies and protecting them from intruders.

WHAT IS THE DIFFERENCE BETWEEN AN ALLIGATOR AND A CROCODILE?

There are three crocodilian families: crocodiles, alligators (including caimans), and gharials. Their jaws are the best way to tell them apart. Crocodiles have narrower, more V-shaped jaws than broad-nosed alligators, and some teeth are visible even when the jaws are closed. Gharials have very slender jaws.

Crocodile

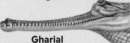

Alligator

Gharial

HOW POWERFUL IS A CROCODILE'S BITE?

One of the largest crocodile species may have the strongest bite of any living animals. The Nile crocodile's bite is 30 times that of a human. Only a great white shark might have a stronger bite, but this is uncertain, because no one has yet measured a living shark's bite!

WHAT ARE CROCODILE TEARS?

We say that someone weeps crocodile tears when they cry but are not actually sad. In fact, crocodiles produce tears like other animals to help keep the eyes clean and free from grit—but saltwater crocodiles also use them to get rid of excess salt.

CROCODILES:

Large, thick-skinned reptiles with powerful jaws that spend much of their lives in water

HOW MANY TEETH DO CROCODILES HAVE?

Most crocodiles have 60 to 70 teeth at any one time—but the number varies from species to species. Fish-eating gharials have more than 100. Crocodiles replace their teeth whenever they drop out, so they can go through thousands in a lifetime.

Saltwater crocodiles can reach 23 ft (7 m) in length.

Webbed feet used for paddling in water.

Conical teeth for gripping prey are up to 5 in (13 cm) long.

Hooked barbules

Main shaft

Barbs branch from shaft.

IT'S A MYSTERY!

Why don't birds have teeth?
The dinosaur ancestors of birds had teeth, but birds evolved to have beaks and no teeth. Scientists have many theories, including diet and the time it takes to grow teeth, but they don't really know.

HOW DO FEATHERS KEEP BIRDS DRY?

Feathers have barbs on either side of the main shaft that interlock with minute hooks. Birds use their bill to smear the feathers with oil from a gland at the base of their tail, zipping the barbs together. The oil helps make the plumage waterproof, so when it rains, water droplets run right off.

WHY ARE EGGS EGG-SHAPED?

The typical egg shape—with one end more pointed than the other—may help eggs pack together in a nest for incubation without rolling away. Some birds, such as owls, lay round eggs in tree holes, where rolling is less of a problem.

Long-eared owl eggs

BIRDS: Animals with warm-blooded bodies covered in feathers; a toothless beak; scaly, clawed feet; and wings

Flight feathers extend from rear side of wing.

WHY DO BIRDS HAVE FEATHERS?

Birds are the only feathered animals today. Multitasking feathers evolved from the scales of reptile ancestors. By trapping air close to the skin, downy feathers keep the body warm, while stiff flight feathers help lift a bird into the air in flight. Colored feathers can also be useful for showing off to mates or as a disguise for camouflage.

Ostrich's big toe carries most of the weight.

HOW MANY TOES DO BIRDS HAVE?

Most birds have four-toed feet, usually with three toes pointing forward and one back. But some birds, such as emus and bustards, have three toes in total and ostriches have just two— all the better for running.

Flight feathers of tail connect behind wings.

Tail feather

Wing feather

Body feather

Down feather

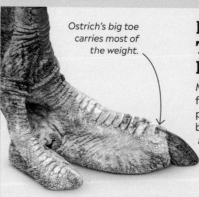

WHY DO PARROTS SPEAK SO WELL?

Many birds are natural mimics. Starlings, mockingbirds, and lyrebirds can all copy sounds. Copying calls from others can help birds sing more elaborate songs to attract mates. Parrots are possibly best known for copying human speech, but are not among the birds that typically mimic in the wild, and no one knows why.

HELLO

WHY DO SOME BIRDS DANCE?

Whereas many mammals rely on scent to attract mates, birds use more visual signals. Some use flamboyant plumage, while others perform acrobatic displays in flight or as a dance. And some—such as birds of paradise—do both together. It is often the male of the pair, such as this magnificent riflebird (male on the left), that puts on a dazzling performance to attract a female.

Lilac-breasted roller

HOW DO BIRDS FLY?

A flying bird must push forward and upward to overcome gravity. The push (thrust) comes from flapping its wings. A streamlined body helps it cut through the air. The shape of the wings and their long flight feathers provide lift. A lightweight skeleton, efficient lungs, and fast conversion of food into energy all help, too.

WHICH BIRD BUILDS THE BIGGEST NEST?

Different kinds of birds build different nests. Some build delicate cups from grass and moss, while others build sturdy platforms from sticks, or elaborate shapes from mud. The huge communal nest of a sociable weaver—accommodating hundreds of birds—is one of the biggest.

Covert feathers help air flow smoothly over wings.

Moving tail helps steer and brake.

DO ALL BIRDS EAT WORMS?

Some birds eat insects, worms, or the meat of bigger animals. Others eat fruit, nectar, or leaves. The shape of a bird's bill is adapted to its diet.

Insect eater
Thin, pointed bill snatches insects, spiders, and worms.

Seed eater
Wide, stubby bill crushes hard seeds and nuts.

Fish eater
Saw-edged bill grabs slippery fish.

Meat eater
Hooked bill kills prey and shreds the meat.

Filter feeder
Specialized bill strains tiny algae or shrimp from water.

Probe feeder
Long bill reaches deep into mud for buried animals.

DO PENGUIN DADS RAISE THE CHICKS?

In most penguins, both parents share the responsibility of raising chicks over a single summer. It takes longer for big emperor penguins, so each father incubates a single egg and cares for the chick through the bitter Antarctic winter while the mothers feed at sea. They return in springtime to help feed both the chick and the father.

Fluffy down helps trap body heat.

FAST FACTS

Emperor penguins can live in **-40°F** (-40°C) temperatures.

Galápagos penguins can live in temperatures as high as **86°F** (30°C).

Emperor penguins weigh up to **100 lb** (46 kg).

Little penguins weigh just **4.6 lb** (2.1 kg).

WHY ARE PENGUINS BLACK AND WHITE?

This coloring helps protect penguins in waters patrolled by predatory sharks and leopard seals. A dark back helps them blend into the ocean when viewed from above, while a white belly blends with the bright surface when viewed from below.

Gentoo penguins can be recognized by a white spot behind their eye.

PENGUINS: Flightless birds that live in the southern hemisphere, with wings shaped like flippers for swimming

WHY DO PENGUINS HUDDLE TOGETHER?

To stay warm in the freezing Antarctic, emperor penguins huddle together on the ice. The ones on the outside of the huddle trap the body heat of those in the middle, warming them up. They keep moving so each gets a turn in the center.

WHY CAN'T PENGUINS FLY?

Antarctic predators live in the ocean rather than on land, so penguins have evolved to avoid capture underwater. Instead of wings for flying, they have flipperlike wings for swimming.

Small, scaly feathers work like a wetsuit.

Flipperlike wings are too small to provide lift.

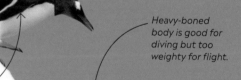

Heavy-boned body is good for diving but too weighty for flight.

ARE THERE DIFFERENT TYPES?

There are nearly 20 species of penguins, ranging in size from the little penguin of Australasia to the emperor penguin of Antarctica. The six shown here represent the main groups. Just a few of these live on Antarctica. Most live on shores and islands farther north.

Emperor penguin

Chinstrap penguin

Little penguin

Rockhopper penguin

Humboldt penguin

Yellow-eyed penguin

Fish-eating osprey flies over lakes with its strong wings to scan for prey.

HOW DO RAPTORS HUNT?

Raptors (also known as birds of prey) rely on super-senses to locate their prey. Those that hunt during the day, including hawks, falcons, and ospreys, can see prey from high in the sky. Night-hunting owls listen to prey moving in the dark.

Tail feathers fan out in flight.

WHY DO SOME RAPTORS LIVE IN CITIES?

Like other animals such as foxes, raptors have made a home in cities, because the living is easy. Peregrine falcons prey on trash-eating city pigeons. Cliff-nesting raptors such as red-tailed hawks (below) nest on building ledges.

Bill is used to tear fish apart.

DO ALL RAPTORS HUNT PREY?

Almost all raptors are meat-eaters, but not all attack moving prey. Some scavenge from carcasses of dead animals. The Egyptian vulture has a fondness for eggs—and is skilled at throwing down stones to shatter their shells.

Curved talons and spiky soles help grip slippery fish.

RAPTORS:

Meat-eating birds with a hooked bill and taloned feet for killing prey

Osprey turns fish to face direction of flight so it is streamlined.

HOW DO OWLS SEE AT NIGHT?

Because all eyes must be stimulated by light rays to work, no animal can see in pitch darkness. But owls have extra-sensitive eyes for working in very low light. Owl eyes are so big that they can collect the dimmest rays.

Eyes cannot roll in sockets, so owl must move its entire head to look around.

Maximum wingspan: 10.5 ft (3.2 m)

Typical human armspan: 5.3 ft (1.6 m)

QUICK QUIZ!

HOW DOES THE SECRETARY BIRD KILL PREY?

a: Throws mice from sky

b: Harpoons fish

c: Stomps on snakes

WHAT IS THE BIGGEST BIRD OF PREY?

South America's Andean condor is the world's largest living raptor. Out of all birds, only albatrosses and pelicans have bigger wingspans. The condor soars as it scans the mountains for meat, flapping its wings as little as it can to save energy.

WHAT'S THE SMALLEST MAMMAL?

The smallest mammals are bats, shrews, and mice—and there are many different species of them all. The tiniest by weight, just 0.04 oz (1.2 g), is the Etruscan shrew; the smallest by length, from 1.1 in (28 mm) long, is Kitti's hog-nosed bat (left).

Tiny head has smallest skull of any mammal.

DO ALL MAMMALS GIVE BIRTH?

Most mammals give birth to live young, producing well-developed babies after long pregnancies. Marsupials, with short pregnancies, give birth to underdeveloped babies. A tiny minority of species, called monotremes, lay eggs.

Placentals
These mammals—including humans—nourish babies in the womb with a placenta for varying lengths of time.

Marsupials
Found in Australasia and America, marsupials include opossums, possums, quolls, kangaroos, and bandicoots.

Monotremes
Confined to Australasia, monotremes include echidnas and platypuses.

HOW MANY BABIES CAN A RABBIT HAVE?

Most mammals produce more than one baby at a time, in litters. The record number of rabbit babies in a single litter is 24. The biggest litters of all (up to 36) are produced by hedgehoglike Madagascan mammals called tenrecs.

Domesticated rabbits are born different colors.

QUICK QUIZ!
WHICH OF THESE MAMMALS IS TOOTHLESS?

a: Giant anteater

b: Armadillo

c: Aardvark

MAMMALS:
Warm-blooded, furry animals that feed their young from the mother's milk

WHY DO SOME MAMMALS LIVE IN THE SEA?

The first mammals lived on land, but some evolved ways of getting food underwater and flippers for swimming. Today, some—such as whales and unrelated dugongs—spend their whole lives in water. Others, such as seals and sea lions, live on land and in water.

Dugongs have paddlelike forelimbs and a dolphinlike tail.

FAST FACTS

- There are **6,459** known **species** of mammals.

- **Rodents** are the biggest mammal group, making up **41%** of species.

- The second largest mammal group, **bats** make up **23%** of species.

- All mammals have **hair**, but **whales** only have a **few strands** before they are born.

Tiny dormouse hibernates in dead leaves in winter.

WHY DO MAMMALS HIBERNATE?

It takes a lot of food to fuel warm-blooded mammals, so many survive cold winter months, when food is scarce, by hibernating. They become inactive and their body temperature and heart rate drop, so they need less fuel to stay alive.

WHAT IS A MONOTREME?

Monotreme means "one hole"—and refers to the fact that these animals pee, poop, and lay eggs through one opening, called a cloaca. This is the same as in reptiles. Monotremes are the only mammals that lay eggs. Although they do feed their young with milk, like other mammals, they lack nipples. Instead, mothers "sweat" milk onto a belly patch for the babies, called puggles, to drink.

Dense, waterproof fur provides insulation.

Platypus stores fat reserves in its broad, flat tail.

ARE THERE ANY VENOMOUS MAMMALS?

Some shrews and slow lorises have a toxic bite that can immobilize prey. But male platypuses, uniquely among mammals, have a venomous spine on their hind ankles—used in defense and when fighting their own kind. A stab is excruciatingly painful. Male echidnas have an ankle spine, too—but it lacks venom.

Platypus propels itself through water with webbed limbs.

Lines of electric receptors detect signals created by prey's muscular activity.

Touch sensors detect water movement.

WHY DO PLATYPUSES HAVE DUCK BILLS?

All monotremes have a bill covered with sensitive rubbery skin. This is a pointed bill in echidnas to probe for ants or worms, and a wide duck bill in platypuses for sweeping through water. The platypus bill has touch and electric sensors that detect prey, such as insect larvae and crayfish.

Echidna egg is laid and then kept in a pouch until it hatches.

WHY DO MONOTREMES LAY EGGS?

Monotremes belong to a group of mammals that split away at the time of the dinosaurs and kept the egg-laying behavior of their reptile ancestors right up to the present day. All other mammals evolved to give birth to live young.

HOW MANY TYPES OF MONOTREMES ARE THERE?

There just five species of monotremes alive today: one species of platypus and four types of echidna—three long-nosed and one short-nosed. All live in either Australia or the island of New Guinea.

Short-nosed echidna rolls into a spiny ball when danger threatens.

Echidna

MONOTREMES:
Mammals with some primitive reptilelike features, including laying hard-shelled eggs

ELEPHANTS:

Enormous, plant-eating animals with a long, muscular snout called a trunk

FAST FACTS

Asian and African elephants can **live** for up to **70 years** in the wild.

African elephants **drink** around **10 buckets** (32 gallons/120 liters) of water a day.

Asian elephants live in **13 countries** but are **extinct** in many regions.

DO ELEPHANTS LIVE IN THE JUNGLE?

There are three species of elephants, and their names offer clues about where they live. African bush elephants live in grasslands and deserts, while rarer African forest elephants roam in rainforests, or jungles. Asian elephants (right) live in both grasslands and forests across South and Southeast Asia. All elephants avoid steep areas, as flatter land is easier to travel across.

CAN ELEPHANTS GET A SNOTTY TRUNK?

Just like a human's nose, the trunk has a lining of mucus to stop dust and germs from reaching the lungs. When an elephant is ill, its trunk gets snotty, just like our noses do. The elephant can suck up water and blow this out along with the mucus to clear its trunk.

The trunk is packed with muscles and lacks bone, making it very flexible.

Long eyelashes protect the eye from dust.

African elephant tusks measure around 6 ft (2 m) long.

Tip of trunk can be used like fingers to pick up objects. African elephants have two "fingers."

DO ALL ELEPHANTS HAVE TUSKS?

All African elephants have tusks, but only some male Asian elephants. The tusks are large teeth that grow outside the mouth. They have many uses, from clearing a way through forests to fighting for mates.

Skull of a male Asian elephant

Tusks grow throughout the elephant's life.

HOW BIG IS AN ELEPHANT?

The African bush elephant is the world's largest living land animal. The Asian elephant is not as big and can be told apart by its smaller ears. Four pillarlike legs support an elephant's massive bulk. The legs are straighter than those of other animals to carry the body weight, and the leg bones are solid for extra strength.

African bush elephant 6.6 tons (6 tonnes)

Asian elephant 5.5 tons (5 tonnes)

WHY DO RODENTS HAVE TAILS?

Not all rodents have tails, but those that do use them for a range of activities, from swimming to climbing. Tails also help with balance, temperature, and communication.

Beaver's tail
This flat tail works as a paddle when swimming and can be slapped on the water to warn other beavers of danger.

Black rat's tail
This rat's long, thin tail moves from side to side for balance. The furless tail also loses heat to keep the rat cool.

Red squirrel's tail
A squirrel also uses its tail for balance and to regulate its temperature. In the cold, the tail can give extra warmth.

Harvest mouse's tail
This tail can grasp plant stalks as the mouse climbs.

DO MICE REALLY EAT CHEESE?

If cheese is on offer, a house mouse might have a nibble, because it is tempted by any food in a home. However, most of the more than 1,000 mouselike rodents forage outdoors, eating a mixture of plants and animals, including grasses, grains, seeds, fruit, bark, insects, and worms.

QUICK QUIZ!

WHAT IS THE BIGGEST RODENT?

a: Squirrel

b: Capybara

c: Beaver

Large ears aid hearing and help the mouse cool down.

Wood mouse has a white belly (house mouse is more gray-brown).

Tail is roughly the same length as the body.

Large back feet help the mouse leap.

RODENTS: Mammals with four continuously growing front teeth used for gnawing

WHY DO RODENTS HAVE SUCH BIG TEETH?

Rodents gnaw, which wears down the teeth, so the teeth are always growing. They lack canine teeth but have cheek teeth (premolars and molars).

Silvery mole rat

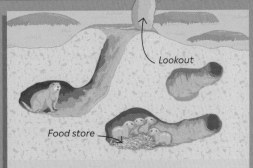

Lookout

Food store

WHICH RODENTS LIVE IN BURROWS?

Prairie dogs, like many rodents, live in groups underground. They dig large burrow systems with rooms for sleeping and food storage, all connected by tunnels. Above ground, lookouts alert the colony to danger.

DO YOU GET HAMSTERS IN THE WILD?

Yes! There are 18 wild hamster species living in Europe and western Asia. Hamsters sleep in burrows during the day and forage for food at night. The food is stuffed into cheek pouches and brought back to the burrow to eat later.

Black-bellied hamsters live in central and eastern Europe.

PRIMATES:

Big-brained mammals with grasping hands, such as lemurs, monkeys, and apes, including humans

Ring-tailed lemurs can climb trees but spend a lot of their time on the ground.

DO MONKEYS EAT ONLY BANANAS?

Many primates have a sweet tooth and enjoy eating fruit such as bananas, although they are not a staple. Monkeys have a mainly vegetarian diet and eat a wide variety of foods, from nuts and seeds to leaves and flowers. Gelada monkeys are grass-eaters, spending most of their day grazing like cows. Marmosets gnaw holes in trees with their sharp teeth to find and eat tree sap.

DO ALL PRIMATES LIVE IN TREES?

Many different primates live and sleep in trees, but not all do. Some, such as the patas monkey, are ground-dwellers that live in grassland habitats. Most lemur species spend their time up in the trees, but ring-tailed lemurs spend about 40 percent of their time on the ground.

Silverbacks get their name from the silvery patch of fur on their backs.

WHAT TYPES ARE THERE?

There are 520 known species of primates, which are grouped into two main categories: prosimians and anthropoids (resembling a human being).

Prosimians
This group includes lemurs, tarsiers, and lorises. Prosimians tend to be nocturnal and have long snouts and wet noses. They also have a special claw, often on the second toe, for grooming.

Anthropoids
Also known as "higher primates," this group includes monkeys, apes, and humans. Most anthropoids are larger than prosimians, are active during the day, and have good color vision.

HOW STRONG ARE GORILLAS?

As the world's largest living primate species, gorillas have immense muscle strength. The silverback gorilla can be more than 10 times stronger than the average human and can bite with more force than a bear!

WHY DO MANDRILLS HAVE COLORFUL BUMS?

Male mandrills have brightly colored faces and bums to help attract a potential mate. The more vibrant their red and blue colors, the higher the male's rank in the social group. Female mandrills have been observed to prefer the most brilliantly colored males.

Gorillas only stand when fighting—they typically knuckle-walk on all fours.

AM I AN APE?

Yes! Humans are primates and—alongside orangutans, gorillas, bonobos, and chimpanzees—belong to a primate subgroup called the Hominidae, also known as the great apes. Chimps are the closest living relatives of humans. Although the human brain is about three times as big as a chimpanzee's, we share 98.8 percent of our DNA.

Rounded braincase allows for a larger brain than any other ape.

Human skull

Chimps have a smaller braincase and low foreheads.

Chimpanzee skull

Gorillas bare their long, sharp canines when they feel threatened.

A gorilla's hands look similar to a human's but are a lot stronger.

Muscular arms are used for gathering foliage, as well as defense.

Gorillas have long, thick, and dark coats of hair.

Opposable big toes help grasp and grip tree branches.

Highly mobile wrists allow gibbons to pivot from arm to arm.

WHICH PRIMATE IS THE KING OF THE SWINGERS?

White-handed gibbons are some of the fastest swingers, moving at speeds of up to 35 mph (56 km/h). They travel using brachiation: swinging through the trees, alternating from one handhold to the other, and hanging by the arms.

HOW CLEVER ARE PRIMATES?

Primates are highly intelligent, with larger brains than other mammals. In particular, chimps are good problem-solvers, using tools for different tasks and even treating their wounds using crushed insects!

Chimps use sticks to probe for insects inside a log.

QUICK QUIZ!

HOW DO JAPANESE SNOW MONKEYS STAY WARM IN WINTER?

a: Hot food

b: Hot drinks

c: Hot baths

WHY CAN'T APES TALK?

This question is hotly debated by scientists. For a long time, they thought our primate cousins' voice boxes were not developed for speech. Now, researchers think it is because an ape's brain cannot send the right signals to its voice box. Instead, primates use a range of facial expressions, body language, gestures, and calls to communicate with one another.

IT'S A MYSTERY!

Where were wolves domesticated?
It is thought that wolves may have started living and feeding at the edge of settlements thousands of years ago before being tamed to protect humans—but no one is sure where this first happened.

A dense layer of fur under the outer coat keeps a wolf warm.

DO PET DOGS COME FROM WOLVES?

The gray wolf is the ancestor of all pet dogs, which means that although dogs can look very different, they are all the same species. People selected dogs to breed for a job, such as herding livestock, guarding, or catching small animals. This, over many years, created different breeds of dogs.

DO WOLVES LIVE IN PACKS?

Although some wolves are solitary, most wolves live in packs of around 20. One pair of wolves leads the pack. These are the parents of the rest of the pack, some of which are young adults. The adults rear the pups together and defend territory as a group.

Gray wolves have long, bushy tails that are often black-tipped.

Adult gray wolves have 42 teeth and keen senses.

WOLVES: Large members of the dog family that live and hunt in packs

White-furred Arctic wolves are a type of gray wolf.

HOW DOES A PACK HUNT?

Wolves hunt in packs, tracking prey with their keen sense of smell and hearing. If the prey is large, the pack separates to surround it, then the wolves close in and attack, working together to take it down. This can be dangerous if the prey has antlers or hooves that can injure a wolf.

WHY DO WOLVES HOWL?

Gray wolves howl to communicate with other wolves. A pack's howls announce to rival packs that the territory is taken—it's a warning to stay away. This helps avoid clashes between packs. Howls can be heard at distances of up to 6 miles (10 km). Not all wolves howl though—maned wolves bark.

WHY DO WOLVES HAVE SUCH BIG TEETH?

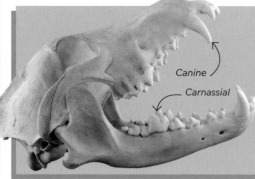

Canine

Carnassial

Wolves are meat-eaters and have canines (large, pointed teeth) to grip and bite into their prey. These teeth can be a huge 2.5 in (6 cm) long. Broader carnassial teeth at the back of the jaw are sharp and work like scissor blades, slicing meat from the bone.

WHY DO PANDAS EAT SO MUCH?

Pandas live in forests of bamboo that grow all year round in China. Their ancestors were meat-eaters, but they may have started to eat bamboo because meat was hard to find and there was a lot of bamboo. However, a panda's body cannot digest bamboo as well as other plant-eaters, so the panda has to eat a lot and often, munching for around 14 hours a day.

Polar bear cubs are born in a den dug in the snow.

DO BEARS SLEEP THROUGH WINTER?

Bears in cool climates snuggle down in dens when food is hard to find. Their breathing and heart rate slow, and they may not eat or drink for 100 days. Bears can wake up to avoid danger or feed if needed.

DO BEARS EAT HONEY?

If there's honey around, bears will eat it, as well as the bees and their larvae. Bears eat other insects, too. Polar bears eat mainly meat, while black and brown bears and sun bears eat a more varied diet of meat, plants, and insects. Pandas eat mainly plants.

Sloth bear uses sharp claws and long snout to catch termites.

DO BEARS CLIMB TREES?

The smaller the bear, the better it can climb a tree to find fruit, nuts, and honey and escape danger. Although their young are able to climb trees, adult polar and brown bears cannot because they are so heavy.

Asiatic black bear cub has sharp claws for grip.

BEARS: Heavy-bodied mammals with short tails that walk on the soles of their five-clawed feet

Human 6 ft (1.8 m) tall

Polar bear

Kodiak bear

Spectacled bear

Sun bear

QUICK QUIZ!

HOW MANY CUBS CAN A BEAR HAVE IN A YEAR?

a: 1–3

b: 4–6

c: 7–10

HOW BIG IS A BEAR?

The biggest bears are the polar bear and the Kodiak (a type of brown bear). Both are around 10 ft (3 m) long. They live in cold places, where their large bodies help them generate and retain body heat. The smallest bear is the sun bear, which lives in tropical Southeast Asia.

LIONS:

Big cats that live in groups, called prides, in Africa and a small area of India, with males that usually have manes

WHY DO LIONS LIVE IN PRIDES?

Most big cats work alone to ambush prey, relying on the forests or hills for cover, but on Africa's open plains, lions need other tactics. Living and hunting in prides, they work together to bring down prey.

HOW DO LIONS HUNT?

Lions kill prey as big as buffaloes and with as much speed and stamina as zebras, so they need to work fast to minimize the risk of injury from horns and hooves. Pride members hunt together—some run ahead to cut off the escape route, while others attack, jumping up to topple the victim and strangling prey by biting its neck.

Mane hairs can grow up to 7 in (16 cm) long.

IT'S A MYSTERY!

Why are some male lions maneless?

Some male lions never grow a mane. In the Tsavo part of Tanzania, maneless males are common. Lacking a mane may help the lions cope with heat, but no one is sure.

ARE LIONS KING OF THE JUNGLE?

Lions are Africa's top predators, so that could make them monarchs of their natural world. But they stick mainly to open grassland with scattered trees, while "jungle" means dense thickets of vegetation between trees—places that lions usually avoid.

WHY DO LIONS ROAR?

Male lions roar to show their power and to defend territory and scare off intruders. Most big cats roar but cannot purr, while small cats can purr but not roar. Cats can also make other sounds; cheetahs, for example, can chirp.

CAN A LION LICK YOUR SKIN OFF?

No! All mammal tongues have tiny bumps, called papillae, for carrying taste buds. But cats also have lots of spiny papillae for grooming or for licking meat from bones. The small tongue of a domestic cat just feels rough. A lion's tongue has spines big enough to scratch your skin—but not to lick it off.

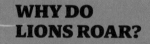

TIGERS:

The world's biggest cats, recognizable by their camouflage stripes

DO TIGERS SWIM?

Tigers live in habitats with swamps, lakes, and rivers. In the tropics, they enjoy a cooling dip and can swim across broad stretches of open water. Like other cats, they have webs of skin between their toes, which helps the paws paddle forward.

ARE TIGER STRIPES ALL THE SAME?

No. Like human fingerprints, every tiger's pattern of stripes is unique. Conservationists can identify individual tigers by their stripe pattern. This helps track and count endangered tigers. The largest population in the wild is in northern India and Nepal, where protected areas have helped restore numbers.

Striped markings on the head are different for each individual.

WHY DO TIGERS HAVE SUCH BIG PAWS?

Paws are used to help a cat with hunting—unlike dogs, cats can twist their forelimbs to help grab prey. They also have extendable claws to grip and tear. Tigers use their enormous paws to bring down prey as big as wild oxen.

ARE LIONS OR TIGERS BIGGER?

Tigers vary a lot more in size than lions. The smallest tigers in tropical Sumatra are smaller than the average lion, but tigers in cold Siberia are much bigger, and the biggest of all cats.

Lion: up to 8.2 ft (2.5 m) long

Tiger: up to 9.5 ft (2.9 m) long

Leopard

Cheetah

Jaguar

Tiger

WHY DO TIGERS HAVE STRIPES?

A patterned coat—such as a leopard's spots—helps break up the outline of a body. Black stripes on a brown-orange background are perfect for concealing a tiger among Asian forests as it creeps up on prey.

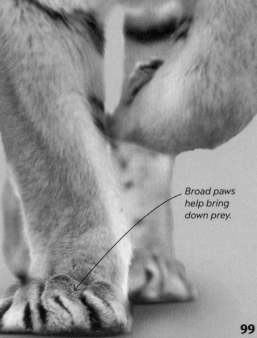

Broad paws help bring down prey.

GIRAFFES: Tall, hoofed African mammals with long necks, long legs, and short coats

DO GIRAFFES SLEEP STANDING UP?

Giraffes usually stand when they sleep and may lean against a tree for support—this way, they can react quickly to danger. They can sleep lying down, too, by folding their legs under their body, but it takes time to get up again. Sleeping happens in short bursts that can add up to less than 10 minutes a night.

WHY DO GIRAFFES HAVE LONG NECKS?

A giraffe's long neck allows it to eat from treetops that are out of reach for most animals. At such heights, it can also spot danger from afar. Males wrestle with their necks to fight for territory or females.

QUICK QUIZ!

HOW TALL IS A GIRAFFE?

a. Up to 6 ft (2 m)

b. Up to 13 ft (4 m)

c. Up to 20 ft (6 m)

CAN GIRAFFES RUN FAST?

Giraffes can reach a top speed of 37 mph (60 km/h) over a short distance. Over a longer distance, they can run at an average speed of 10 mph (16 km/h).

Bony bumps on the head are called ossicones.

Long skull means eyes are far away from thorny trees when eating.

Eyeballs are the size of golf balls, with excellent vision.

Dark color of the tongue is thought to prevent sunburn while eating.

WHAT NOISES DO GIRAFFES MAKE?

Giraffes are mostly silent, but they may snort and hiss in warning, and mothers whistle or bellow to their young. At night, giraffes hum—no one knows why—but the sound is too low for people to hear.

WHAT DO GIRAFFES EAT?

The leaves of the acacia tree are a giraffe's favorite food. The tongue and lips of the giraffe have extra-thick skin to stop the tree's thorns digging in. The 18-in (45-cm) long tongue wraps around a branch and pulls it into the mouth, where teeth strip off the leaves.

ARE THERE ANY WILD HORSES?

The only surviving species of wild horse is the Przewalski's horse, which lives in Mongolia. Most other horses that exist in the wild are feral horses descended from domestic horses that escaped or were released into the wild.

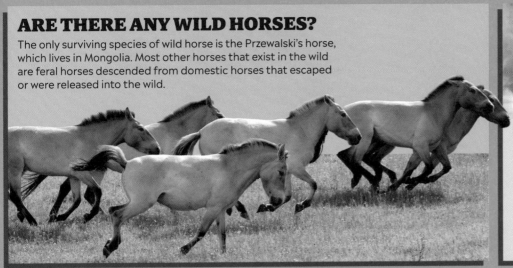

WHY DO HORSES WEAR SHOES?

Horses' hooves are made of keratin, the same substance in human hair or nails. Steel shoes strengthen and protect the hooves on hard ground. Nailing them in position doesn't hurt the horse.

HOW DO HORSES MOVE THEIR EARS?

A horse's ear has 10 muscles and can move 180 degrees back and forth. One ear can move in a different direction to the other.

One ear forward and the other back to listen in two directions at once

HOW MANY KINDS OF DOMESTICATED HORSES ARE THERE?

All domestic horses belong to one species, which has around 400 breeds of different shapes and sizes. Donkeys and zebras look like horses but are instead close relatives.

African wild donkey
This donkey is the ancestor of the domestic donkey.

Mountain zebra
Each zebra has its own unique pattern of stripes.

Thoroughbred horse
The fastest domestic horse breed is the Thoroughbred.

HORSES:
Plant-eating animals with one toe on each foot

WHAT IS THE SMALLEST HORSE?

The smallest horse breed is the Falabella miniature, at an average of 7.2 hands (29 in/73 cm), but the smallest living male horse is a miniature Appaloosa named Bombel. A horse's height is measured in "hands" from its hooves to its shoulders ("withers"). One hand is the width of an adult's hand, equal to 4 in (10 cm).

Spotted coat pattern is typical of Appaloosas.

Bombel is just 5.6 hands (22.36 in/56.7 cm) tall. His tiny stature is due to dwarfism.

The color of this horse is bay, which is a brown coat with a darker mane and tail.

WHALES:
Warm-blooded ocean mammals, some of which are the world's biggest animals

WHY ARE WHALES SO BIG?

Blue whales are the biggest animals ever to have lived. Animals can grow bigger in the ocean because the water around them supports their weight. And because ocean plankton is especially rich and productive, the biggest whales that consume this food source can grow into real giants.

Blue whale: up to 107 ft (32.6 m) long

Boeing 737-7: over 115 ft (35 m) long

DO DOLPHINS PLAY TOGETHER IN THE WILD?

Dolphins are a group of small, toothed whales. Smart and social, they can often be seen playing together in the wild. Spinner dolphins jump and spin in the air, spinning up to seven times on one leap, and bottlenose dolphins (below) have been spotted playing ball with an inflated pufferfish.

WHY DO NARWHALS HAVE HORNS?

It looks like a horn, but male narwhals actually have a spiral tooth poking out of their upper lip. These tusks could be used to attract a mate or to sense temperature changes in the Arctic waters.

DO WHALES HAVE BELLY BUTTONS?

Whales give birth to live young just like other mammals. A whale calf is attached to its mother (known as a cow) by an umbilical cord in the womb. The cord delivers oxygen and nutrients to the growing fetus. After birth, it drops off, leaving a belly button. Whale cows even produce milk and nurse their babies like humans.

A whale's belly button is in the middle of its abdomen.

FAST FACTS

Cuvier beaked whales can **hold** their **breath** for over **3 hours** when deep diving.

Most whales live in the **oceans**, but there are several **river dolphin** species.

Bowhead whales can **live** for over **200 years**.

DO WHALES HAVE TEETH?

Whales are split into two main groups, depending on whether they have teeth or not. Toothed whales include dolphins, porpoises, and orcas, which use their teeth to attack prey. Baleen whales do not have teeth, instead sieving krill (tiny shrimp) from seawater through filters called baleen plates.

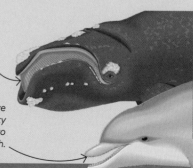

Baleen whales use comblike baleen plates to filter out seawater and keep krill in their mouth.

Toothed whales have small and pointy cone-shaped teeth to catch slippery fish.

ARE HIPPOS DANGEROUS?

Although they are plant-eaters and do not hunt for food, hippos are the deadliest land mammal other than humans, killing an estimated 500 people each year in Africa. They are aggressive when threatened and can crush people with their enormous bulk. Surprisingly for their size, hippos can reach speeds of up to 30 mph (48 km/h) on land in short bursts.

CAN HIPPOS SWIM?

Hippos spend a lot time in the water, but they cannot swim. Due to their dense bones, hippos sink to the riverbed and slowly gallop forward using their legs. They can hold their breath for up to five minutes and, to keep water out, their eyes and nostrils shut tight. Despite not being able to swim, hippos can sleep underwater by using a reflex that allows them to rise to the surface, take a breath, and sink back down—without waking up.

HOW HUNGRY ARE HIPPOS?

Hippos are herbivores that mainly feed on grass, but they also eat fruit and leaves. They are most active at night and if grazing from dusk until dawn, a hippo can eat a whopping 88 lb (40 kg) of grass—a similar weight to four large watermelons. This is equivalent to only around 2 percent of its body weight.

4 large watermelons   **88 lb (40 kg) of grass**

HIPPOS: Large, semiaquatic mammals with huge mouths

WHY DO HIPPOS WALLOW IN MUD?

This helps protect their hairless, sensitive skin, which needs constant access to moisture to prevent it from drying out and cracking. Hippos also secrete an oily fluid from glands in their skin, which acts as both a sunscreen and an antibiotic. Nicknamed "blood sweat," it is initially colorless before turning orange-red.

Sharp canine teeth can reach 20 in (50 cm) in length and are used when fighting other hippos.

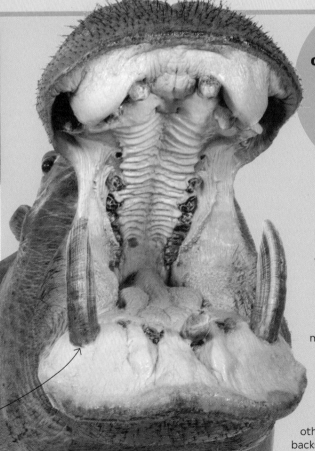

WHICH ANIMALS ARE HIPPOS MOST CLOSELY RELATED TO?

a: Whales

b: Pigs

c: Crocodiles

QUICK QUIZ!

WHY DO HIPPOS HAVE SUCH BIG MOUTHS?

Hippos have incredibly large mouths that can open to almost 180 degrees and span about 4 ft (1.2 m) in adult males. This is important for "gaping," a display behavior where hippos meet nose-to-nose with their mouths wide open to size each other up. Unless the smaller hippo backs down, a fight typically ensues!

ENDANGERED ANIMALS:

Animal species that are at risk of going extinct and being lost forever

Endangered Darwin's frog broods tadpoles in its vocal sac.

WHY ARE AMPHIBIANS SO VULNERABLE?

Around two-fifths of the world's 8,740 or so species of amphibians are under threat of disappearing. Their soft, moist skin—which helps them absorb oxygen—makes them especially vulnerable to polluted air, global warming, and disease. Habitat loss is also a factor.

FAST FACTS

🌿 **12%** of **bird** species are **threatened.**

🌿 **26%** of **mammal species** are threatened.

WHAT IS BIODIVERSITY?

This is a measure of the natural world's diversity in terms of different types of habitats and the species that live there. Some habitats, such as tropical ocean reefs and rainforests, have so many different species that they are known as biodiversity "hotspots." The loss of endangered species is affecting biodiversity.

WHICH ANIMALS ARE ON THE BRINK?

Many species and subspecies are known from just a few individuals or isolated spots, so they could easily disappear when habitats are lost. Fewer than 100 Amur leopards (above) are left in the wild, and Javan rhinos, Sunda tigers, mountain gorillas, and the Yangtze finless porpoise are all at risk of extinction.

On Fiji's reefs, coral species support more than 2,000 fish species—but global warming threatens reefs.

HOW MANY SPECIES ARE THREATENED?

FISHES	3,551
AMPHIBIANS	2,606
INSECTS	2,345
REPTILES	1,842
BIRDS	1,400
MAMMALS	1,340

An organization called the International Union for Conservation of Nature (IUCN) runs a database known as the Red List that monitors threatened species. Each is studied and ranked according to the level of threat, from "least concern" to "critically endangered." Nearly a third, or 44,000, of the species studied are judged to be threatened.

CAN SPECIES BE BROUGHT BACK FROM THE BRINK?

Species can be saved from extinction by conservation measures, such as protecting their habitats in reserves. Grand Cayman blue iguanas had dwindled to near-extinction, but numbers have been restored to over 1,000 by a breeding program on the island.

HOW CAN WE PROTECT ANIMALS IN THE OCEANS?

By limiting fishing, banning whaling, and reducing levels of pollution, countries around the world are helping conserve marine life. Creating protected marine areas can help preserve endangered species such as giant manta rays (right). We can also help by keeping coastlines free from trash.

WHY ARE SO MANY SPECIES ENDANGERED?

Over hundreds of years, humans have changed so much natural habitat that just a quarter of Earth's wilderness and wild places are left. And all around the world, even the remotest places can be affected by pollution and climate change.

Habitat change
Forests and other natural habitats are cleared and broken up to make way for farmland, cities, roads, and industry.

Overharvesting
If animals are hunted and fished faster than they can reproduce, their numbers decline.

Invasive species
Some species, such as pigeons, have spread to places where they don't live naturally and are killing native species.

Pollution
Our homes, agriculture, industry, and transportation generate waste that poisons the air, water, and land.

Climate change
Pollutants include greenhouse gases, such as carbon dioxide, that trap the Sun's heat and warm the planet.

WHAT IS REWILDING?

Efforts are being made to reintroduce animals to natural habitats where they once lived. This can go hand in hand with rewilding land by letting nature run its course. Although there is sometimes conflict, wild animals and humans can be neighbors. Beavers reintroduced to the UK are now breeding, and their dams are even helping to reduce seasonal flooding.

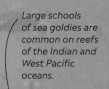

Large schools of sea goldies are common on reefs of the Indian and West Pacific oceans.

Purple male sea goldies guard large groups of orange females.

CAN EXTINCT SPECIES BE BROUGHT BACK TO LIFE?

Scientists are attempting to recover lost species by cloning from specimens or by trying to breed their characteristics into related species still alive today. But, sadly, many extinct animals like the dodo are probably lost forever.

SCIENCE

ATOMS: Extremely tiny particles that combine to form all the matter in the world around us

WHAT IS INSIDE AN ATOM?

Although they are minuscule, atoms are composed of even tinier particles. Two types of these particles, called protons and neutrons, huddle together at the center (nucleus) of the atom. Meanwhile, electrons whiz around the edges.

Atoms of different elements have different numbers of particles.

Protons (shown in blue) are positively charged.

Neutrons (shown in red) have no electrical charge.

The center of the atom is called the nucleus.

Negatively charged electrons orbit (circle around) the nucleus in layers called shells.

Carbon atom

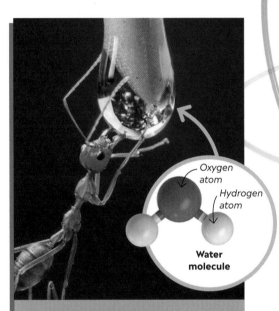

Oxygen atom

Hydrogen atom

Water molecule

IS EVERYTHING MADE FROM ATOMS?

Atoms are the building blocks of all the stuff around us in the Universe. Different types of atoms bond together into molecules, forming an incredible variety of substances—even plants, animals, and minerals. Water is made from two atoms of hydrogen bonding with one of oxygen.

IT'S A MYSTERY!

What does the inside of an atom really look like?
Pictures like the one above are simplified. In reality, the nucleus is around 10,000 times smaller than the rest of the atom! The inside of the atom is far too small to see directly.

HOW BIG IS AN ATOM?

Different types of atoms have varying sizes and masses, but around 5 million of the smallest atoms could fit on the tiny tip of a pin!

IF ATOMS ARE SO SMALL, HOW DO WE KNOW THEY ARE THERE?

It is impossible to see an atom with the human eye alone. However, the most powerful microscopes can magnify individual atoms more than 500,000 times. These work by using a beam of electrons instead of light.

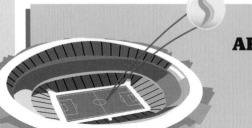

IS IT TRUE THAT ATOMS ARE MOSTLY EMPTY SPACE?

To understand the scale of an atom, imagine the nucleus is the size of a marble and placed at the center of a huge sports stadium. The electrons would be tiny dots sitting in the farthest seats, with masses of empty space in between them!

WHAT IS AN ELEMENT?

Elements are pure substances that make up all the other substances around us. This shiny lump is the element calcium. It is made of calcium atoms only. If calcium atoms join with atoms of another element, they form substances called compounds.

Pure calcium is soft and shiny.

Calcium

CAN SCIENTISTS MAKE NEW ELEMENTS?

Scientists predict there are more elements than we currently know, but that these are too unstable to exist naturally on Earth. One way they try to create these new elements is by smashing particles together in machines called particle accelerators. This one in Germany is being carefully checked by a technician.

FAST FACTS

⚛ The rarest natural element on Earth is **astatine.** Only 1 oz (25 g) exists in Earth's crust.

⚛ **Helium** was first discovered in the Sun before it was found on Earth.

⚛ There are **118** known elements in total, with **94** of them occurring naturally.

WHICH ELEMENTS AM I MADE OF?

Ninety-nine percent of your body is composed of just six chemical elements—oxygen, carbon, and hydrogen, along with smaller amounts of nitrogen, calcium, and phosphorus. The final 1 percent is made from a range of other elements, including sulfur, potassium, sodium, chlorine, and magnesium.

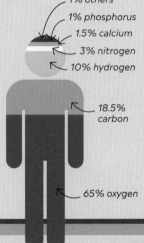

1% others
1% phosphorus
1.5% calcium
3% nitrogen
10% hydrogen
18.5% carbon
65% oxygen

ELEMENTS: Pure substances, which are each made from only one type of atom

WHICH ELEMENT IS THE MOST COMMON?

Hydrogen is the most common element in existence—making up more than 70 percent of the Universe, and most commonly found on Earth in water. It also has the simplest atomic structure, with each atom containing just one proton.

When an electric current is passed through it, colorless hydrogen gas glows purple.

ARE WE ALL MADE OF STARDUST?

Elements found naturally on Earth are created in the centers of stars. When a supermassive star dies in a brilliant supernova explosion (see page 14), the elements are scattered far and wide. So elements that make us and Earth may have originally come from far across the Universe!

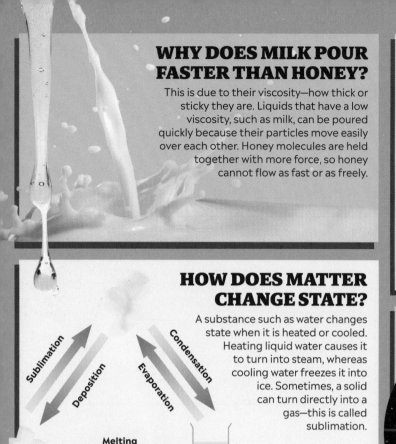

WHY DOES MILK POUR FASTER THAN HONEY?

This is due to their viscosity—how thick or sticky they are. Liquids that have a low viscosity, such as milk, can be poured quickly because their particles move easily over each other. Honey molecules are held together with more force, so honey cannot flow as fast or as freely.

WHAT IS THE DIFFERENCE BETWEEN WATER, ICE, AND STEAM?

Ice is the solid form of water—the particles are packed tightly together in a rigid pattern. Liquid water has more loosely arranged particles that touch but tumble over each other. In steam (water vapor), the particles are widely spaced apart, moving at random.

Solid   **Liquid**   **Gas**

HOW DOES MATTER CHANGE STATE?

A substance such as water changes state when it is heated or cooled. Heating liquid water causes it to turn into steam, whereas cooling water freezes it into ice. Sometimes, a solid can turn directly into a gas—this is called sublimation.

Sublimation

Deposition

Condensation

Evaporation

Melting

Freezing

WHAT IS PLASMA?

Often known as the fourth state of matter, plasma is like a gas made of electrically charged particles. It is the most common state of matter in the universe—found in the Sun, stars, and even the tails of comets.

Like other similar stars, the bright star Vega is made of plasma.

MATTER: Everything that makes up all living and nonliving things in the world around us

IT'S A MYSTERY

How many states of matter are there?
Researchers are constantly discovering new, rare states of matter. So far, more than 15 have been demonstrated in labs, but we don't know how many more may reveal themselves!

WHY DOES ICE FLOAT?

Because it is a hard solid, you might expect ice to be heavier than liquid water. But water breaks all the rules! In ice, there is a greater distance between the water molecules than in liquid water, making it less dense and causing it to float (see page 118).

These shards of ice on Lake Michigan have been pushed up by the motion of the water beneath.

WHAT CAUSES EXPLOSIONS?

Explosions are a type of exothermic reaction—a reaction that gives out heat as it happens. Fireworks produce a type of exothermic reaction when explosive chemicals inside the firework's shell are ignited. The resulting reactions create a dazzling display of color—and a bang!

CHEMICAL REACTIONS:

When chemical substances are broken apart and changed into different ones

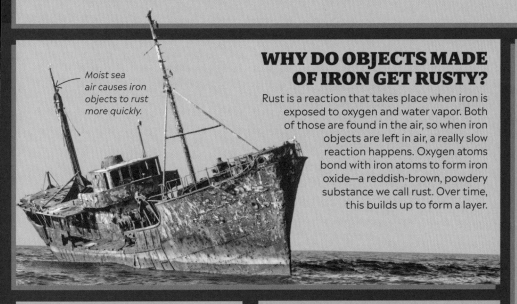

Moist sea air causes iron objects to rust more quickly.

WHY DO OBJECTS MADE OF IRON GET RUSTY?

Rust is a reaction that takes place when iron is exposed to oxygen and water vapor. Both of those are found in the air, so when iron objects are left in air, a really slow reaction happens. Oxygen atoms bond with iron atoms to form iron oxide—a reddish-brown, powdery substance we call rust. Over time, this builds up to form a layer.

Reactant 1 **Reactant 2**

Reactants
The separate substances involved in a reaction are called reactants.

Reaction
When the reactants combine, a reaction takes place. Sometimes, reactants are heated to give them the energy they need to react.

Product
New substances formed by the chemical reaction are known as products and may have completely different properties from the initial reactants.

HOW MANY REACTIONS TAKE PLACE INSIDE MY BODY?

Around a billion biochemical reactions occur in each body cell every second, and we have many trillions of cells. The human body is constantly breaking down molecules and building new ones, using the energy it gets from food. These reactions keep your body working.

IS COOKING A REACTION?

Yes! Some reactions can be reversed, but when you bake a cake, this is an irreversible reaction. The ingredients—such as butter, eggs, and flour—are your reactants, and adding heat from the oven helps the reaction take place. The resulting cake cannot be changed back into its ingredients.

WHAT IS A REACTION?

A reaction is a process where two or more substances are changed into different ones. During this process, the chemical bonds between the atoms of each substance break and the atoms are reorganized into new, often completely different substances.

WHAT IS A FORCE?

A force is a push or a pull that changes an object's speed, direction, or shape—either increasing or reducing its speed, sending it down a different path, or squashing or stretching it. The amount an object is affected depends on the size of the force applied and how heavy the object is.

Changing direction
Hitting a ball with a tennis racket will change its direction, sending it back the way it came.

Changing speed
As a golf club connects with a ball, it pushes it forward, increasing its speed from zero to a speedy zip along the course.

Changing shape
Pushing and pulling forces can change the shape of objects by bending or stretching them.

IF I KICKED A BALL IN SPACE, WOULD IT KEEP GOING FOREVER?

On Earth, air resistance slows down moving objects. In the empty vacuum of space, there is no air, so there is nothing to cause friction or air resistance. Once kicked, a ball would keep on going in the same direction until it hit another object or met the gravity of a planet or moon.

On the Moon, a ball would travel farther than on Earth, but the Moon's gravity would eventually pull it back down.

WHY IS ICE SO SLIPPERY?

When shoes move across the ground, the tiny, rough bumps on each surface rub against each other, creating a force called friction. This force gives you grip. Ice, however, has a smooth surface covered in a very thin film of liquid water. This watery layer reduces the amount of friction, making it slippery. When you wear skates with a thin blade, friction is reduced further, so you can glide across the ice!

FORCES: Pushes and pulls that can change an object's speed, direction, or shape

ARE FORCES INVISIBLE?

The forces that happen all around us are invisible! We can't always see a force, such as gravity, but in some cases we can see the effect of forces on objects. If you pull on an elastic band or squash a foam ball, they will become a different shape due to the forces acting on them.

The ball becomes slightly compressed, changing shape and showing a force is acting upon it.

HOW DO YOU WIN A TUG OF WAR?

In a tug of war, two pulling forces are acting in opposite directions. If each team pulls with roughly the same force, the forces are balanced and the knot at the center hardly moves. To win, a team must exert more force than the other side, making the forces unbalanced. The rope will then move toward the side where the force is stronger.

SPEED: The rate at which an object is moving, measured by how far it can travel in a given time

WHAT IS THE FASTEST CAR?

Jet- and rocket-powered cars are the ones setting the pace! On October 15, 1997, this ThrustSSC supersonic car, driven by Andy Green, reached a speed of 763 mph (1,228 km/h)—quicker than the speed of sound. It set the current World Land Speed Record.

WHY CAN PLANES TRAVEL FASTER THAN BOATS?

As planes and boats propel themselves forward, they are both slowed down by a force called drag. In the sky, this is called air resistance and is the force of all the air particles the plane passes through pushing back against it. When traveling through water, boats face water resistance, but water is denser than air and so produces a stronger force.

HOW MUCH ACCELERATION CAN HUMANS WITHSTAND?

When our bodies accelerate in a car or on a rollercoaster, the effects they feel can be measured in g-force. The effect of gravity pulling us to the ground is 1 *g*, which our bodies can easily deal with. Strong g-forces of more than 6 *g* can cause blood to pool in the legs, leading people to pass out. But trained jet fighter pilots in special suits can cope with up to 9 *g*!

WHAT IS THE DIFFERENCE BETWEEN SPEED AND ACCELERATION?

Speed is a measurement of the distance traveled by an object in a certain time—for example, the number of miles (or km) per hour. But acceleration records an object's change in speed. When a car speeds up, this is called positive acceleration, but if the driver reduces speed, that is negative acceleration. Changes in direction are also a form of acceleration.

FAST FACTS

The fastest speed a passenger train has run is **302.8 mph (487.3 km/h)**, reached by a China Railways train in 2011.

In **1978**, the *Spirit of Australia* reached a speed of **317.58 mph** (511.09 km/h), setting the water speed record.

When boats jump out of the water, they can fly faster due to less drag.

IS THERE ANYTHING FASTER THAN THE SPEED OF LIGHT?

Not that we know of! When traveling in a vacuum (an empty space with nothing in it to slow things down), light zips along at 671 million mph (1,079 million km/h). At this incredible rate, a beam of light could circle the Earth 7.5 times in just one second.

ROCKET SCIENCE:

Creating enough power to overcome the pull of Earth's gravity and launch spacecraft

HOW DO ROCKETS GET OFF THE GROUND?

On the launchpad, a rocket's engine creates a powerful blast of hot exhaust gases that shoot out of nozzles pointed at the ground. This creates an equally strong but opposing reaction—a thrusting force in the opposite direction that lifts the rocket into the air!

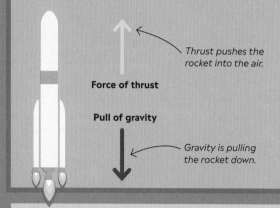

Thrust pushes the rocket into the air.

Force of thrust

Pull of gravity

Gravity is pulling the rocket down.

HOW MUCH DOES IT COST TO LAUNCH A ROCKET?

Sending a rocket into space is not cheap, but the exact cost depends on many things, such as how heavy it is, the amount of fuel it needs, and the amount of cargo it is carrying. European Space Agency rocket Ariane 5 costs around $178 million (£140 million) per launch.

HOW FAST DOES A ROCKET TRAVEL?

To beat Earth's gravitational pull, a rocket needs to reach a speed known as escape velocity, which is 7 miles (11.2 km) per second. This incredible speed, equivalent to more than 25,000 mph (40,000 km/h), is 30 times faster than a passenger jet and blasts the rocket into space in six or seven minutes.

HOW IS A ROCKET TRANSPORTED TO THE LAUNCHPAD?

Rockets are often enormous, with the biggest—Space X's Starship—more than 400 ft (122 m) tall. Once their parts have been assembled, the largest rockets can only be moved by specially designed vehicles, such as NASA's crawler transporters (see page 132). Even using these giant machines, it often takes two or more hours for rockets to travel just 1.7 miles (2.7 km) from the final assembly building to the launchpad.

Launch towers pull away as the rocket begins to fire.

HOW MUCH FUEL DOES IT TAKE TO LIFT OFF?

A rocket, such as the Falcon Heavy (left), burns millions of tons of fuel to achieve liftoff! Much of the fuel is usually contained in two boosters on either side of the main rocket. When the fuel in them burns at launch, it generates more than 22 million newtons of thrust—a force that could lift approximately 18 regular aircraft!

Protective sections separate to reveal the payload (cargo) inside.

Second stage engine ignites after first stage separation.

The payload, such as a satellite, is delivered into orbit.

Solid rocket boosters separate and fall away when their fuel is spent.

Second stage separates and the third stage engine takes over.

First stage separates and falls into the ocean.

WHAT CAN A ROCKET CARRY?

Some rockets can carry more than 22 tons (20 tonnes) in their payload area. Rockets deliver a wide variety of machines into orbit, including weather monitoring and communication satellites, space telescopes, other spacecraft, and even parts intended for the International Space Station.

WHY DO ROCKETS BREAK APART?

This rocket is not broken! Rockets carry many tons of fuel, which is why they are built from sections called stages. As soon as the heavy fuel on board each stage is used up, that stage falls away. This reduces the overall weight of the rocket, allowing it to accelerate further.

All stages of a rocket are fixed together at launch.

Huge amounts of hot gas are generated by a rocket launch.

QUICK QUIZ!

WHEN WAS THE FIRST ROCKET LAUNCHED?

a: 1926

b: 1940

c: 1957

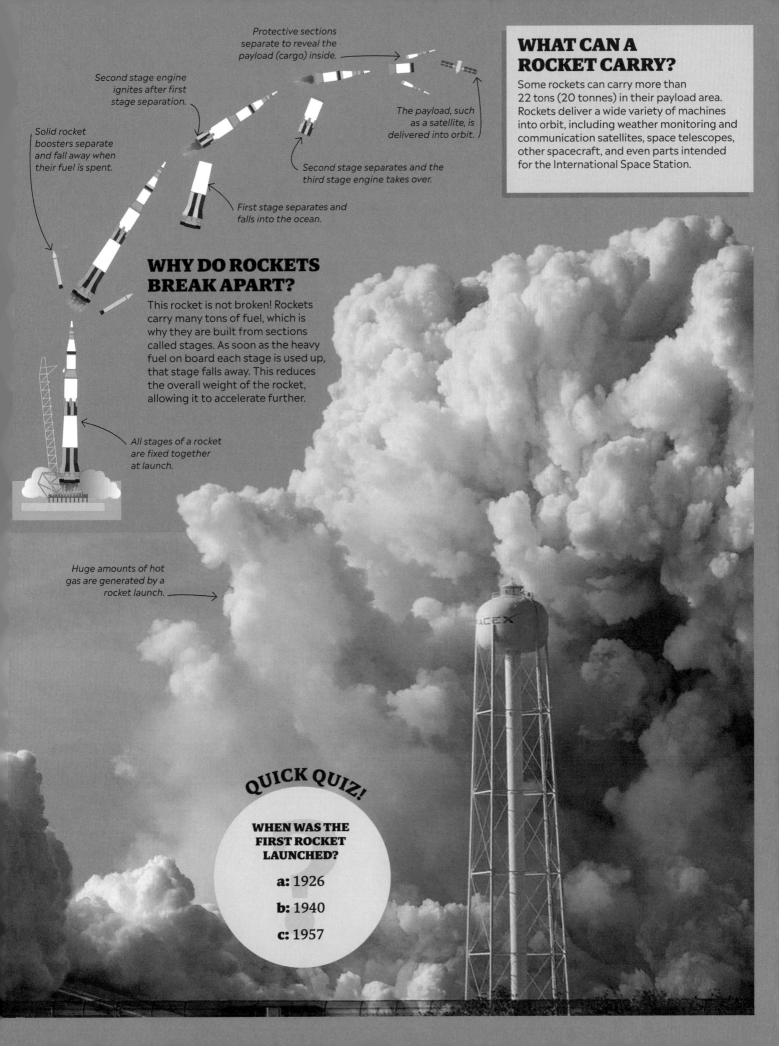

GRAVITY:

The invisible force of attraction between objects that brings us down to Earth

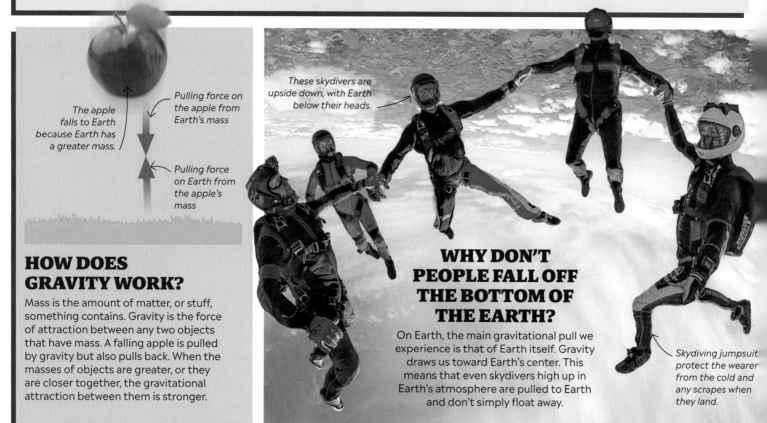

The apple falls to Earth because Earth has a greater mass.

Pulling force on the apple from Earth's mass

Pulling force on Earth from the apple's mass

These skydivers are upside down, with Earth below their heads.

Skydiving jumpsuit protect the wearer from the cold and any scrapes when they land.

HOW DOES GRAVITY WORK?

Mass is the amount of matter, or stuff, something contains. Gravity is the force of attraction between any two objects that have mass. A falling apple is pulled by gravity but also pulls back. When the masses of objects are greater, or they are closer together, the gravitational attraction between them is stronger.

WHY DON'T PEOPLE FALL OFF THE BOTTOM OF THE EARTH?

On Earth, the main gravitational pull we experience is that of Earth itself. Gravity draws us toward Earth's center. This means that even skydivers high up in Earth's atmosphere are pulled to Earth and don't simply float away.

With enough speed, a satellite can pull away from Earth's gravity.

Without enough speed, a satellite will fall to Earth.

At the right speed, satellites are held in orbit by Earth's gravity.

WHY DON'T SATELLITES FALL TO EARTH?

Without Earth's gravity, satellites would travel through space in a straight line. But because gravity pulls on them, they travel around Earth in a path called an orbit. Their speed is not enough to break away from Earth's gravity but is enough to keep them from falling.

WHY DO ASTRONAUTS FLOAT IN SPACE?

This spacecraft is in orbit. It is moving forward and falling toward Earth at the same time. The astronauts feel weightless because they are falling at the same speed as the spacecraft. Although floating astronauts are sometimes said to be in "zero gravity," they are actually still being pulled on by gravity.

WHY DO PEOPLE WALK MORE SLOWLY ON THE MOON?

Due to its smaller mass, the Moon has only one-sixth of Earth's gravity. This weaker pulling force gives astronauts less grip on the Moon's powdery surface, making walking around half as quick. Astronauts' bulky spacesuits are also very hard to move in, which slows them down further.

HOW DID THE INVENTOR OF THE CLOCK KNOW WHAT TIME IT WAS?

Telling the time is at least 5,000 years old and began way before modern clocks! People in ancient Egypt and Mesopotamia set up tall pointers over a dial. As the Sun moved across the sky, the pointer cast shadows over the dial, showing what time of day it was.

Hours are marked around the edge of the sundial.

Shadow cast by the Sun

WHY ARE THERE 60 MINUTES IN AN HOUR?

As early as 2000 BCE, the ancient Sumerians and Babylonians realized that 60 is a great counting number. It can be easily divided by lots of other numbers—such as 1, 2, 3, 4, 5, 6, 10, 12, 15, 20, and 30—so an hour with 60 minutes in it can be evenly broken into lots of smaller chunks. This system worked so well that we still use it today!

IS IT ALWAYS THE SAME TIME IN DIFFERENT PLACES?

Clocks do not show the same time around the world, because in some places it would be dark when the clock says it is midday. To fix this, the world is divided into time zones. These are based on the time in Greenwich, London, UK—the times in the zones to the west are earlier and to the east the times are later.

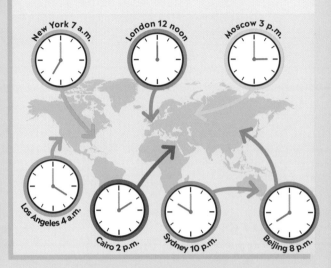

New York 7 a.m.
London 12 noon
Moscow 3 p.m.
Los Angeles 4 a.m.
Cairo 2 p.m.
Sydney 10 p.m.
Beijing 8 p.m.

TIME: How we measure the passing of years, months, weeks, days, hours, minutes, and seconds

A wormhole could hypothetically connect two faraway points in space and time.

QUICK QUIZ!

HOW MANY TIME ZONES DOES THE WORLD HAVE?

a: 12

b: 24

c: 48

Caesium reacts when exposed to air, so it is stored in a tube.

WHAT'S THE MOST ACCURATE CLOCK?

Most modern clocks keep time using a quartz crystal, which vibrates at a precise number of times per second when an electrical current passes through it. Even more accurate are atomic clocks. These use the element caesium and track the tiny energy changes in its atoms, which happen at a regular frequency.

IS TIME TRAVEL POSSIBLE?

This image is pure science fiction, and all the ideas scientists have about time travel are highly theoretical. Some theories suggest that wormholes—tunnels that fold time and space so that you can travel instantly between two different points in time—could exist, but none has ever been detected!

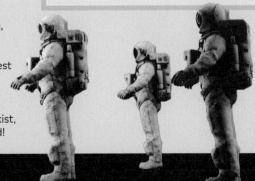

HOW DO SUBMARINES GO UP AND DOWN?

Submarines regularly dive to depths of 1,310 ft (400 m). When it needs to dive, a submarine fills its ballast tanks with water to become denser than the seawater around it.

Floating
With air filling its ballast tanks, the submarine floats on the surface of the water.

Diving
The submarine begins to fill its ballast tanks with water, making it heavier, so it can dive.

Rising
To rise back up, the submarine pumps air into the ballast tanks to push water out.

QUICK QUIZ!

WHICH ANCIENT GREEK FIRST EXPLAINED BUOYANCY?

a: Pythagoras

b: Aristotle

c: Archimedes

Warm air fills the balloon, causing it to rise.

CAN YOU FLOAT IN AIR?

You can in a hot air balloon! Using a burner, you can heat the air inside the balloon, which makes it less dense than the cooler air outside it (meaning it has less matter crammed into the same space). This allows the balloon—and the passengers in the basket below—to rise and float upward.

WHY DO SOME THINGS FLOAT?

Objects in water displace (push aside) an amount of water equal to their volume. This creates an upward force called upthrust. The greater the volume of water displaced, the greater the upthrust. If the object has the same density as water, the upthrust will balance its weight. Objects less dense than water float on the surface, and denser objects will sink.

Weight

Upthrust

Rubber ducks are not very dense, so upthrust is bigger than weight.

A heavy treasure chest is denser than water and sinks.

FLOATING: When an object is suspended in or rests on the surface of a liquid or a gas

HOW DO ARMBANDS HELP YOU FLOAT?

Armbands are made from light, thin plastic and filled with air, making them less dense than water. Wearing them on your arms pulls your arms up, allowing your head to stay above the surface of the water.

WHY DON'T MASSIVE BOATS SINK?

Big ships might not seem like they should float, because they are made out of heavy materials such as steel. But they also have massive spaces for air inside them. This makes the ships less dense than a block of pure steel, allowing them to float, while the block would sink.

CAN A HELICOPTER FLY UPSIDE DOWN?

Some can! A helicopter is lifted into the air by rotor blades as they spin. Some stunt helicopters use special rotor systems—and exceptionally skilled pilots—to constantly change the angle of the rotor blades until the machine is flying upside down.

Small rotors on the tail counteract the main rotors so that the helicopter's body does not spin around as well.

The blades of a helicopter can spin around more than 400 times every minute.

WHY DON'T PLANES FALL OUT OF THE SKY?

The power of an aircraft's engine produces thrust to push it forward and the air pushes back against it as drag. Air flowing over the wings as the aircraft moves gives the plane lift, which balances its weight. When the plane is cruising at a steady speed, each pair of forces is balanced.

The four forces of flight are balanced.

Lift

Drag

Thrust

Weight

WHAT IS THE FASTEST AN AIRPLANE CAN FLY?

On October 3, 1967, a rocket-powered, experimental aircraft known as the North American X-15 reached a speed of 4,534 mph (7,297 km/h). This remains the world record for the fastest speed a pilot has flown a powered aircraft.

FLIGHT: The process of moving through the air, often by powered means such as engines

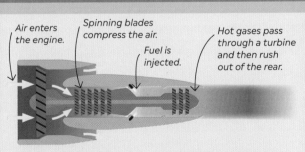

Air enters the engine.

Spinning blades compress the air.

Fuel is injected.

Hot gases pass through a turbine and then rush out of the rear.

HOW DO JET ENGINES WORK?

Jet engines work by compressing air, putting it under pressure. The compressed air is mixed with a spray of fuel and set alight by electric sparks. As the gases burn, they expand and blast out through a nozzle at the back of the engine, pushing it forward.

WHY DON'T PLANES FLAP THEIR WINGS LIKE BIRDS DO?

Birds flap their wings for thrust, while planes use engines, but both use wings to generate lift. Wings have a shape called an aerofoil. When angled correctly, they push more air under the wing than over it. The air below moves more slowly, creating an area of high pressure, which lifts the plane upward!

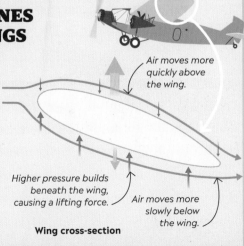

Air moves more quickly above the wing.

Higher pressure builds beneath the wing, causing a lifting force.

Air moves more slowly below the wing.

Wing cross-section

WHAT MAKES BULLETPROOF GLASS STRONG?

Although it can't stop everything, bullet-resistant glass is tougher and more elastic than ordinary glass. It is made of multiple layers of different types of glass or transparent plastic. These layers allow it to flex instead of shatter when a bullet hits it.

WILL WE RUN OUT OF ANY MATERIALS?

Possibly. While there are huge amounts of raw materials on Earth, some are rarer than others. Some rare metals are increasingly used in computers, smartphones, and electric cars, and as a result are becoming scarcer.

Minerals such as cobalt calcite contain the rare metal cobalt, used to make lithium-ion batteries.

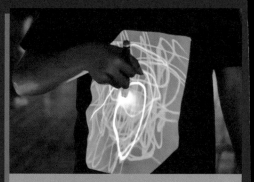

HOW CAN SOME MATERIALS CHANGE COLOR?

Some materials, such as those in this t-shirt (above), react when ultraviolet light (see page 128) is passed over them. Others are thermochromic, meaning they contain a substance, such as a dye, that changes colour at different temperatures.

WHERE DO MATERIALS COME FROM?

All materials begin with nature. We extract useful elements, such as metals, from minerals in Earth's crust. Plants, trees, and animals also produce materials we rely on. Synthetic, or human-made, materials are created by chemically changing natural materials.

SYNTHETIC

Graphene
Tough substance made of carbon.

Nylon
Artificial fibers used to make fabrics.

NATURAL

Cotton
Fibers derived from the cotton plant.

Rubber
Comes from the liquid sap of certain trees.

WHAT WAS NYLON FIRST USED TO MAKE?

a: Toothbrush bristles

b: Umbrellas

c: Stockings

QUICK QUIZ!

MATERIALS:

Natural and human-made substances used to make the things we need

ARE HUMAN-MADE MATERIALS BETTER THAN NATURAL ONES?

Not always, but scientists are often inspired by nature when creating new materials. For example, shark skin is covered in toothlike scales that reduce drag forces in water, and some scientists have developed synthetic swimsuit materials that behave in the same way—designed to improve swimmers' performance.

WHAT IS PLASTIC?

There are many types of plastics used for different things because they are so lightweight and easily molded. They are made by joining small molecules called monomers into long chains called polymers.

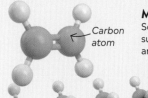

Monomer
Some small molecules, such as ethylene (left), are known as monomers.

Carbon atom

Hydrogen atom

Polymer
Using a chemical reaction, lots of monomers can be combined to form one large molecule, such as polyethylene (above).

WHEN WAS PLASTIC FIRST USED?

In 1907, Belgian chemist Leo Baekeland created a hard, moldable plastic named Bakelite. This was one of the most popular early plastics, used in many products in the 1920s and 1930s, from jewelry to casings for telephones and radios.

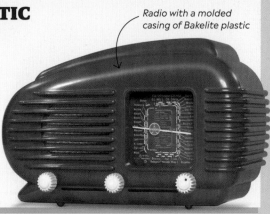

Radio with a molded casing of Bakelite plastic

HOW ARE PLASTICS RECYCLED?

Before recycling, plastic materials need to be sorted into different types of polymers. They are then shredded, washed, and melted down to form small pellets. These pellets are transported to different factories, where they can be molded into new plastic products.

Hard plastics, such as those used to make bottles, are recycled differently to plastic film and foamlike polystyrene.

HOW LONG DOES IT TAKE FOR PLASTIC TO BREAK DOWN?

Plastic waste takes a long time to decompose. Before then, it gets broken into smaller and smaller pieces. Some polymers decompose after 20 years, while the plastics in bottles, toothbrushes, and diapers may take more than 500 years to decompose.

Plastics break down into tiny pieces called microplastics, which have been found in environments all over Earth.

HOW MUCH PLASTIC POLLUTION IS THERE?

Each year, we produce about 440 million tons (400 million tonnes) of plastic waste, with around 8 million pieces of plastic alone ending up in the ocean and causing harm to marine life. A lot of plastic is used to make food or drink packaging, 85 percent of which ends up in landfills.

IT'S A MYSTERY!

Can plastics harm our health?
Some studies have linked microplastics being in the human body with worse health outcomes. However, we still don't know what levels of these are a risk or the long-term effects of such plastics.

Each day, around 60 million plastic bottles are sent to landfills.

PLASTICS:
Synthetic materials constructed from long molecules called polymers

As the diver moves through the air, he has kinetic energy.

Stored potential energy in the board is transferred into kinetic energy to help lift the diver into the air.

ARE THERE DIFFERENT TYPES OF ENERGY?

Energy can never be created or destroyed. Scientists consider all energy the same, but it can be stored in different ways and transfer from one store to another.

Kinetic energy
Things in motion have kinetic energy, otherwise known as movement energy.

Electrical energy
The movement of charged particles in an electric current is a form of energy.

Potential energy
This is the energy stored in a raised or stretched object such as a coiled spring.

Sound energy
The vibration of an object or substance travels in waves as sound energy.

Nuclear energy
The energy stored in tiny atoms, which can be released when they are split apart in reactions.

Chemical energy
Substances store energy in the chemical bonds that hold them together.

WHAT IS ENERGY?

Anything that can make a change has energy. Whenever some kind of change happens, energy is being transferred. For example, the stored energy in this flexible diving board is transferred to the diver springing off it.

ENERGY: Something that can be stored and transferred, that makes things happen all around us

We can hear a splash as the diver reaches the water as some kinetic energy transfers to sound energy!

DO WE NEED THE SUN TO PROVIDE ENERGY?

Plants use energy in sunlight to create their food, which is passed up the food chain—as chemical energy—to animals that eat plants and to animals that eat animals. Without the Sun, we would lose our food energy, the world's heat energy, and the light that enables us to see.

WHERE DOES ENERGY GO?

The total amount of energy in existence always remains the same, but it is constantly transferring from one energy store to another. As this boy uses his own chemical energy to pull the elastic part of his slingshot back as far as possible, the energy becomes stored as elastic potential energy. When he lets go, this transfers to kinetic energy—stored in the now moving ball.

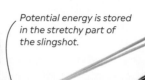

Potential energy is stored in the stretchy part of the slingshot.

Kinetic energy is stored in the slingshot's missile.

HEAT: The energy stored in the jiggling particles that make up all matter

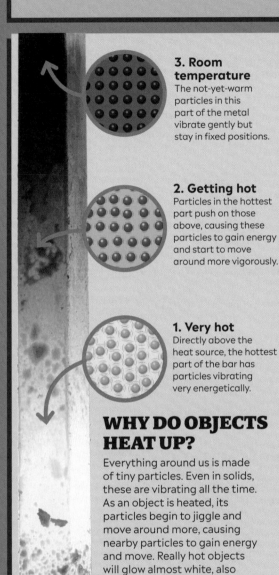

3. Room temperature
The not-yet-warm particles in this part of the metal vibrate gently but stay in fixed positions.

2. Getting hot
Particles in the hottest part push on those above, causing these particles to gain energy and start to move around more vigorously.

1. Very hot
Directly above the heat source, the hottest part of the bar has particles vibrating very energetically.

WHY DO OBJECTS HEAT UP?

Everything around us is made of tiny particles. Even in solids, these are vibrating all the time. As an object is heated, its particles begin to jiggle and move around more, causing nearby particles to gain energy and move. Really hot objects will glow almost white, also emitting light energy.

Convection
In fluids, hotter parts rise away from the heat source and then cool and fall, causing currents that heat up the whole substance.

Conduction
Objects in direct contact with something hot, such as this flame, heat up by conduction.

Radiation
Heat radiates out as waves when traveling through gases such as the air.

HOW DOES HEAT TRAVEL?

Heat energy can be passed on in three main ways: radiation, convection, and conduction. A source of heat, such as a gas stove, radiates thermal energy upward toward this pan of cool water, which gets warmer and warmer.

QUICK QUIZ!

WHAT IS ABSOLUTE ZERO— THE COLDEST TEMPERATURE?

a: -245.2°F (-154°C)

b: -459.4°F (-273°C)

c: -751°F (-435°C)

WHY DO MATERIALS MELT AT DIFFERENT TEMPERATURES?

Materials with heavier particles and stronger bonds between them require more heat energy to break them apart. Tungsten only melts at temperatures of above 6,192°F (3,422°C), whereas others such as mercury (below) are liquid at room temperature.

WHERE IS THE HOTTEST PLACE ON EARTH?

On July 10, 1913, the hottest ever air temperature of 134.1°F (56.7°C) was recorded at Furnace Creek in Death Valley in California. This area sees some of the highest temperatures in the world, as the bare desert plains are heated by the Sun and mountains on either side trap the hot air.

STOP
Extreme Heat Danger
Walking after 10 AM not recommended

Dusty deserts can get extremely hot in the daytime, so any visitors must take care!

HOW HOT IS TOO HOT FOR A HUMAN?

When temperatures soar to between 103°F (39°C) and 124°F (51°C), the human body stops working as it should. People may suffer from dehydration, painful cramps, and heat exhaustion. But too much cold can also be deadly, leading to frostbite and a condition called hypothermia.

ELECTRICITY:

A way of transferring energy caused by charged particles

IS ELECTRICITY A FORCE OF NATURE?

The dramatic flashes of lightning that strike the ground in a storm are a form of naturally occurring electricity. Each bolt happens when negatively charged particles that have built up in a cloud shoot down to the ground toward areas of positive charge. The electricity that flows through wires and into our homes is also the movement of charged particles.

WHY DON'T ELECTRIC EELS SHOCK THEMSELVES?

They often do! While most of the electricity eels generate flows through the water to stun predators or prey, some does pass through their body. Luckily, most of their important organs are squished toward their front, away from the electricity-producing cells and protected by thick, insulating fat.

The eel's shocks can deliver up to 860 volts of electricity.

QUICK QUIZ!

WHEN WAS THE FIRST RECHARGEABLE BATTERY INVENTED?

a: 1759

b: 1859

c: 1959

HOW DO WE GET POWER FROM ELECTRICITY?

Atoms (see page 108) contain tiny particles called electrons. In substances such as metal wire, these electrons are free to move around. When connected to a battery, they all flow in the same direction—creating an electric current that can pass through and power objects such as light bulbs.

The bulb lights up when the battery is switched on.

Electrons all move in the same direction when a current is flowing.

HOW DOES ELECTRICITY GET TO OUR HOMES?

The electricity we use in our homes is generated in power stations, where huge steam-powered turbines drive generators to create a continuous supply of electricity. Power lines carry the high-voltage electricity to smaller substations, which convert it to the lower, safer form we use in our homes.

WHY DOES STATIC ELECTRICITY MAKE YOUR HAIR STAND UP?

When two materials rub together, electrons move from one material to the other. A balloon rubbed on someone's hair gains electrons, becoming negatively charged. The hair loses electrons and is positively charged. Objects with the same charge repel each other, so your hairs stand on end!

Each hair is repelling the others around it.

WHO DISCOVERED THAT THE EARTH IS MAGNETIC?

Although compasses had been used since around 200 BCE, nobody knew why they pointed north. English physicist William Gilbert was the first to propose that this was because Earth itself was magnetic. After carrying out experiments, he published his ideas in a book in 1600.

The magnetic north pole is a few degrees away from the North Pole.

The geographical North Pole is at the very top of Earth.

Earth generates a magnetic field as if it had a giant bar magnet inside it.

The magnet's south pole

The magnet's north pole

WHICH SUBSTANCES STICK TO A MAGNET?

The most common magnetic materials are metals, but only a few metals are magnetic. Anything containing iron, nickel, and cobalt will be attracted to a magnet, but other metals, such as gold and silver are not magnetic.

The nails are attracted to the magnet.

IT'S A MYSTERY!

Why do Earth's magnetic poles swap around?
Changes to the flow of magnetic materials in Earth's core causes the poles to flip—183 times in the last 83 million years! But scientists cannot predict when this might happen next.

Iron is one of several metals that are magnetic materials.

MAGNETISM:
A force produced by magnets that pulls on magnetic materials or other magnets

DO OPPOSITES REALLY ATTRACT?

Yes! When opposite poles of magnets are put close together, they attract each other. The opposite effect happens when the same poles of two bar magnets are close—they push each other away. This is because around each bar magnet are invisible lines of force that form a magnetic field. Whether these point in the same direction or not determines if poles attract.

Like poles repel each other.

Opposite poles attract each other.

HOW DO WE USE MAGNETS?

Some materials become electromagnets when electricity is passed through them. We can control the strength of electromagnets by increasing or decreasing the electrical current and we can switch them on and off! This makes them ideal for lifting heavy loads of metal.

Scrap metal is attracted to the large, round electromagnet and pulled out of the pile.

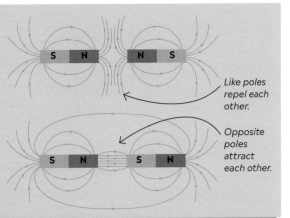

WHAT IS THE WORLD'S STRONGEST MAGNET?

Huge stars called magnetars are the most magnetic objects in the Universe. They have a powerful magnetic field, shown in this artist's impression (left). On Earth, the strongest magnets we use are made from the metal neodymium. While an average fridge magnet has a strength of 0.001 Teslas (T), a neodymium magnet can create magnetic fields of 1.4 T—1,400 times stronger!

ENERGY RESOURCES:

Fuels and other sources of power that are used to generate electricity

Turbine blades can be as long as 430 ft (130 m).

Each turbine can rotate between 15 and 20 revolutions per minute.

WHAT ARE FOSSIL FUELS?

Fossil fuels form over millions of years—deep underground or under the sea bed—from the decomposing remains of plants and animals, and release energy when burned. Coal, oil, and natural gas are examples of fossil fuels. Machines drill through layers of rock to extract oil and gas, and coal is dug from mines deep underground. Fossil fuels are nonrenewable, because they are not being replaced as we use them up.

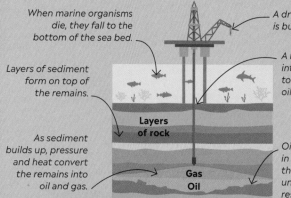

When marine organisms die, they fall to the bottom of the sea bed.

A drilling platform is built at sea.

Layers of sediment form on top of the remains.

A hole is drilled into the sea bed to extract the oil or gas.

Layers of rock

As sediment builds up, pressure and heat convert the remains into oil and gas.

Gas
Oil

Oil and gas collect in spaces between the rock, forming underground reservoirs.

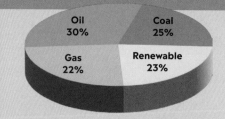

Oil 30%

Coal 25%

Gas 22%

Renewable 23%

HOW MUCH OF THE ENERGY WE USE COMES FROM FOSSIL FUELS?

Almost 80 percent of the world's energy is still generated by burning coal, oil, and natural gas. Iceland is leading the way in cleaner power, getting almost all of its energy from renewable sources.

WHAT IS RENEWABLE ENERGY?

Natural sources of energy are known as renewables, because—unlike fossil fuels—they will never run out. These different energy sources are mostly ways of turning huge turbines that convert motion into electrical power.

Wind energy
Large turbines on land or at sea are pushed around by the power of the wind.

Solar energy
Large panels absorb energy from the Sun and convert it into electricity.

Tidal energy
The power of the tides can turn underwater turbines.

Hydroelectric energy
Dams capture water, which is directed through turbines to make electricity.

Geothermal energy
Heat energy from rocks deep underground can be used for power.

Biomass energy
Decomposing plant and animal material produces energy-rich methane gas.

WHY ARE WIND TURBINES SO BIG?

Offshore wind turbines can be as tall as 850 ft (260 m). Longer blades capture more wind, and generate more electricity, even in regions that are less breezy.

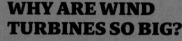

WHAT IS A NUCLEAR REACTION?

When the nucleus (core) of an atom is split, some of the energy that holds the atom together is released. Splitting atoms in a controlled way can trigger a chain reaction involving billions of atoms colliding and splitting to release huge amounts of energy.

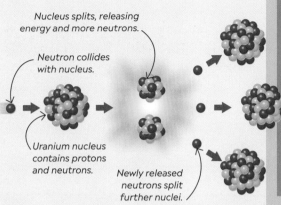

Nucleus splits, releasing energy and more neutrons.

Neutron collides with nucleus.

Uranium nucleus contains protons and neutrons.

Newly released neutrons split further nuclei.

IS NUCLEAR ENERGY DANGEROUS?

The waste produced by nuclear reactions is radioactive and hazardous to health, so it must be stored securely. Power plants have extensive safety procedures to stop radiation from leaking into the environment. There have been some reactor accidents, but the risk of these happening is usually low.

HOW MANY NUCLEAR POWER STATIONS ARE THERE?

There are around 400 nuclear reactors operating in 32 countries around the world, which is far fewer than the 2,400 coal-fired power stations still active. With over 90 nuclear power plants, the US has the most, while France and China both operate more than 50 reactors.

WHAT DO WE DO WITH NUCLEAR WASTE?

Nuclear waste can cause harm to people and must be disposed of safely. Wastes that stay radioactive the longest are stored deep underground, and less hazardous wastes are sealed in concrete. Some waste can remain radioactive for up to 10,000 years!

NUCLEAR ENERGY:
The energy released when atomic particles smash together and split apart

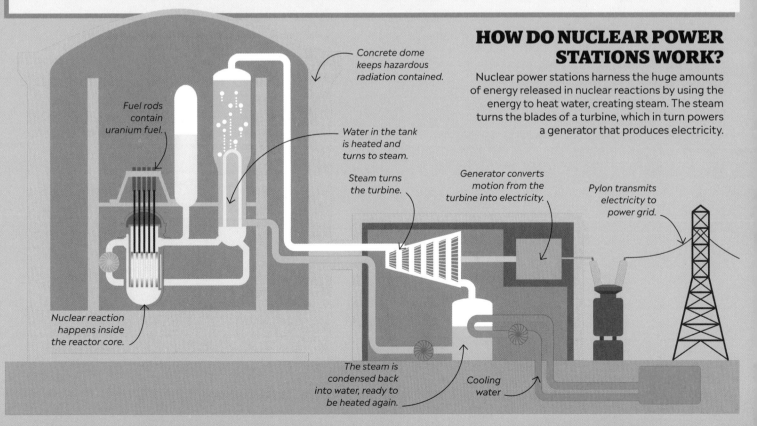

HOW DO NUCLEAR POWER STATIONS WORK?

Nuclear power stations harness the huge amounts of energy released in nuclear reactions by using the energy to heat water, creating steam. The steam turns the blades of a turbine, which in turn powers a generator that produces electricity.

Concrete dome keeps hazardous radiation contained.

Fuel rods contain uranium fuel.

Water in the tank is heated and turns to steam.

Steam turns the turbine.

Generator converts motion from the turbine into electricity.

Pylon transmits electricity to power grid.

Nuclear reaction happens inside the reactor core.

The steam is condensed back into water, ready to be heated again.

Cooling water

LIGHT: A form of electromagnetic radiation (energy that travels in waves) that makes it possible for humans to see the world around us

WHERE DOES LIGHT COME FROM?

On Earth, the Sun is our main source of natural light. Reactions in its core generate masses of light energy, which travel through space to light our planet (see page 13). But light is also generated in other ways, using electricity, or by chemical reactions such as fire. Fire dancers (right) can speedily move their torches (light sources) around to create patterns against a dark sky.

(see page 13)

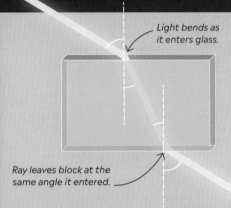

Light bends as it enters glass.

Ray leaves block at the same angle it entered.

DOES LIGHT TRAVEL IN A STRAIGHT LINE?

Light always moves in a straight line, but it travels at different speeds through different materials. When it passes from the air into water or a glass block (above), it slows down. This change in speed causes the light ray to bend—a process called refraction. When leaving the material, it speeds up and returns back to its original path.

IT'S A MYSTERY!

Why do scorpions glow in the dark?
A scorpion's exoskeleton contains a layer that shines blue-green under ultraviolet light. But scientists have no idea why it glows this color or how this helps the scorpion!

Radio waves

Microwaves

Infrared

Visible light

Ultraviolet rays

X-rays

Gamma rays

WHAT IS LIGHT?

Light is a type of radiation—a wave that transfers energy. It is part of a spectrum of other waves that have longer or shorter wavelengths, known as the electromagnetic spectrum. Only a very small part of this spectrum is visible to the human eye.

All the light and colors we see make up a small part of the spectrum.

X-rays pass through the soft parts of our bodies, making them useful for medical imaging.

Gamma rays have the shortest wavelengths and can be harmful to humans.

HOW POWERFUL ARE LASERS?

Lasers emit a concentrated, powerful beam of single-color light. They can be strong enough to cut and engrave metals, but are also used in healthcare, scientific research, and even technology to scan barcodes!

IS THERE ANY WAY TO SEE IN THE DARK?

In dim light, night vision goggles can enhance what you see. These convert small amounts of light into particles called electrons, which are then multiplied. This greater number of electrons is then converted back into a stronger visible light in shades of green. Green is used because the human eye is more sensitive to this color.

The swirling paths of the flames are captured by the camera.

WHAT ARE FIBER OPTICS?

Optical fibers are tiny threads of transparent glass or plastic and are used to send data over huge distances in the form of light. Each thread has a mirrorlike coating inside, allowing light to speedily bounce through it. The internet, TV, and telephone services all rely on fiber optic cables running through the ground and even under the sea.

The mirror version of you is flipped.

WHY DOES A PHOTOGRAPH OF ME LOOK DIFFERENT TO MY REFLECTION?

We see things because light reflects off objects and travels to our eyes. When you look into a mirror, you see yourself flipped because of the way light bounces off it. The left side of your face appears on the left of the mirror, but this is actually the right side of the person shown in the mirror. A photograph, however, shows you how you look to other people.

COLOR: The appearance of an object due to the way it reflects or transmits light

WHY DO OBJECTS LOOK DIFFERENT COLORS?

White light is a mix of colors, and each one of these has a different wavelength. Objects that appear to be different colors are actually just reflecting certain wavelengths and absorbing others. The ones that they reflect bounce back and into your eyes, where they are detected by specialized light-sensitive cone cells.

White T-shirt
The fabric appears white because it reflects all the colors in light.

Green T-shirt
This fabric appears green, because it reflects only the green part of visible light.

WHY IS THERE NO COLOR BLACK IN THE RAINBOW?

To our eyes, a beam of light appears white. But when it passes through a prism (right), it slows and bends in a process called refraction. This separates it into the colors of the visible spectrum (see page 128)—those found in a rainbow. This does not include black, which is an absence of light instead of a color.

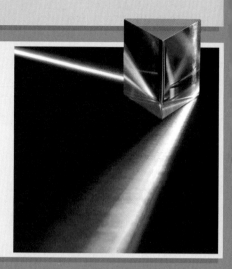

WHAT DOES IT MEAN TO BE COLOR-BLIND?

Color-blind people usually see objects clearly, but they cannot fully see the difference between some colors. Difficulty distinguishing between red and green is the most common type. This Ishihara image (left) tests for color-blindness. If you can spot a bird shape in red, you are not color-blind.

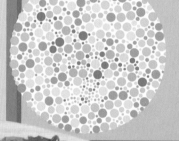

QUICK QUIZ!

WHICH OF THESE ANIMALS CAN SEE ULTRAVIOLET LIGHT ?

a: Humpback whales

b: Chimpanzees

c: Bees

WHY IS BLUE SO RARE IN NATURE?

Colored substances called pigments are what reflect wavelengths and give an object its color. But there isn't a true blue pigment in nature. Animals and plants that appear blue instead mix other pigments or have unique structures that can bend the light.

Tiny scales on this blue morpho butterfly bend light to give it its color.

WHY DOES MIXING ALL COLORS TOGETHER MAKE BROWN?

Different-colored paints can be mixed together to produce other colors, such as mixing blue and yellow to create green. Mixing more paints together increases the wavelengths they will absorb, producing a darker color—usually a brown or blackish shade.

WHAT'S THE LOUDEST SOUND EVER MADE?

The intensity, or loudness, of sounds is measured in decibels. In 1883, the volcanic eruption of Mount Krakatoa in Indonesia was heard more than 3,000 miles (5,000 km) away. The sound measured between 230 and 300 decibels—probably one of the loudest noises ever heard!

Volcano erupting
The blast of lava and ash out of a volcano can create sounds of 180 decibels or more.

Howler monkey
Thought to be the loudest land animal, these monkeys' calls are up to 140 decibels.

Plane taking off
A plane's jet engines make sounds of around 140 decibels when taking off.

WHAT MAKES SOME SOUNDS HIGHER THAN OTHERS?

The difference between higher-pitched sounds and lower-pitched sounds is due to their wavelength. This is the distance between the crests of the wave. A shorter wavelength means a higher frequency of waves (more waves per second). Sounds with a higher frequency produce higher-pitched noises.

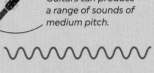

The low-pitched rumble of thunder is due to low frequency waves.

Guitars can produce a range of sounds of medium pitch.

High-frequency sound waves are produced by a mouse's squeak.

CAN ANYONE HEAR YOU SCREAM IN SPACE?

No! Sound waves travel as a series of vibrations. When sound passes through air, the air particles vibrate, which passes on the sound. Space is a vacuum, which means there is no air, so there is no way for sound waves to travel.

SOUND: Vibrations that travel as waves through materials—including the air—to reach our ears

HOW FAST DOES SOUND TRAVEL?

Although sound travels incredibly fast—moving through the air at around 1,130 ft (345 m) per second—it still moves a million times slower than light. When a balloon is popped, the air inside it rapidly expands, vibrating the air particles. This causes the particles next to them to vibrate, and the vibration is passed on like this until it reaches your ears as a noisy bang.

Our body reacts to the loud sound almost instantly.

As the pencil pierces the balloon, it makes a loud bang.

The big ears of a fennec fox radiate heat in the desert.

DO BIG EARS HELP YOU HEAR BETTER?

The external, flappy part of our ear called a pinna helps channel sound waves into the inner parts of the ear. Larger pinnas do amplify sound slightly more, but not enough to make a huge difference!

WHAT ARE SIMPLE MACHINES?

There are six main types of simple machines that transfer a force and movement from one place to another, magnifying them at the same time.

Inclined plane
Pushing a heavy load up a ramp requires less force than lifting it upward.

Wedge
A force applied to the thick end of a wedge is concentrated into the thin, cutting end—used in tools such as axes.

Wheel and axle
A wheel can turn around a central rod, or axle. Spinning the wheel turns the axle with more force.

Screw
When turning a screw, a rotating force is turned into a downward force.

Pulley
Pulling down on the rope of a pulley changes the direction of a force—lifting a load upward.

Lever
A lever moves on a fulcrum. Applying force at one end can move objects at the other.

A mobile launcher stretching 380 ft (116 m) into the sky can sit atop the 26 ft (8 m) crawler to support rockets being moved.

HOW BIG CAN MACHINES GET?

NASA's massive crawler-transporter is one of the biggest machines around—measuring 131 ft (40 m) long and 114 ft (35 m) wide. It transports rockets to and from the launchpad and weighs in at almost 3,300 tons (3,000 tonnes).

HOW DID THE WHEEL CHANGE THE WORLD?

First used on roads in ancient Mesopotamia as early as 3500 BCE, wheels revolutionized transportation and also led to advances in agriculture when used in farming machines. Initially solid discs of wood (above), they were later designed with gaps to become lighter.

WHY DO BIKES HAVE GEARS?

Gears help the rider keep a steady pedaling speed, whether cycling uphill or on flat ground. Going uphill, using a low gear, the rider turns the pedals many times for each rotation of the wheel to maximize power. In a high gear, the pedals turn the wheels further than in a low gear, which increases speed.

Changing gear shifts the chain from one toothed wheel to another.

Chain transmits the turning force from the pedals to the wheel.

Rider applies a turning force by pushing pedals.

Eight huge tread belts propel the machine along.

When were the first machines used?
Our ancient ancestors used really simple machines such as hand axes—the oldest dating back more than two million years! But we don't know what other devices they could have used that have not been preserved.

IT'S A MYSTERY!

MACHINES:
Human-designed devices that can apply forces to make a task easier

ENGINES:
Machines that use the energy from a power source to do some kind of work

WHEN WERE THE FIRST ENGINES INVENTED?

The very first engines were invented in the 17th century to pump water out of underground mines and were powered by steam. More steam engines followed, including English inventor Thomas Newcomen's 1712 beam engine (below). Later engines were soon being used to power cars, trains, and ships!

The engine is more than 43 ft (13 m) high and bigger than an average three-bedroom house.

WHAT IS THE BIGGEST ENGINE?

Designed to propel gigantic container ships across the ocean, the Wärtsilä-Sulzer RTA96-C is a colossal engine. Weighing 2,535 tons (2,300 tonnes)—as much as 20 blue whales—it is also incredibly powerful and fuel efficient.

The piston moves up and down, driven by steam under pressure.

The beam rocks back and forth, powering the wheel.

WHY DO PLANES HAVE JET ENGINES?

Jet engines, such as this one being tested in Minnesota, emit huge amounts of thrust to power faster journeys through the sky. They also help planes vibrate less and contain fewer moving parts than other engines, making them more reliable.

DO ELECTRIC CARS HAVE AN ENGINE?

Yes, but this is different to those in gas cars. In an electric car, batteries power an electric motor. Modern electric cars can travel between 150–300 miles (241–483 km) before they need to recharge the batteries at charging stations (below).

QUICK QUIZ!

WHEN WAS THE FIRST ELECTRIC CAR BUILT?

a: 1832

b: 1968

c: 1994

HOW DOES A CAR ENGINE WORK?

Cars that run on gas or diesel fuel use an engine called an internal combustion engine. Inside this, the fuel combusts (burns), producing gases that push against pistons. Through a system of connecting gears, this movement drives the car's wheels.

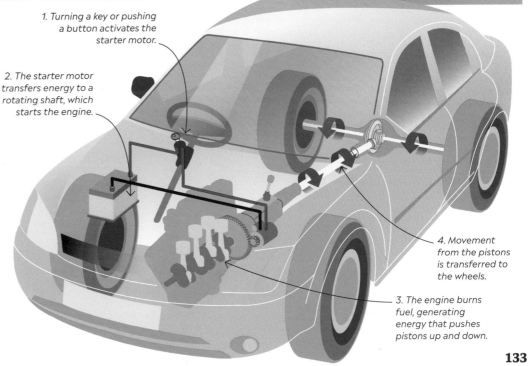

1. Turning a key or pushing a button activates the starter motor.

2. The starter motor transfers energy to a rotating shaft, which starts the engine.

4. Movement from the pistons is transferred to the wheels.

3. The engine burns fuel, generating energy that pushes pistons up and down.

133

ROBOTS:

Machines that can be programmed to complete tasks set by humans and that are sometimes designed to resemble humans themselves

WHAT IS A ROBOT?

The term robot comes from *robota*, a word from the Czech language that means "hard, boring work." This is because many robots are automatic machines that are designed to do repetitive, tedious, or physically difficult jobs that humans don't want to do! Some robots, however, are made to interact and work alongside humans.

ARE ROBOTS DANGEROUS?

You might have seen a film where robots take over the world, but this is still science fiction. While robots using AI (see page 143) can learn and adapt to their environments, they are not sentient (self-aware with thoughts and feelings like humans). Robots may malfunction and make mistakes or biased choices, but they cannot cause us intentional harm.

WHEN WERE THE EARLIEST ROBOTS?

As far back as ancient times, people made machines that could move by themselves, powered by clockwork or water. But it was not until the mid-20th century that engineers designed complicated programmable robots. These included the first industrial robot, which began work in a car factory in New Jersey in 1961.

ARE THERE ROBOTS IN MY HOUSE?

If you have a vacuum cleaner that zooms around on its own or washes the floor, robots are living alongside you! There are lots of domestic robots that can feed and take care of pets, play games, and even keep us company.

WHAT JOBS DO ROBOTS DO?

More than 90 percent of robots do hazardous or difficult jobs in factories, building other machines, such as cars and electronic goods. Robots are now so common that in these industries there is approximately one robot for every 80 human workers. Robotic arms are used to lift, weld, and paint metal parts.

A locomotor controls the overall movement of the robotic arm.

Robotic arms have rotating joints and other flexible parts.

Robotic hand can grasp, turn, and set down objects with precision.

CAN ROBOTS THINK FOR THEMSELVES?

Thanks to advanced programming and AI, some robots can do complex jobs that involve making humanlike decisions, such as assessing whether a product is faulty or fine. However, although these robots appear to be thinking for themselves, they are still following an algorithm—a set of steps and rules created by humans.

HOW DO HUMANS CONTROL ROBOTS?

Some controllers have buttons that can change a robot's direction.

Some robots are controlled using a remote, while others are automated, which means they can work on their own once they have their instructions. Humans teach them using programming languages such as Python. Automated machines then get on with their jobs, using sensors to understand their surroundings.

HOW DO YOU BUILD A ROBOT?

Making a robot merges complex engineering—making its parts work together so it can move—and computing power, which gives the robot the ability to process information received by its sensors. Some robots, such as humanoid robots intended to resemble us, also have complex external designs. Robots such as this one (left), made by the company Engineered Arts, have faces created from 3D scans of real people and can make a huge range of realistic facial expressions.

This Mesmer robot has humanlike hair, skin texture, and facial expressions.

An electronic "brain" can be programmed and controlled from any location.

SUPER STRUCTURES:

Large structures designed by architects and engineers

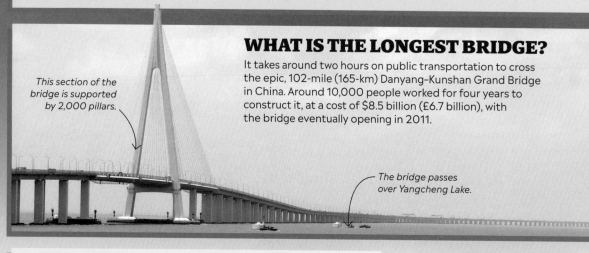

This section of the bridge is supported by 2,000 pillars.

WHAT IS THE LONGEST BRIDGE?

It takes around two hours on public transportation to cross the epic, 102-mile (165-km) Danyang–Kunshan Grand Bridge in China. Around 10,000 people worked for four years to construct it, at a cost of $8.5 billion (£6.7 billion), with the bridge eventually opening in 2011.

The bridge passes over Yangcheng Lake.

There are 163 floors in the building.

Cables connected to towers hold up the main bridge deck.

Weight is spread out along an arch's curve.

Arch

Cable-stayed

WHAT MAKES A STRONG BRIDGE?

The strongest bridges are made from strong materials, such as iron, steel, and concrete, and have a structure that distributes stress. Some bridges were built as arches because an arch is a strong shape, while others use cables for support.

WHAT IS THE TALLEST BUILDING?

Constructed between 2004 and 2010, the Burj Khalifa in Dubai, UAE, remains the planet's tallest building. It soars to the dizzying height of 2,700 ft (828 m). The building narrows as it rises, making it more stable and resistant to wind.

HOW MUCH OF A BUILDING IS UNDERGROUND?

Buildings can stretch high up into the sky, but they also extend underground—with deep concrete foundations to support them. Skyscrapers need bigger foundations than smaller buildings to support their tall vertical load.

Shanghai Tower, China, is 2,074 ft (632 m) high.

Foundations extend 102 ft (31 m) below ground.

There are six tiers to the pyramid.

WHY WERE ANCIENT MONUMENTS OFTEN PYRAMID-SHAPED?

A pyramid is a very stable shape as the greatest load is toward the bottom. It would have been an easy to way to build a tall structure. The pyramid of Djoser in Saqqara, Egypt (above), was built more than 4,500 years ago and still stands today!

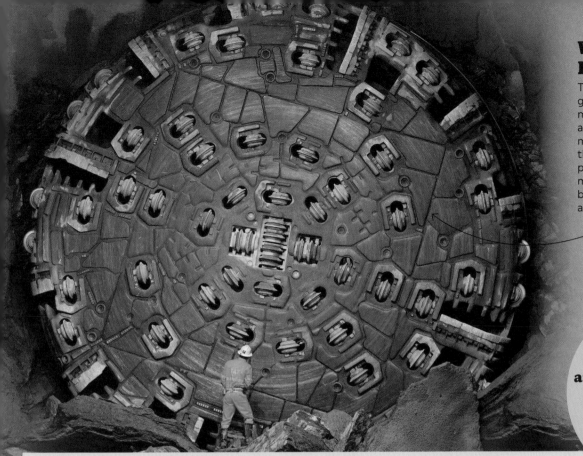

WHAT MACHINE DIGS TUNNELS?

Tunnel boring machines are like giant mechanical worms that make modern tunneling faster and safer. At the front, they have many rotating disks that cut into the rock face, while powerful pneumatic jacks push the machine forward. Conveyor belts carry rock fragments away from the front.

Drilling machine Sissi, shown here constructing a railroad in Switzerland, can cut through 50–65 ft (15–20 m) of rock a day.

WHAT WAS THE FIRST UNDERWATER TUNNEL?

a: Elbe Tunnel, Germany

b: Thames Tunnel, UK

c: Holland Tunnel, US

QUICK QUIZ!

TUNNELS:

Long passages under roads, under water, and even through mountains

HOW DO TUNNELS PASS THROUGH MOUNTAINS?

When tunneling through rock, engineers often use controlled explosions to shatter and break down the rock before sending in hue boring machines. The tunnel that passes through Zion National Park, Utah (below) travels through more than a mile of solid sandstone rock.

ARE THERE TUNNELS UNDER THE SEA?

There are many! This photo shows the construction of the Channel Tunnel, which opened in 1994. Linking the UK and France, it took six years to build. One of the tunnel boring machines used was too big to back out, so was buried in the ground!

WHY DON'T TUNNELS COLLAPSE?

As the head of a boring machine makes its way underground, the open area behind it is lined and reinforced with curved, concrete segments that fit together—like pieces in a jigsaw puzzle—to form tight rings. Steel frames and bolts also add support.

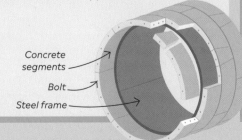

Concrete segments

Bolt

Steel frame

WHERE IS THE LONGEST TUNNEL?

The world's longest tunnel is also the deepest! The Gotthard Base Tunnel is just over 35 miles (57 km) long and lies at a depth of 7,546 ft (2,300 m). It provides a rail link through the Alps between Switzerland and Italy.

WHAT'S THE FASTEST CAR?

If you blink, you might miss the Koenigsegg Jesko Absolut as it zooms by. This Swedish-built car can reach the eye-watering speed of 330 mph (531 km/h), making it the world's speediest road car available to buy. It even beats the fastest official speed reached by a Formula 1 racing car—247 mph (397 km/h).

HOW DO TRAINS RUN ON MAGNETS?

Maglev trains have magnets on their underside. The base of the train carriage wraps around a guiding rail, in which electromagnets produce a magnetic field (see page 125). This alternately attracts and repels the magnets on the train, propelling the train along.

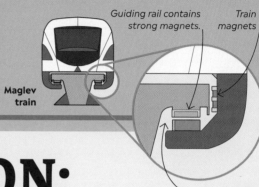

Guiding rail contains strong magnets.

Train magnets

Maglev train

Train levitates as the two magnets repel each other.

TRANSPORTATION:

Methods of moving people and cargo from place to place

This jet suit has multiple engines.

HOW MANY PEOPLE CAN FIT ON A CRUISE SHIP?

As many as a small town! The *Icon of the Seas* cruise ship (below) is so massive that it needs a crew of 2,350 people to run and sail it. The maximum number of passengers is 7,600, meaning it can hold 9,950 people on board in total.

Swimming pools and lounging areas adorn the top deck.

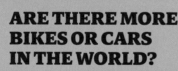

HOW DOES A JET PACK WORK?

Just like a rocket engine, a jet pack mixes liquid fuel with oxygen. The powerful chemical reaction between the two causes super-hot gas to push out through nozzles, lifting the wearer into the air. Most current jet pack models are only tested for short flights.

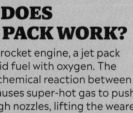

ARE THERE MORE BIKES OR CARS IN THE WORLD?

In many parts of the world, bicycles are the main mode of transportation. Denmark's capital, Copenhagen, is a cycling hot spot, where the 675,000 bikes outnumber cars by more than five to one. Globally, more than 100 million bikes are made each year, compared to around 80 to 90 million cars.

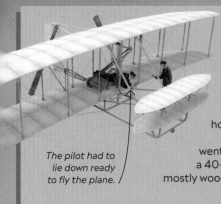

The pilot had to lie down ready to fly the plane.

WHO FLEW THE FIRST PLANE?

US brothers Wilbur and Orville Wright spent four years studying gliders in the hope of developing the world's first powered aircraft. They went on to build the *Wright Flyer*, a 40-ft (12-m) long plane made of mostly wood and cloth. On December 17, 1903, it made its first flight.

WILL CARS EVER FLY?

Flying cars may sound like science fiction, but engineers are working hard to get them off the ground. Called vertical take-off and landing aircraft (VTOL), these designs could become air taxis or even personal vehicles. Some companies are planning to launch prototypes in the next few years!

QUICK QUIZ!

HOW LONG DID THE FIRST-EVER POWERED FLIGHT LAST?

a: 12 seconds

b: 22 seconds

c: 32 seconds

NORTH AMERICA
Vancouver
Emeryville
Toronto
Chicago
ASIA
Moscow
EUROPE
AFRICA
Vladivostok
Lhasa
Shanghai
Dibrugarh
Kanyakumari
SOUTH AMERICA
AUSTRALIA
Perth
Sydney

HOW FAR CAN A TRAIN TRAVEL?

Some stretches of track are so long that trains can run across them for days! The Trans-Siberian Railway spans across Russia from Moscow to Vladivostok—a distance of more than 5,771 miles (9,288 km). This map shows the world's six longest train routes.

Six speedy waterslides make up a mini waterpark on board.

More than 2,000 cabins fit into the ship, some with ocean views.

THE INTERNET:

A huge network linking computers all around the world, allowing easy access to information

HOW OLD IS THE INTERNET?

The internet as we know it today is about 30 years old. It began in the 1960s as a system called ARPANET, which connected universities across the US. But it wasn't until the 1990s that it grew into a worldwide network and became accessible to the general public.

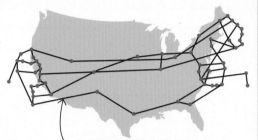

By 1977, the ARPANET network had grown to connect many computers across the US.

HOW DOES THE INTERNET WORK?

The internet is a global network of computers that exchange and share information thanks to a technology called packet switching, which breaks data into small chunks called packets and sends these separately. Internet signals are sent around the world via satellites.

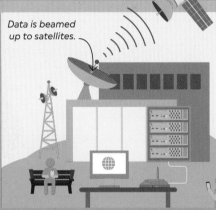

Data is beamed up to satellites.

HOW MANY PEOPLE HAVE ACCESS TO THE INTERNET?

Around the world, an estimated 5.3 billion people can connect to and use the internet. That is roughly 66 percent of Earth's population. People use the internet to work, communicate, research, and even play games in giant e-sports tournaments like the one pictured below.

IS THE INTERNET THE SAME AS THE WORLD WIDE WEB?

The internet is what connects computers and devices together, but the World Wide Web is all the webpages you view on it. British scientist Tim Berners-Lee (above) invented the World Wide Web, launching the first ever webpage in 1991.

WHAT IS THE INTERNET OF THINGS?

The internet of things is where technology such as cars, TVs, and even refrigerators can connect and share data. They can then be controlled remotely through smartphones.

WHAT DO SATELLITES DO?

Satellites are put onto different paths, or orbits, around the planet, depending on their purpose. Some satellites transmit global communications or GPS signals, while others monitor weather and climate, map Earth's surface, track missiles, study the Sun, or look deeper into space.

A geostationary orbit is circular and often used by telecommunications satellites.

Highly elliptical orbits (HEOs) are stretched and oval-shaped.

Satellites in geostationary orbits are always directly above the same point on Earth.

Satellites used to capture images use low Earth orbits (LEOs).

Sensing and communications satellites often use HEOs.

SATELLITES: Spacecraft that orbit Earth to observe our planet or transmit communications

HOW MANY SATELLITES ARE THERE?

There are currently more than 9,000 active satellites, with hundreds more launched each year. When no longer in use, some reenter Earth's atmosphere, but around 3,000 disused satellites are still in orbit. Along with old spacecraft parts and other debris, these contribute to the huge amount of space junk floating around Earth (shown left).

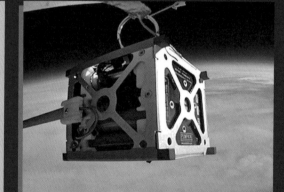

WHAT ARE CUBESATS?

CubeSats are a type of microsatellite that are so small, you could hold them in your hands! They measure around 3.9 in (10 cm) in height, width, and depth, weighing no more than 4 lb (2 kg). They perform tasks such as measuring the weather and sending communications.

HOW DOES GPS WORK?

A Global Positioning System (GPS) uses satellites to pinpoint the precise location of an object or person. A receiver (on the ground) can pick up signals from multiple satellites, measuring the distance between you and them. Because it knows the exact positions of these satellites, it can then work out your location.

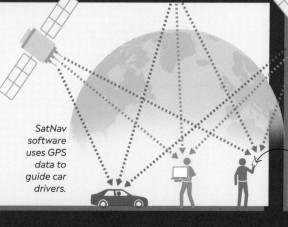

SatNav software uses GPS data to guide car drivers.

Getting signals from three satellites gives a specific point on Earth.

WHEN WERE THE FIRST COMPUTERS?

The earliest types of computers were mechanical calculating machines, such as this "Difference Engine" designed by English mathematician Charles Babbage in 1832. Early electronic computers were developed during World War II to translate coded messages. These were so big, they could take up whole rooms!

The machine was designed to add and subtract faster than humans.

The wheels could be turned to input digits.

Japanese chess-playing robot arm faces Tatsuya Sugai, a professional player.

IT'S A MYSTERY!

Are there any ancient computers?

In 1901, an ancient Greek device known as the Antikythera Mechanism was discovered. Because gears were found inside, it is thought to have been used to make astronomical calculations, but scientists don't know how!

IS A COMPUTER MORE POWERFUL THAN MY BRAIN?

Powerful supercomputers can do calculations incredibly quickly, allowing them to speedily analyze thousands of chess moves to beat world-class chess players! However, the brain is far more complex than a computer and can do a wider range of tasks. It is also more efficient, using less power.

COMPUTERS:
Machines that can store and process information or data

Microprocessor from a laptop

HOW DID COMPUTER PARTS BECOME SO TINY?

Computers used to take up lots of space because they involved lots of large components connected together. Since the late 1950s, it has been possible to etch tiny components and electrical circuits onto a single chip of silicon. These circuits, known as microchips, were first used in computers in 1975. They contain microprocessors—tiny computers that perform the main operations of a laptop or PC.

Apple iPhone

HOW FAST ARE COMPUTERS DEVELOPING?

Over the last 50 years, the speed and memory of computers has doubled every year or two. Today's mobile phones have 100,000 times more data processing power than the computer on board the Apollo spacecraft that took astronauts to the Moon in 1969!

Apollo Lunar Module

HOW SMALL IS THE SMALLEST COMPUTER?

Scientists have developed a computerized microdevice that is just 0.01 in (0.3 mm) wide—smaller than a grain of rice! Designed to operate inside the human body, the tiny computer has been used to find new ways to monitor and treat cancer.

Grain of rice   Computer

AI:
Short for artificial intelligence—technology that can complete tasks that usually require human intelligence

QUICK QUIZ!

WHICH SCIENTIST INVENTED A WAY TO TEST IF AI CAN THINK LIKE A HUMAN BEING?

a: Charles Babbage

b: Grace Hopper

c: Alan Turing

WHAT IS ARTIFICIAL INTELLIGENCE?

AI is technology that allows a machine or computer to carry out complex tasks or solve problems that would normally require human intelligence. AI can do a wide range of tasks—from diagnosing medical conditions, to facial recognition and tracking used in social media filters.

AI can add digitally generated layers onto your face, adding glasses or changing features.

HOW DOES AN AI LEARN?

Many AIs are trained on huge sets of data. They use this information to identify patterns that help them generate their own responses. Popular AI chatbot ChatGPT was trained on 560 gigabytes of data from the internet—equivalent to more than 1.3 billion books!

CAN AI BE YOUR DOCTOR?

AIs have many medical uses. They can analyze scans of the body to spot conditions and can also be used in defibrillators—medical devices used to revive a person whose heart has stopped beating regularly. In some types of defibrillators, AI technology is used to work out exactly when it is safe to shock the patient.

An AI defibrillator is tested on a training dummy.

HOW DO I KNOW IF I'M TALKING TO AN AI?

Many websites now use chatbots powered by AI to talk to us and answer our questions. Signs that you are chatting to an AI include getting a long reply instantly and the language being overly formal, clunky, or repetitive.

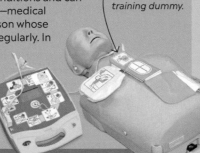

COULD AI HARM US?

AI may soon influence many areas of our life—both online and in the physical world, as AI-run, driverless cars (left) could dominate our roads. If these malfunction or are hacked, this could lead to accidents. There are also risks that AI could take human jobs and generate content that is harmful or inaccurate. As the use of AI increases, we will need to ensure it is carefully regulated.

FAST FACTS

Around **35 percent** of businesses now use AI in some way.

77 percent of electronic devices feature some form of AI technology.

Fully **self-driving cars** could be available by the year **2035**.

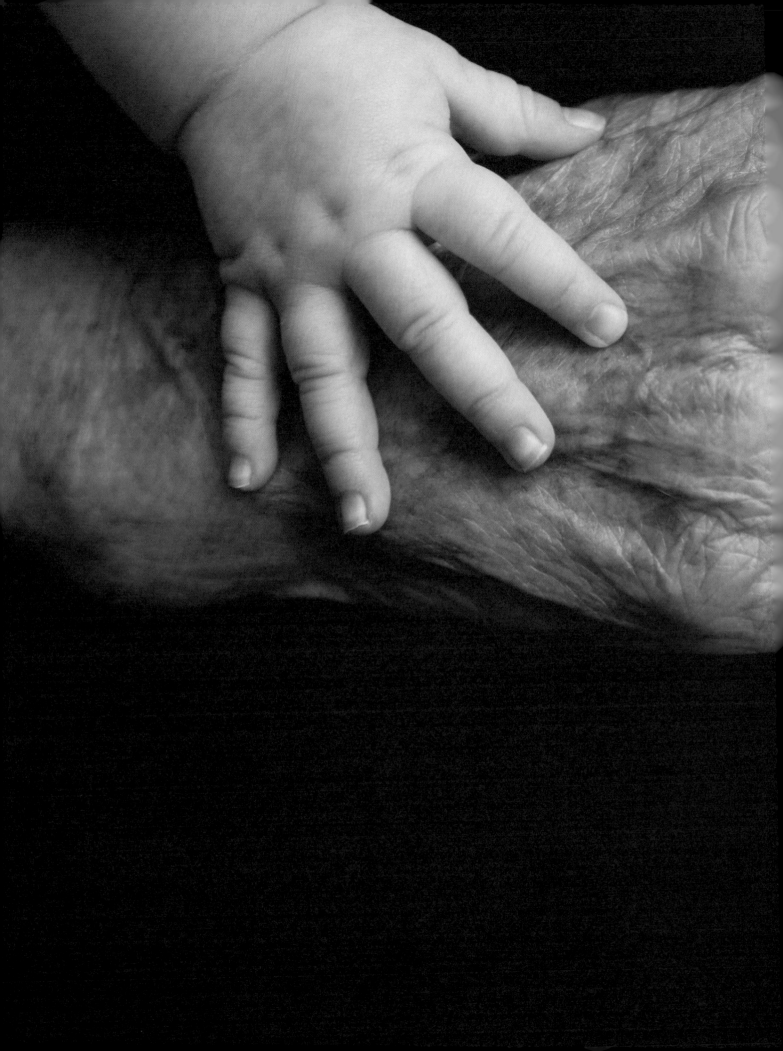

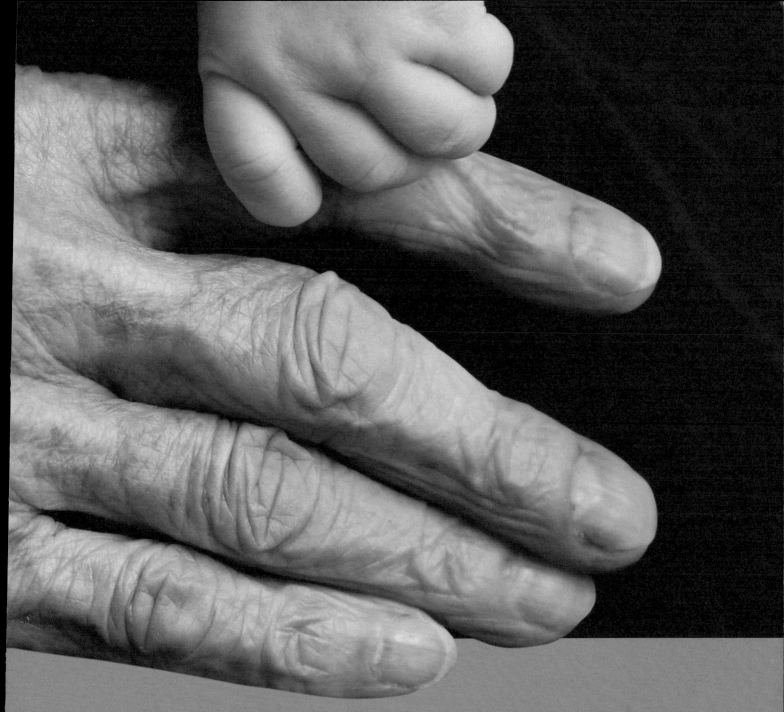

HUMAN BODY

DNA: Stands for deoxyribonucleic acid—a molecule inside body cells that contains coded instructions that control how cells work

HOW DO WE KNOW ABOUT DNA?

In the 1950s, scientists knew DNA existed, but little else about it. Then British scientist Rosalind Franklin found a way to photograph it. From this, researchers Francis Crick and James Watson (left) worked out the molecule's shape and function.

Pairs of chemicals called bases make the "rungs" of the ladder. The order of these pairs forms a code that tells cells what to do.

The long, thin outer strands of DNA are known as the backbone.

DO WE REALLY SHARE 50 PERCENT OF OUR DNA WITH BANANAS?

Yes, we do! Many of the same genes that are necessary for cells to function are the same in plants (including bananas) as in animals like us. We share 60 percent of our DNA with chickens and fruit flies, too!

IT'S A MYSTERY!

Why is a DNA strand so long?
About 98 percent of a DNA strand is a mystery to us. It is not used for genes, and scientists don't know yet what it does! One theory is that this DNA used to have a purpose but doesn't any more.

WHAT IS DNA ?

DNA is a chemical code contained in the nucleus of the body's cells. It holds the essential information those cells need to stay in working order. The code is stored in a long, thin molecule, shaped like a twisted ladder, often called the double helix.

HOW MUCH DNA DO I HAVE?

The DNA in your cells is incredibly tightly packed. An unraveled strand would be 6 ft (2 m) long—taller than you! Multiply that by the trillions of cells in your body and your stretched-out DNA would reach to the Sun and back 300 times.

HOW CAN DNA HELP SOLVE CRIMES?

We share 99.9 percent of our DNA with other humans, but that crucial 0.1 percent difference is what makes each of us unique. Analyzing DNA from hair, skin, blood, or saliva left at a crime scene can help identify a suspect.

An electrical current moves the fragments through the jelly.

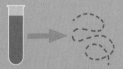

DNA evidence
DNA from a sample is broken down into tiny chemical fragments.

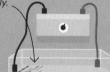

Electric current
The fragments are placed at the ends of a sheet of jelly and left to seep into it.

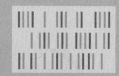

DNA fingerprint
After a few hours, the fragments form themselves into a pattern—a DNA fingerprint.

GENES:
Chemical instructions stored in DNA and passed on from parents to their offspring

Chromosome
Chromosomes are bundles of DNA found in a cell's nucleus. Every chromosome contains hundreds or thousands of genes.

One long strand of DNA, tightly coiled up, forms a chromosome.

WHY DO CHROMOSOMES COME IN PAIRS?
Humans have 23 different types of chromosomes (shown below). We all develop from a single cell that has received 23 chromosomes from each parent, which means all our cells contain two of each type, or 46 in total. Each chromosome pair is a different shape and size.

WHAT'S THE DIFFERENCE BETWEEN A GENE AND A CHROMOSOME?
A gene is a section of DNA that contains a specific set of instructions for a cell to make one of the proteins your body needs to work. Each person has about 20,000 genes. Inside a cell, these genes are grouped into bundles called chromosomes.

Gene
The shaded section shows a single gene, which carries information on how to make one specific protein.

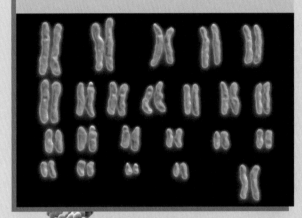

CAN FAULTY GENES BE FIXED?
Scientists are finding new ways to alter the genes that cause some illnesses. In gene editing therapy, a faulty segment of DNA is removed and replaced with a segment containing healthy code. The amended cell is then put back into the body.

A new section is inserted.

Tight coils enable large amounts of data to fit in the cell.

QUICK QUIZ!
THE COMPLETE SET OF THE GENES IN AN ORGANISM IS CALLED THE …?

a: Genome

b: Generation

c: Nucleus

DO GENES CONTROL HOW HEALTHY I AM?
Genes partly determine our future health, but how we live plays a big part, too. For instance, your genes might pass on naturally strong teeth to you. But if you never brush your teeth and eat candy all day, you will have more tooth decay than someone who looks after theirs!

WHAT DO GENES DO?
Genes give the body's cells the "recipe" they need to make proteins, the building blocks of every part of the body. Different genes determine body features, such as the color of your eyes or hair, your blood type, or the size of your ears or nose!

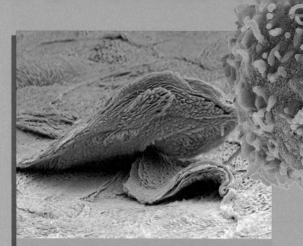

Two "daughter" cells are formed when a "parent" cell divides.

HOW ARE NEW CELLS MADE?

Body cells are being renewed all the time in a process called mitosis, where a cell makes a copy of itself. First, the nucleus, which contains DNA, divides in two. Then the cell pulls apart so that each new cell has its own nucleus. The two half-sized cells quickly grow to full size.

Cytoplasm (cell membrane) pulls apart as cells separate.

The two daughter cells are identical.

WHAT HAPPENS TO OLD CELLS WHEN THEY DIE?

Body cells have a fixed lifespan. Some last for a long time, while others are replaced more frequently. Skin cells live for just a few weeks before dying and then peeling away (shown above). Some nerve cells last many years. Dying cells inside the body shrink and then break down into tiny fragments. These are then devoured by special "cleaner" cells called phagocytes.

QUICK QUIZ!

HOW MUCH OF A CELL IS MADE UP OF WATER?

a: 10%

b: 50%

c: 70%

CELLS: Microscopic building blocks that make up every part of the body

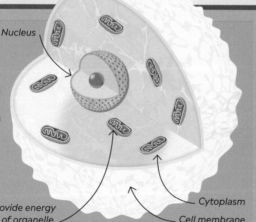

WHAT'S INSIDE A CELL?

Most of the body's cells have the same basic structure. The central nucleus is the control center. Floating in the jellylike cytoplasm that surrounds the nucleus are organelles. There are many different types of organelles, all performing different functions.

Nucleus

Mitochondria provide energy and are a type of organelle.

Cytoplasm

Cell membrane

Fat cells
Store energy as liquid fat.

Muscle cells
Contract and relax to produce movement.

Red blood cells
Carry oxygen around the body.

Intestinal cells
Absorb nutrients from food.

Nerve cells
Transmit and receive electrical signals.

Epidermal cells
Overlap to form the top layer of skin.

CAN SCIENTISTS GROW CELLS IN THE LAB?

Skin sheet

Yes! Stem cells are "blank" cells that can develop into many different kinds of cells. Stem cell technology is developing fast—soon, we may be able to grow new organs for transplants. Even without stem cells, some tissue can be grown artificially. This sheet of skin has been grown from live skin cells and may be used to treat burns and other wounds.

HOW MANY CELLS DO I HAVE IN MY BODY?

The human body is made up of trillions of cells— the latest estimate is 34 trillion! Up to 200 different types of cells perform tasks such as forming tissue, carrying messages to and from the brain, fighting disease, or storing energy. A few of the key types are shown above.

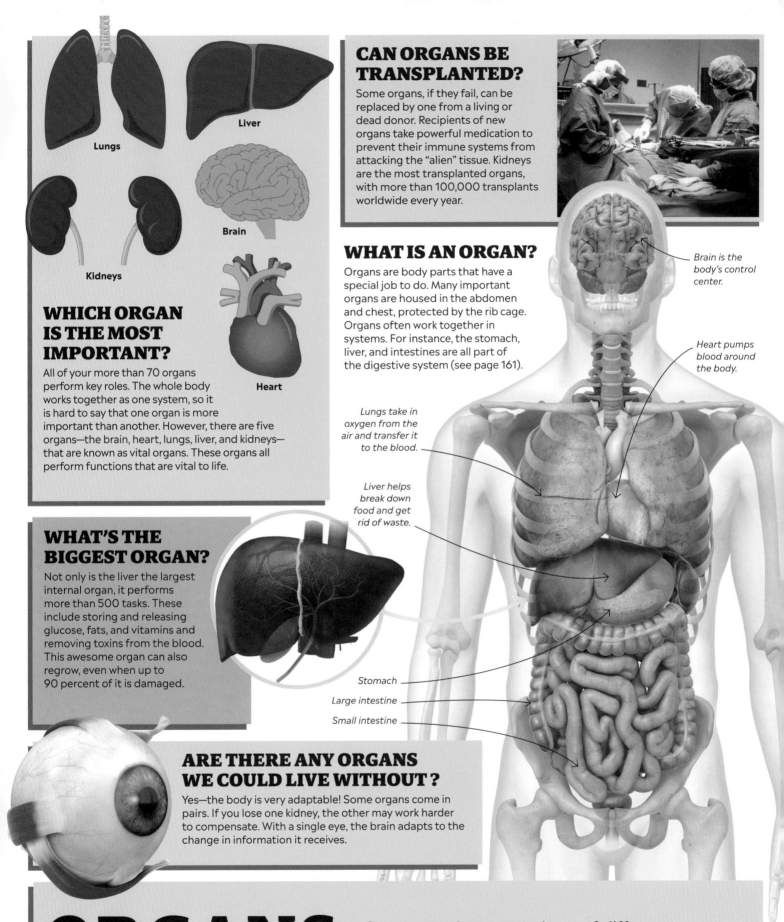

Lungs

Liver

Brain

Kidneys

Heart

CAN ORGANS BE TRANSPLANTED?

Some organs, if they fail, can be replaced by one from a living or dead donor. Recipients of new organs take powerful medication to prevent their immune systems from attacking the "alien" tissue. Kidneys are the most transplanted organs, with more than 100,000 transplants worldwide every year.

WHAT IS AN ORGAN?

Organs are body parts that have a special job to do. Many important organs are housed in the abdomen and chest, protected by the rib cage. Organs often work together in systems. For instance, the stomach, liver, and intestines are all part of the digestive system (see page 161).

WHICH ORGAN IS THE MOST IMPORTANT?

All of your more than 70 organs perform key roles. The whole body works together as one system, so it is hard to say that one organ is more important than another. However, there are five organs—the brain, heart, lungs, liver, and kidneys—that are known as vital organs. These organs all perform functions that are vital to life.

WHAT'S THE BIGGEST ORGAN?

Not only is the liver the largest internal organ, it performs more than 500 tasks. These include storing and releasing glucose, fats, and vitamins and removing toxins from the blood. This awesome organ can also regrow, even when up to 90 percent of it is damaged.

ARE THERE ANY ORGANS WE COULD LIVE WITHOUT ?

Yes—the body is very adaptable! Some organs come in pairs. If you lose one kidney, the other may work harder to compensate. With a single eye, the brain adapts to the change in information it receives.

Brain is the body's control center.

Heart pumps blood around the body.

Lungs take in oxygen from the air and transfer it to the blood.

Liver helps break down food and get rid of waste.

Stomach

Large intestine

Small intestine

ORGANS: Structures that are made up of different kinds of tissue and perform specific tasks within the body

SKIN:

The thin, waterproof, outermost layer of the body that keeps germs and dirt out and helps control body temperature

WHY DOES MY SKIN GET WRINKLY IN THE BATHTUB?

Skin secretes an oily substance called sebum to keep it soft, supple, and waterproof. If you spend a long time in water, this sebum is washed away, allowing the skin to absorb water. This is what makes the skin get wrinkly. It quickly goes back to normal when you get out of the water!

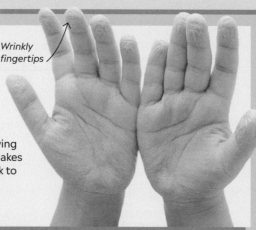

Wrinkly fingertips

WHAT'S INSIDE MY SKIN?

Skin is made up of different layers. The epidermis, or outer layer, is made of flat, dead skin cells that interlock to make a waterproof barrier. The dermis is the thicker lower layer, packed with blood vessels, sweat glands, and touch receptors. Beneath that is an insulating layer of fat.

QUICK QUIZ!

HOW MUCH DOES THE AVERAGE ADULT'S SKIN WEIGH?

a: 4 lb (2 kg)

b: 11 lb (5 kg)

c: 24 lb (11 kg)

WHY DO PEOPLE HAVE DIFFERENT SKIN TONES?

A pigment (colored chemical) called melanin controls skin tone. Made deep inside the skin, it protects against harmful rays from the Sun. People with darker skin have more melanin. How much melanin you have depends mainly on your genes (see page 147).

WHAT ARE FINGERPRINTS FOR?

The raised ridges on our fingertips help us grip things. They form long before we are born, when layers of skin grow at different rates, making ridges and grooves.

Every fingerprint pattern is unique.

WHY SHOULDN'T I PICK A SCAB?

The crust that forms over a cut or graze is the body's way of protecting itself while new skin forms. Picking a scab before it falls off naturally is tempting, but the wound will take longer to heal and may leave a scar, and you risk letting in germs and infections.

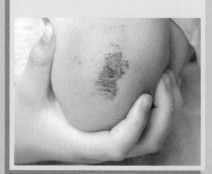

Skin is covered in tiny hairs.

Pores are openings in the epidermis.

Epidermis

Dermis

Layer of fat

Sweat glands release sweat.

Sebaceous glands release sebum.

Blood vessels carry oxygen to cells.

Nerves send information from touch receptors to the brain.

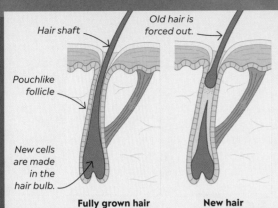

Hair shaft

Old hair is forced out.

Pouchlike follicle

New cells are made in the hair bulb.

Fully grown hair

New hair

HOW DOES HAIR GROW?

Hair grows from a pit in the skin called a follicle. Inside, new cells are produced, pushing the hair upward and making it increase in length. After a certain amount of time, growth stops and the hair stays the same length. When growth starts again, a new hair forms and pushes the old hair out of the follicle.

FAST FACTS

We lose **80–100** hairs from our scalp every day.

Hair grows **faster** in the summer than in winter.

Humans have the same number of hairs as **chimpanzees** do.

WHY DOESN'T A HAIRCUT HURT?

Once a hair emerges from its follicle, the hair cells are dead—that's why having a haircut doesn't hurt. This highly magnified view of a single strand of hair shows the overlapping layers of flat cells.

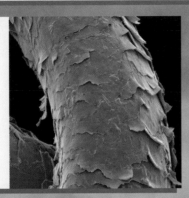

WHY DOES HAIR GO GRAY?

Hair color comes from melanin, a pigment made in the body. Different types of melanin produce blond, brown, black, or ginger hair. As you get older, production of melanin slows, turning hair gray. When it stops completely, hair goes white.

HAIR: Flexible strands made from dead cells packed with a tough substance called keratin

WHAT MAKES HAIR CURLY OR STRAIGHT?

It all depends on the shape of the follicle it grows out of. As a hair grows, it is molded by the follicle into straight, wavy, or curly strands.

Round follicle

Straight hair

Oval follicle

Wavy hair

Flat follicle

Curly or coiled hair

HOW LONG WOULD MY HAIR GET IF I NEVER CUT IT?

Hair can't carry on growing forever. A head hair grows for up to 6 years, then stops and is eventually pushed out by a new hair. Eyebrow hairs only grow for 4 months before they fall out, so they never get a chance to grow over your eyes!

Head hairs grow at about 0.3 in (9 mm) a month.

A hinge joint bends in one direction only.

A ball and socket allows movement in all directions.

Pivot joints allow one bone to swivel around another.

Condyloid joints move side to side and up and down.

HOW DOES THE SKELETON MOVE?

Most bones meet at points called joints, and these are what allow the skeleton to move freely. The different types of joints depend on the shape of the bones that meet. They each allow a different kind of movement. Four common types of joints are shown above.

HOW MANY BONES DO I HAVE?

Babies are born with about 300 bones, but over time, some of these fuse together. An adult's skeleton is made up of 206 bones. This skeleton forms a flexible, mobile framework that enables us to move our bodies in all kinds of ways. Nonmoving bones, such as the skull, protect delicate organs, such as the brain, from damage.

33 interlocking vertebrae form the backbone.

Each hand has 27 bones.

12 pairs of ribs protect the heart and lungs.

BONES: Tough, lightweight structures that give your body shape and anchor your muscles to keep you moving

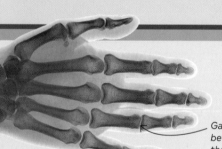

Gaps in between the bones contain cartilage.

WHAT'S IN BETWEEN MY BONES?

The ends of neighboring bones, such as those in the fingers, are covered in a smooth, rubbery substance called cartilage. This allows bones to glide easily against each other when they move.

Malleus (hammer bone)

WHICH IS THE SMALLEST BONE?

Three tiny ear bones take the prize for the smallest named bones— the stapes (stirrup), malleus (hammer), and incus (anvil), all named after their shapes. There are even smaller, sesame-seed-shaped bones embedded in some tendons, which don't have names.

Tibia (shin bone)

WHAT'S INSIDE A BONE?

Under a bone's hard outer layer is spongy bone, which has a honeycomb structure— bars of hard bone with a network of tiny holes between them. Long bones, such as those in the arms and legs, contain jellylike bone marrow.

Blood vessels **Femur**

Spongy bone is strong but light.

Hard compact bone

The outer covering is called the periosteum.

Bone marrow

FAST FACTS

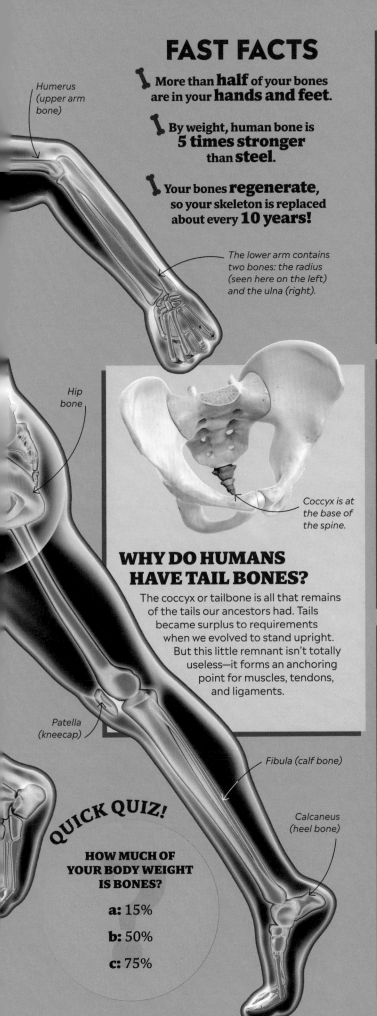

Humerus (upper arm bone)

1️⃣ More than **half** of your bones are in your **hands and feet**.

2️⃣ By weight, human bone is **5 times stronger** than **steel**.

3️⃣ Your bones **regenerate**, so your skeleton is replaced about every **10 years!**

The lower arm contains two bones: the radius (seen here on the left) and the ulna (right).

Hip bone

Coccyx is at the base of the spine.

WHY DO HUMANS HAVE TAIL BONES?

The coccyx or tailbone is all that remains of the tails our ancestors had. Tails became surplus to requirements when we evolved to stand upright. But this little remnant isn't totally useless—it forms an anchoring point for muscles, tendons, and ligaments.

Patella (kneecap)

Fibula (calf bone)

Calcaneus (heel bone)

QUICK QUIZ!

HOW MUCH OF YOUR BODY WEIGHT IS BONES?

a: 15%

b: 50%

c: 75%

WHICH BONE IS THE TOUGHEST?

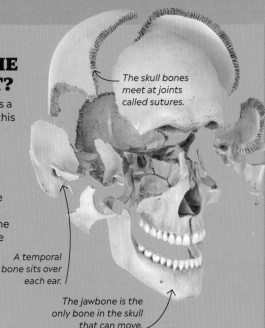

The temporal bone is a good candidate for this award! It is formed by two of the 22 interlocking bones that make up the skull. These bones, which are among the body's densest and strongest, protect the brain's temporal lobe and the delicate inner workings of the ears.

The skull bones meet at joints called sutures.

A temporal bone sits over each ear.

The jawbone is the only bone in the skull that can move.

WHICH IS THE MOST PAINFUL BONE TO BREAK?

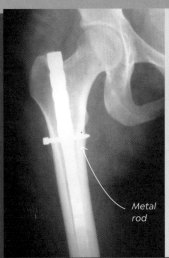

Metal rod

The femur (thigh bone) is one of the strongest bones, so a fracture is usually the result of a significant amount of force. This is likely to be very painful—especially if you have to put weight on the injured leg. Surgery is often needed to reset the bone by inserting a metal rod, so there is postop pain to deal with, too. Try hard not to break this bone!

HOW DO BROKEN BONES HEAL?

When a bone fractures (breaks), the repair process starts almost immediately. After a few months, the bone will have healed fully. If the bone is one that usually moves a lot, a cast might be needed to keep the broken ends together during the healing process.

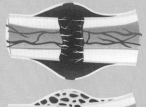

Clot forms
A blood clot forms between the ends of the broken bone to stop the bleeding. White blood cells arrive to destroy germs and prevent infection.

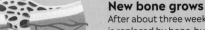

New bone grows
After about three weeks, the blood clot is replaced by bone-building cells, which build a "bridge" of spongy bone to reconnect the two ends.

All healed
After about three months, the bone is almost good as new. Hard compact bone has replaced the spongy bone.

Hard lump gradually disappears.

WHY DOES EXERCISING GIVE YOU BIGGER MUSCLES?

The more you use a muscle, the bigger and stronger it gets. Repetitive exercise causes tiny tears in a muscle's fibers. Then, when you rest after exercise, the body repairs the damage by filling in the tears with new, bulkier muscle fibers, which means that the repaired muscle is larger.

Muscles are bundles of fibers.

Exercising causes tiny tears on the fibers.

Each set of fibers is wrapped in a membrane.

The more you use arm muscles, the stronger and bulkier they become.

WHAT DO MUSCLES DO?

Muscles convert energy from the food we eat into movement. Skeletal muscles are attached to our bones and allow us to move our bodies. Smooth muscle is found in many internal organs—for example, pushing food around the digestive system. Cardiac muscle is what your heart is made from and keeps it beating.

Skeletal muscle　　**Smooth muscle**　　**Cardiac muscle**

MUSCLES:
Bundles of fibers that contract and relax to enable you to move around and to keep body systems working

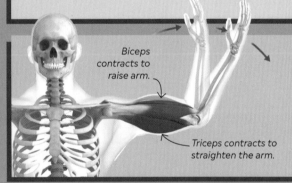

Biceps contracts to raise arm.

Triceps contracts to straighten the arm.

HOW DO MUSCLES HELP US MOVE?

Skeletal muscles work in pairs to move bones. When one muscle contracts, it pulls the bone toward it. Then, when it relaxes and the other muscle contracts, the bone is pulled in the other direction.

QUICK QUIZ!

THE TONGUE IS MADE UP OF HOW MANY MUSCLES?

a: 1

b: 8

c: 140

HOW MANY MUSCLES DO I HAVE?

You have more than 600 skeletal muscles, but you also have a lot of smooth muscle. Each of the 5 million hair follicles in your skin is attached to a tiny muscle called an arrector pili. When you are cold or scared, these muscles contract to pull the hair upright, giving you goosebumps.

WHAT IS THE BIGGEST MUSCLE?

The gluteus maximus, in the bottom, is the biggest muscle, and one of the strongest. It needs to be super strong to work against gravity to move our large leg bones, enabling us to sit, stand, run, jump, or climb.

Gluteus maximus

WHY ARE SOME BODY PARTS SO TICKLISH?

Some areas, such as the feet, are packed with touch-sensitive nerves. When they are touched lightly, they send signals to the hypothalamus, the part of the brain that controls pleasure and our urge to laugh.

WHAT DO NERVES DO?

Nerves are the body's information superhighway. They carry messages between the brain and the body. The brain receives information from your senses about the world around you and sends instructions to your body parts about what to do.

IT'S A MYSTERY!

How many types of neurons are there?
Scientists don't know exactly, but they think there are many hundreds. New neurons in the brain are constantly being found and studied to work out their functions.

The brain is the body's control center.

Spinal cord connects the brain with the rest of the body.

Nerves extend through the whole body.

HOW DO NERVE CELLS SEND AND RECEIVE SIGNALS?

Neurons receive information in their spiderlike arms, called dendrites. They process the data, then send it on via longer arms called axons to the next neuron in the chain.

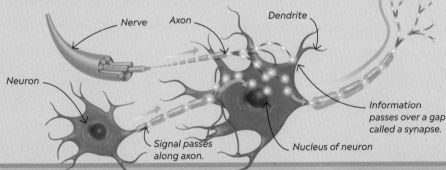

Nerve

Axon

Dendrite

Neuron

Signal passes along axon.

Nucleus of neuron

Information passes over a gap called a synapse.

HOW FAST DO NERVE SIGNALS TRAVEL?

Information travels through neurons via electrical signals called nerve impulses. These signals don't all move at the same speed, but the fastest travel at up to 220 mph (350 km/h)—as fast as a Formula 1 race car!

WHY DO WE FEEL PAIN?

Pain is a useful warning that a body part is at risk of damage. Receptor nerves detect a problem and send a message to the brain. The brain may then direct your muscles to move away from the danger or order the release of endorphins, natural chemicals that lessen painful sensations.

NERVES: Cablelike structures made of cells called neurons, which relay information between the body and the brain

WHAT DOES MY BRAIN DO?

As well as controlling essential functions such as breathing and heartbeat, the brain allows you to see, hear, speak, move, think, remember, and feel emotions. The brain's thinking and feeling center is the cerebrum, which is divided into two halves or hemispheres, each with four lobes. Most actions are controlled by many areas of the brain working together, but each lobe is broadly responsible for different jobs.

BRAIN:
The body's control center, it controls all the body's processes, as well as receiving and processing information from the outside world and telling the body how to respond

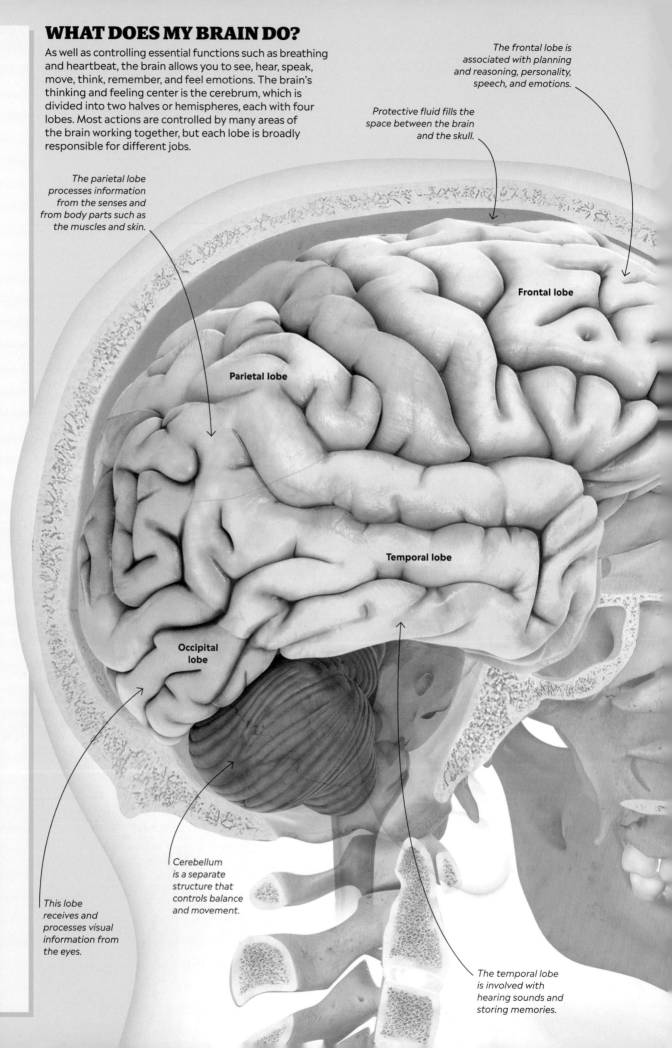

The frontal lobe is associated with planning and reasoning, personality, speech, and emotions.

Protective fluid fills the space between the brain and the skull.

The parietal lobe processes information from the senses and from body parts such as the muscles and skin.

Frontal lobe

Parietal lobe

Temporal lobe

Occipital lobe

This lobe receives and processes visual information from the eyes.

Cerebellum is a separate structure that controls balance and movement.

The temporal lobe is involved with hearing sounds and storing memories.

HOW ARE MY MEMORIES STORED?

When you experience or learn something new, nerve cells link to create paths between an area deep inside the brain called the hippocampus and the cerebral cortex. If you repeat that action, these pathways get stronger. Your experiences then become stored memories that you can recall over a lifetime.

ARE BIGGER BRAINS MORE INTELLIGENT?

A big brain doesn't mean more intelligence—if it did, blue whales would be the smartest animals! If you rated the brain relative to body size, the tiny elephant shrew would be the winner. Most scientists agree that what makes humans the smartest animal is the 16 billion neurons that make up our cerebral cortex—far more than any other species.

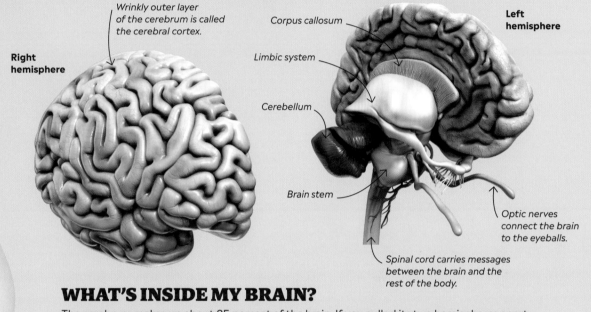

Right hemisphere

Wrinkly outer layer of the cerebrum is called the cerebral cortex.

Corpus callosum

Limbic system

Left hemisphere

Cerebellum

Brain stem

Optic nerves connect the brain to the eyeballs.

Spinal cord carries messages between the brain and the rest of the body.

WHAT'S INSIDE MY BRAIN?

The cerebrum makes up about 85 percent of the brain. If you pulled its two hemispheres apart, you would see other structures deep inside. The limbic system generates emotions and survival instincts such as thirst and hunger. The brain stem controls automatic functions such as heartbeat. The corpus callosum is a bundle of nerve fibers that connects the brain's two hemispheres.

WHAT IS THE BRAIN MADE OF?

The soft, spongy brain is made up mostly of fat. To touch, it would feel like jelly. It contains billions of neurons (nerve cells), as well as blood vessels that supply the cells with oxygen and energy.

WHY IS THE BRAIN SO WRINKLY?

Wrinkles are the brain's secret weapon! They allow more processing power to be packed into the skull. If you stretched an adult's cerebral cortex flat, it would cover an ironing board! A baby's brain is smooth—it starts wrinkling at about 4 months as the brain grows.

WHERE DO THOUGHTS COME FROM?

Many of the brain's functions are still a mystery, and scientists still don't know exactly how the brain generates new thoughts and ideas. What we do know is that they form in the cerebral cortex. This thin outer layer of nerve cells is sometimes called "gray matter."

HOW MUCH ENERGY DOES THE BRAIN NEED?

The brain uses about one-fifth of all the body's energy. That's about the same as it takes to power a 20-watt light bulb. Surprisingly, the brain uses about the same amount of energy whether you are thinking really hard or sleeping. Unlike muscles, the brain can't store energy, so it needs a constant supply of energy and oxygen to function.

WHY DOES MY HEART BEAT FASTER WHEN I FEEL SCARED?

When you feel scared or excited, the body releases a hormone called adrenaline. This chemical messenger tells the heart to beat faster, pumping extra oxygen-filled blood to your muscles. This is so your body can respond to the danger—either by running away or fighting back!

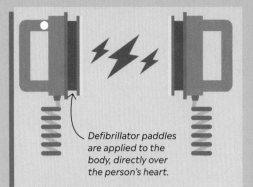

Defibrillator paddles are applied to the body, directly over the person's heart.

CAN YOU RESTART A HEART IF IT STOPS BEATING?

When someone has a heart attack, it means their heart is not beating properly. A defibrillator is a machine that delivers a burst of electrical energy, which can jolt the heart into working again. However, if a heart has stopped altogether, a defibrillator can't restart it.

WHAT MAKES A HEARTBEAT'S SOUND?

The "lub-dub" sound is made by the regular shutting of different valves, which lie across the openings between the heart's chambers. The first, lower-pitched "lub" is made by valves snapping shut in the atria. The second, shorter "dub" is made by the closing of the valves between ventricles and arteries.

HEART: Muscular organ in the chest that beats constantly throughout your life to keep blood pumping around the body

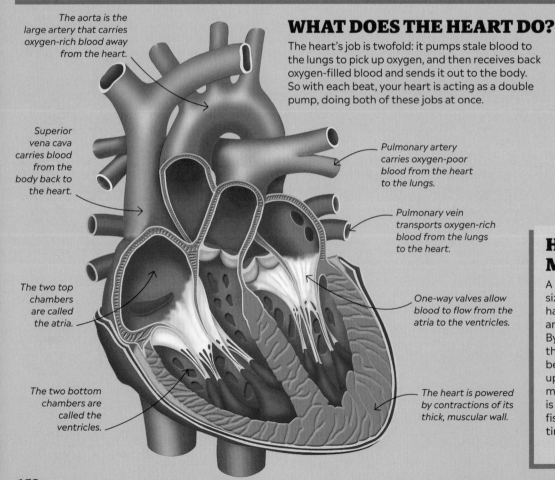

The aorta is the large artery that carries oxygen-rich blood away from the heart.

Superior vena cava carries blood from the body back to the heart.

The two top chambers are called the atria.

The two bottom chambers are called the ventricles.

Pulmonary artery carries oxygen-poor blood from the heart to the lungs.

Pulmonary vein transports oxygen-rich blood from the lungs to the heart.

One-way valves allow blood to flow from the atria to the ventricles.

The heart is powered by contractions of its thick, muscular wall.

WHAT DOES THE HEART DO?

The heart's job is twofold: it pumps stale blood to the lungs to pick up oxygen, and then receives back oxygen-filled blood and sends it out to the body. So with each beat, your heart is acting as a double pump, doing both of these jobs at once.

QUICK QUIZ!

HOW MANY TIMES WILL YOUR HEART BEAT IN YOUR LIFETIME?

a: 1 million times

b: 1 billion times

c: 2.5 billion times

HOW BIG IS MY HEART?

A newborn baby's heart is about the size of a walnut. This tiny organ works hard, beating between 120 and 160 times a minute. By age 10, your heart is the size of your fist and beats more slowly, at up to 100 times a minute. An adult heart is as big as two of your fists and beats 60–90 times a minute.

BLOOD:
Red liquid that carries oxygen and other substances to and from the body's cells

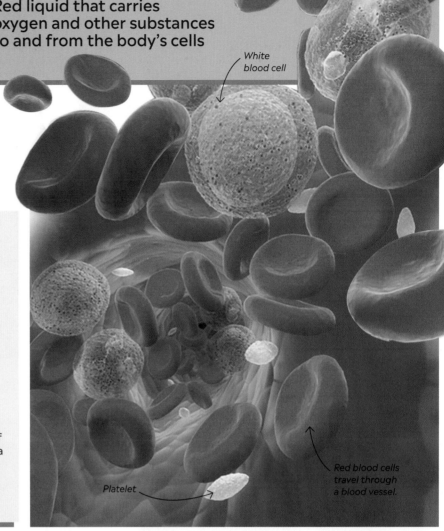

White blood cell

Red blood cells travel through a blood vessel.

Platelet

WHAT MAKES BLOOD RED?

Blood gets its color from its red blood cells, which are packed with iron, a reddish-brown element. The more oxygen it contains, the brighter red the iron becomes. This is why oxygen-poor blood from a vein is a darker red than the oxygen-rich blood in an artery.

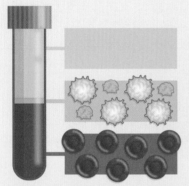

55% is plasma.

1% is white blood cells and platelets.

44% is red blood cells.

WHAT IS BLOOD MADE OF?

Blood is made of three main components. More than half is plasma—a watery, yellowish fluid. Floating in the plasma are red blood cells, which carry oxygen around the body. White blood cells that attack germs and platelets that help heal wounds make up the rest.

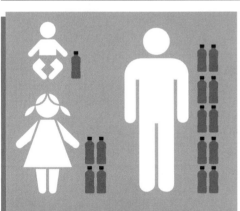

HOW MUCH BLOOD DO I HAVE?

It depends on your age and size. At 1 year old, a baby's body contains about a pint (0.5 liter) of blood. By the age of 10, you will have 4 pints (2 liters). By adulthood, you will have about 10 pints (5.7 liters) of blood, making up around 8 percent of your body weight.

IT'S A MYSTERY!

Why are there different blood types?
There are four blood groups, each with a slightly different type of red blood cell. More than 100 years after blood groups were discovered, scientists still don't really know why they exist.

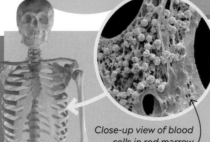

Close-up view of blood cells in red marrow

Bones that make blood cells are shown in pink.

WHAT CAUSES A NOSEBLEED?

The inside of your nose is lined with delicate blood vessels, and if one or more of these bursts, the result is a bloody nose. Nosebleeds can be caused by a cold or allergy, blowing your nose too hard—or too much nose-picking!

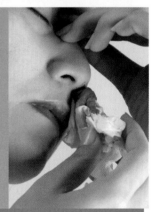

WHERE ARE BLOOD CELLS MADE?

Inside your bones. Bones are filled with a jellylike substance called marrow. There are two types of marrow: yellow and red. Blood cells are only made by red marrow, at a rate of 2 million cells every minute. Babies have red marrow in all their bones, but as you get older, only a few bones can make blood cells.

WHAT MAKES ME SUDDENLY NEED TO PEE?

Urine is collected in the bladder, a stretchy bag that expands as it receives urine from the kidneys. When it fills beyond a certain point, sensors in the bladder wall send nerve signals to the brain that the bag needs to be emptied. The brain quickly responds—and you get the urge to go.

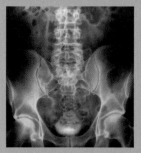

Empty bladder
When the bladder is empty, it does not take up much space in the pelvis.

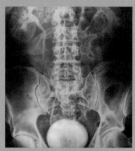

Full bladder
A full bladder can hold over a pint (more than half a liter) of urine.

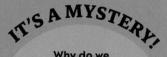

IT'S A MYSTERY!

Why do we have two kidneys?
Humans have two kidneys, but if one is removed, the body can adapt and function well with just one. No one knows precisely why we have two kidneys and two lungs but only one heart and one brain.

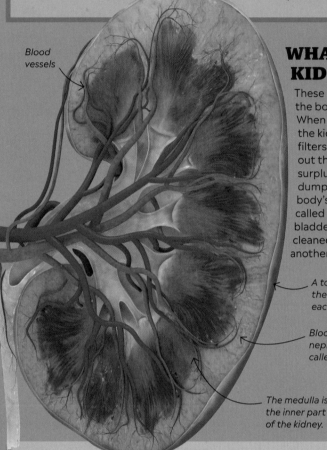

Blood vessels

A tough casing called the capsule protects each kidney.

Blood is filtered by nephrons in a thick layer called the cortex.

The medulla is the inner part of the kidney.

WHAT ARE KIDNEYS FOR?

These hardworking organs are the body's filtration stations. When blood passes through the kidneys, millions of tiny filters called nephrons strain out the toxic chemicals and surplus water that have been dumped in the blood by the body's cells. The waste fluid, called urine, drains into the bladder, while the newly cleaned blood sets off for another lap around the body.

HOW DOES THE URINARY SYSTEM WORK?

The kidneys are part of the body's liquid waste disposal system, the urinary system. Urine is made by the kidneys and flows through tubes called ureters into the bladder, then out of your body through another tube, the urethra. Blood vessels carry blood to and from the kidneys.

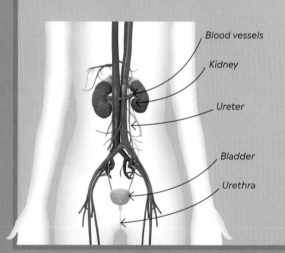

Blood vessels

Kidney

Ureter

Bladder

Urethra

KIDNEYS: Organs that keep the blood clean by filtering out toxins and excess water, making them into a waste product called urine

WHAT IS URINE MADE OF?

More than 90 percent of urine is water. Dissolved in the water are substances including urea, a waste product made when the liver breaks down proteins; excess sodium (salt); and traces of up to 3,000 chemicals, including potassium and calcium.

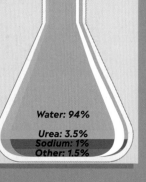

Water: 94%
Urea: 3.5%
Sodium: 1%
Other: 1.5%

WHY IS URINE YELLOW?

The color comes from a chemical called urochrome, produced when old blood cells are recycled. Urine that contains a lot of water looks pale yellow, whereas urine with less water in it looks darker. Very dark yellow urine is a sign that the body is dehydrated.

Dark yellow urine means drink more water!

HOW DOES MY BODY GET ENERGY FROM FOOD?

The digestive system is a giant food processor. It breaks down everything we eat into units small enough to be absorbed by villi (shown below)—tiny, fingerlike projections on the surface of the small intestine. Blood vessels then carry the nutrients to cells, which turn them into energy.

HOW LONG DOES FOOD TAKE TO DIGEST?

From entering the mouth to being processed into nutrients and passed out of the body as poop, food travels about 30 ft (9 m) through the body's winding digestive system. This epic journey takes an average of 24 hours or so to complete, but it can take as long as three days.

Food is chewed in the mouth.

Chewed food travels down the gullet, or esophagus.

It takes just seconds for food to pass down the throat and arrive at the stomach.

Layers of muscle

The innermost layer is lined with thick mucus.

The stomach churns food to a thick liquid; this takes 2–3 hours.

The liquid then arrives in the small intestine, which absorbs the nutrients.

Over 12–24 hours, the large intestine absorbs water from the undigested waste that remains.

The rectum stores waste until it is passed out of the body as poop.

WHY DOESN'T THE STOMACH DIGEST ITSELF?

The stomach acid that breaks down food is strong enough to destroy metal. The stomach's walls are protected by thick, slimy mucus, which forms a barrier that prevents the acid from digesting the stomach as well as the food.

DIGESTION: The process by which food is broken down into nutrients that can be used by the body's cells

WHY IS POOP BROWN?

No matter what color food you eat, healthy poop is always a brown color, because it contains bile and bilirubin. Greenish-brown bile helps the body digest fatty foods. Reddish-yellow bilirubin is produced when red blood cells break down. Mixed in the gut, they turn feces (poop) brown.

FAST FACTS

🍴 Your gut contains more than **100 trillion** bacteria.

🍴 Most people fart **12–25 times** a day.

🍴 There are about **5 million** villi in the small intestine.

WHY DO FARTS SMELL?

Bacteria in your gut break down food in a process called fermentation, producing gases as part of the process. These gases pass out of your body as farts. Most farts don't smell, but eating foods rich in sulfur—such as some vegetables, meat, or dairy—can create farts with a "rotten eggs" aroma.

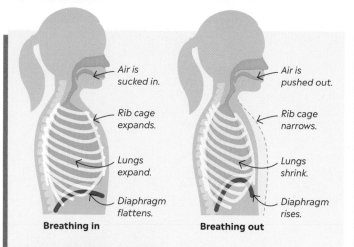

Air is sucked in.

Rib cage expands.

Lungs expand.

Diaphragm flattens.

Breathing in

Air is pushed out.

Rib cage narrows.

Lungs shrink.

Diaphragm rises.

Breathing out

HOW DOES AIR GET INTO MY LUNGS?

Breathing is controlled by muscles in the chest, including a curved sheet of muscle called the diaphragm. When the diaphragm tenses up (contracts), it flattens, making the lungs expand and suck in air. When it relaxes, it rises, making the lungs smaller and pushing air out of them.

WHY DO I GET OUT OF BREATH WHEN I RUN?

When you exercise, your muscles have to work harder and need more oxygen to fuel them. The brain responds by making you breathe faster and more deeply, and the extra effort can make you feel breathless.

HOW LONG CAN A PERSON HOLD THEIR BREATH?

Most people can only hold their breath for a minute or so. However, in the sport of freediving (diving without breathing apparatus), the world record for staying underwater on a single breath is a lung-busting 24 minutes 37 seconds!

BREATHING: Moving air in and out of the lungs to bring oxygen into the body and carry waste gases away

WHAT DO MY LUNGS DO?

The lungs contain a huge network of tiny tubes that deliver air to pockets called alveoli. Oxygen passes through the walls of the alveoli and into the blood, while waste carbon dioxide travels in the opposite direction to be breathed out. This process is called gas exchange.

Bronchi are the two tubes that connect the trachea to the lungs.

Bronchi branch into smaller tubes called bronchioles.

Diaphragm is the sheet of muscle that contracts to inflate the lungs.

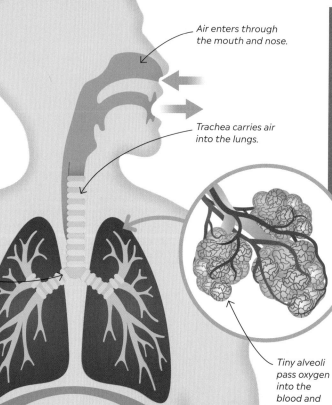

Air enters through the mouth and nose.

Trachea carries air into the lungs.

Tiny alveoli pass oxygen into the blood and take carbon dioxide out.

WHY DON'T I FORGET TO BREATHE?

Your brain controls your breathing without you having to think about it. This is why you carry on breathing even when you are asleep. However, you can override this automatic process—for example, to slow down your breathing when practicing yoga.

QUICK QUIZ!

HOW MANY BREATHS DOES AN ADULT TAKE PER DAY?

a: About 2,000

b: About 22,000

c: About 220,000

MOUTH:
The start of the digestive system, where the body begins the process of breaking down food

How many bacteria are in my mouth?

There are billions of bacteria in a human mouth—so many, it is impossible to estimate accurately. However, it's no mystery that if you don't brush your teeth, the number will increase!

IT'S A MYSTERY!

HOW MANY TEETH DO PEOPLE HAVE?

Babies are usually born with no teeth. Over about three years, a set of 20 "milk teeth" comes through. Around the age of 6, these start to fall out and be replaced by permanent teeth. An adult has 32 teeth, which have different jobs according to their shape and position in the mouth.

Canines are pointed to grip and pierce food.

HOW DOES MY TONGUE DETECT TASTES?

Sensors on the tongue's surface, called taste buds, detect chemicals that are released when you chew food. Taste buds can detect five tastes: sweet, salty, bitter, sour, and umami (which is the savory taste of foods like mushrooms or cheese).

Taste bud

Incisors have sharp edges to slice food.

Molars are wide and grooved for grinding.

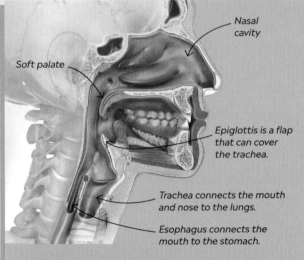

Nasal cavity

Soft palate

Epiglottis is a flap that can cover the trachea.

Trachea connects the mouth and nose to the lungs.

Esophagus connects the mouth to the stomach.

ARE MY MOUTH AND NOSE CONNECTED?

Yes! The upper part of the throat, the nasopharynx, connects the nasal cavity and the mouth. A flap called the soft palate stops food from entering the nasal cavity when you swallow. A separate flap called the epiglottis stops food from going down the wrong way.

WHAT MAKES TEETH SO HARD?

The top part of a tooth is covered with enamel, the hardest substance in the human body. It has to be tough to protect the soft parts of the tooth and to withstand acids and other chemicals in the food we eat.

Enamel coating protects the tooth's upper part, or crown.

The root of the tooth contains blood vessels and nerves.

HOW MUCH SALIVA DOES MY MOUTH MAKE?

The average person produces up to 3 pints (1.5 liters) of saliva every day—enough to fill 150 bathtubs in a lifetime! Saliva is essential for digestion—it moistens food, making it easier to swallow. It also contains chemicals called enzymes that help break down food.

HOW DO I HEAR SOUNDS?

A sound causes waves of vibrations that travel though the air. The external ear collects these vibrations and funnels them through to the inner ear. Here, they are turned into nerve signals, which are then sent to the brain to decode.

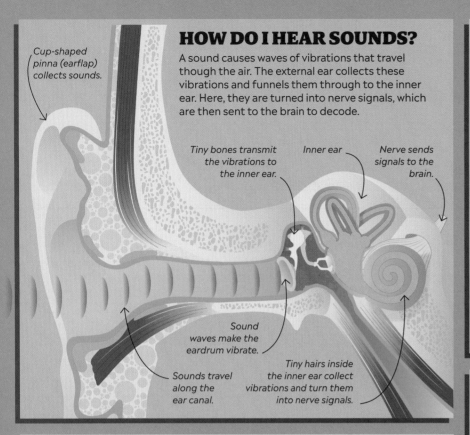

Cup-shaped pinna (earflap) collects sounds.

Tiny bones transmit the vibrations to the inner ear.

Inner ear

Nerve sends signals to the brain.

Sound waves make the eardrum vibrate.

Sounds travel along the ear canal.

Tiny hairs inside the inner ear collect vibrations and turn them into nerve signals.

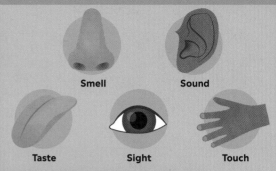

Smell   Sound

Taste   Sight   Touch

HOW MANY SENSES DO WE HAVE?

The five main senses shown here were first described in ancient times. Scientists today have identified more than 15 other senses, including proprioception, which is the body's ability to sense movement and location. Proprioception is what helps you keep your balance—and touch your nose with your eyes closed!

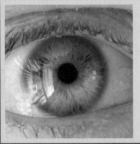

WHY DO PEOPLE HAVE DIFFERENT EYE COLORS?

Eye color comes from a pigment called melanin, and the amount of melanin is determined by our genes. In most people, both eyes are the same color, but a harmless gene mutation can give different colored eyes—or even different colored parts within the same eye.

HOW MANY SMELLS CAN THE HUMAN NOSE DETECT?

The nose contains 1,000 tiny odor receptor cells, which can detect a trillion different smells. These receptors are located in the nasal cavity, the space that links the nose to the throat. Odor sensors work closely with the tongue's taste receptors, helping us discern the flavors in our food.

The leaf reflects light rays toward the eye.

SENSES: The ways in which the body collects information about its environment, then transmits it to the brain

WHAT ARE BOOGERS FOR?

Boogers are a mix of bacteria, dead skin cells from inside the nose, and dried mucus (the slimy fluid that keeps the lining of your nose moist). They are useful, because together with nose hairs, they stop dust, pollen, and germs from reaching our delicate lungs.

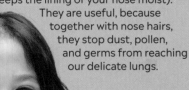

Nose-picking transfers bacteria from your nose to your fingers!

FAST FACTS

Your sense of **smell** is heightened when you are **hungry**.

A child has about **10,000 taste buds**, while an old person may only have 5,000.

One fingertip contains about **3,000 touch receptors**.

HOW DOES MY SENSE OF TOUCH WORK?

The 5 million touch receptors in your skin detect sensations as they happen, and then relay this information to the brain. The brain then works out whether the things touching us are hard or soft, wet or dry, hot or cold—and much more.

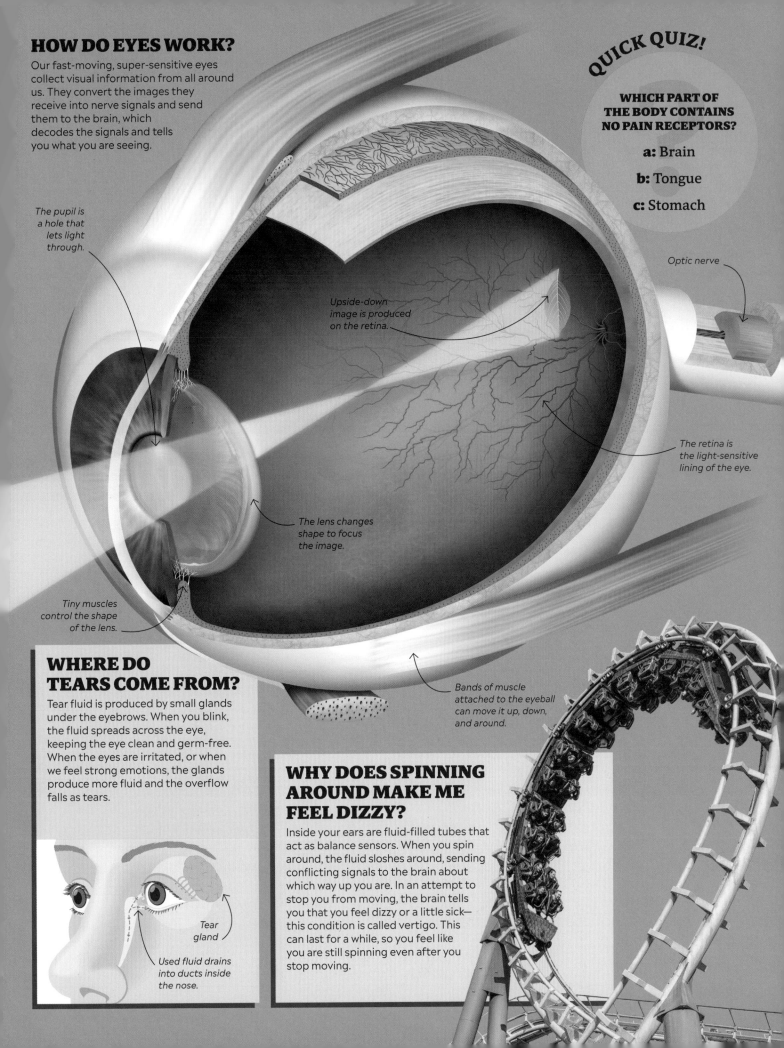

HOW DO EYES WORK?

Our fast-moving, super-sensitive eyes collect visual information from all around us. They convert the images they receive into nerve signals and send them to the brain, which decodes the signals and tells you what you are seeing.

The pupil is a hole that lets light through.

Tiny muscles control the shape of the lens.

Upside-down image is produced on the retina.

The lens changes shape to focus the image.

Bands of muscle attached to the eyeball can move it up, down, and around.

Optic nerve

The retina is the light-sensitive lining of the eye.

QUICK QUIZ!

WHICH PART OF THE BODY CONTAINS NO PAIN RECEPTORS?

a: Brain

b: Tongue

c: Stomach

WHERE DO TEARS COME FROM?

Tear fluid is produced by small glands under the eyebrows. When you blink, the fluid spreads across the eye, keeping the eye clean and germ-free. When the eyes are irritated, or when we feel strong emotions, the glands produce more fluid and the overflow falls as tears.

Tear gland

Used fluid drains into ducts inside the nose.

WHY DOES SPINNING AROUND MAKE ME FEEL DIZZY?

Inside your ears are fluid-filled tubes that act as balance sensors. When you spin around, the fluid sloshes around, sending conflicting signals to the brain about which way up you are. In an attempt to stop you from moving, the brain tells you that you feel dizzy or a little sick—this condition is called vertigo. This can last for a while, so you feel like you are still spinning even after you stop moving.

HOW ARE BABIES MADE?

Every person who ever lived started out when two tiny sex cells joined together. The sperm cell burrows through the egg cell's tough outer case to merge its genetic material with that of the egg in a process called fertilization.

HOW DO TWINS AND TRIPLETS HAPPEN?

After the egg is fertilized, cell division starts. Sometimes, the clump of cells splits into two or more identical clumps. If each one continues to develop, the result will be identical twins, triplets, quadruplets—or more! Nonidentical siblings happen when two or more eggs are fertilized at the same time, but by different sperm.

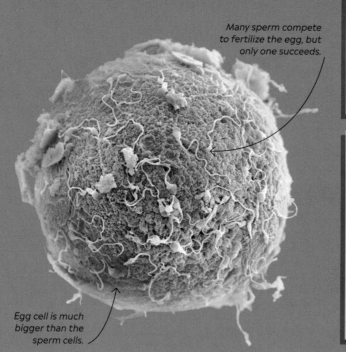

Many sperm compete to fertilize the egg, but only one succeeds.

Egg cell is much bigger than the sperm cells.

HOW QUICKLY DOES A FETUS GROW?

It takes between 38 and 42 weeks for the fetus to reach full size. In that time, it grows rapidly. At eight weeks after fertilization, the fetus is the same size as a kidney bean. By 12 weeks, it is lime-sized. By 20 weeks, the fetus is as long as a banana, and at 27 weeks, it's the size of a cauliflower. After 38 weeks, the fetus is watermelon-sized—and ready to be born!

WHAT HAPPENS AFTER THE EGG IS FERTILIZED?

The fertilized egg splits into two identical cells. Those cells then continue splitting to make four, eight, sixteen, and so on until a tiny cluster of cells called an embryo forms. After about eight weeks, the embryo starts to look like a baby and is now called a fetus.

Outer cells attach to the uterus lining.

Yolk sac nourishes the embryo before the placenta takes over the job.

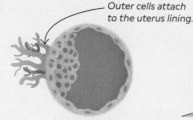
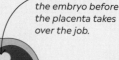
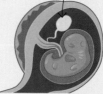

4 days old
The fertilized egg has divided into a clump of 32 cells and become an embryo.

1 week old
The embryo attaches itself to the wall of the uterus. Pregnancy has begun.

4 weeks old
The embryo now has a beating heart, a head, and buds that will develop into arms and legs.

HOW DOES THE MOTHER'S BODY MAKE ROOM FOR A BABY?

The baby develops inside the mother's uterus, a muscular organ usually about the size of a lemon. It can stretch up to many times its original size to accommodate the growing fetus. As it takes up more and more space, the mother's abdominal organs get squeezed together. With her stomach and bladder squashed almost flat, a mother may have to eat smaller meals and urinate more often.

HOW DOES THE BODY KNOW WHEN A BABY IS READY TO BE BORN?

When fully grown, the fetus produces special proteins to signal it is ready to be born. The mother's brain picks up these messages and releases hormones that start the birth process. Her uterus starts to contract very strongly, pushing the baby down the birth canal (vagina) and out into the world.

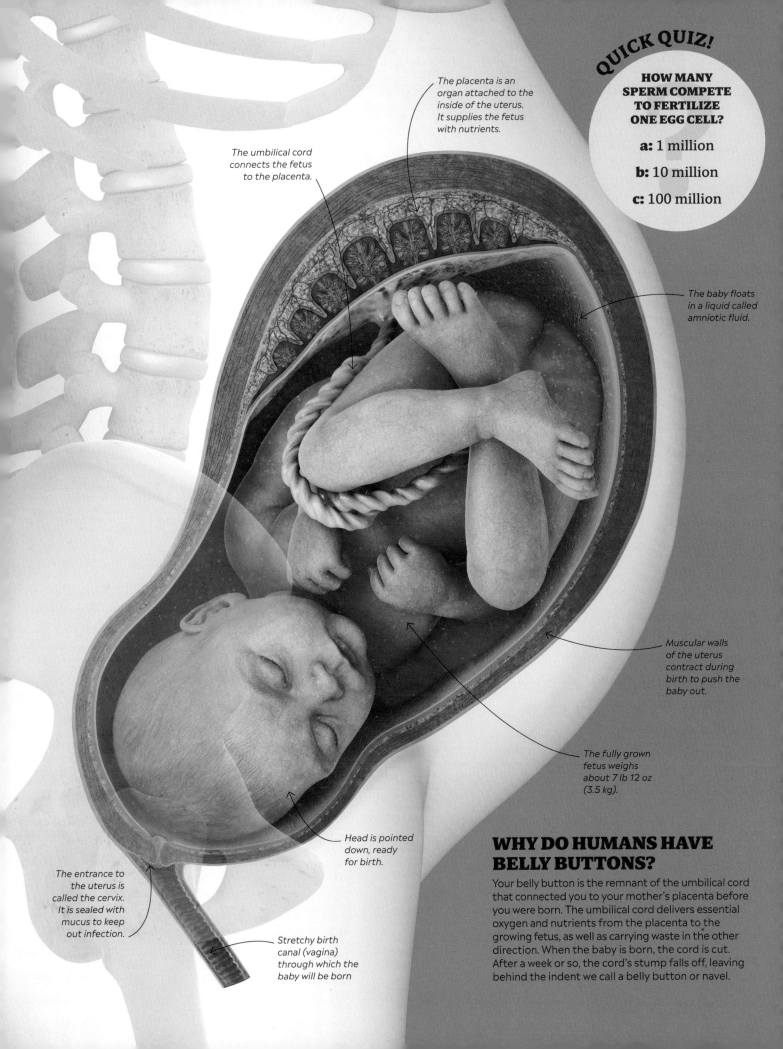

QUICK QUIZ!

HOW MANY SPERM COMPETE TO FERTILIZE ONE EGG CELL?

a: 1 million

b: 10 million

c: 100 million

The placenta is an organ attached to the inside of the uterus. It supplies the fetus with nutrients.

The umbilical cord connects the fetus to the placenta.

The baby floats in a liquid called amniotic fluid.

Muscular walls of the uterus contract during birth to push the baby out.

The fully grown fetus weighs about 7 lb 12 oz (3.5 kg).

Head is pointed down, ready for birth.

The entrance to the uterus is called the cervix. It is sealed with mucus to keep out infection.

Stretchy birth canal (vagina) through which the baby will be born

WHY DO HUMANS HAVE BELLY BUTTONS?

Your belly button is the remnant of the umbilical cord that connected you to your mother's placenta before you were born. The umbilical cord delivers essential oxygen and nutrients from the placenta to the growing fetus, as well as carrying waste in the other direction. When the baby is born, the cord is cut. After a week or so, the cord's stump falls off, leaving behind the indent we call a belly button or navel.

WHY ARE TEENS SO MOODY?

During puberty, big changes are happening in the brain. The area of the brain that creates feelings develops earlier than the thinking regions. This means that teens often feel intense emotions but don't have the ability to keep them under control or stop themselves from acting on impulse.

DO GIRLS HIT PUBERTY BEFORE BOYS?

Most girls start puberty around the age of 10, up to two years earlier than boys. This means they are often taller than boys their own age. Once boys start puberty, they quickly catch up and usually end up taller than girls.

WHY DOES PUBERTY HAPPEN?

Puberty is a time when the body changes rapidly in order to become sexually mature. The process is driven by hormones. In the brain, the hypothalamus sends a signal to the tiny pituitary gland to release a hormone that triggers the start of puberty.

WHY DO BOYS' VOICES CHANGE?

During a boy's puberty, the hormone testosterone makes the vocal cords in the larynx (voice box) grow longer and thicker. This means the cords vibrate much more slowly, producing a lower pitch.

The enlarged larynx makes a bulge called the Adam's apple.

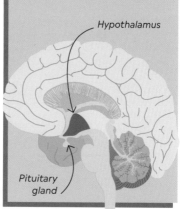

Hypothalamus

Pituitary gland

PUBERTY:

The process humans go through to become adults with bodies mature enough to reproduce

IT'S A MYSTERY!

Why are children hitting puberty earlier?

Studies have shown that today's children begin puberty up to five years earlier than children did 100 years ago. It might be due to changes in our diet, but no one knows for sure.

Inflammation makes the surface of the pimple red and painful.

Pus is a mixture of sebum, white blood cells, dead skin cells, and bacteria.

White blood cells attack the bacteria.

WHY DO TEENAGERS GET PIMPLES?

Puberty causes the sebaceous (oil) glands in the skin to start producing more oil, especially on the face, back, and chest. The oil can sometimes get trapped within a hair follicle instead of draining out properly, and this blocks the pore. If bacteria breed in the oil, the area gets inflamed and a pimple is born.

Sebaceous gland, which produces oily sebum, has been invaded by bacteria.

Hair growing within a hair follicle

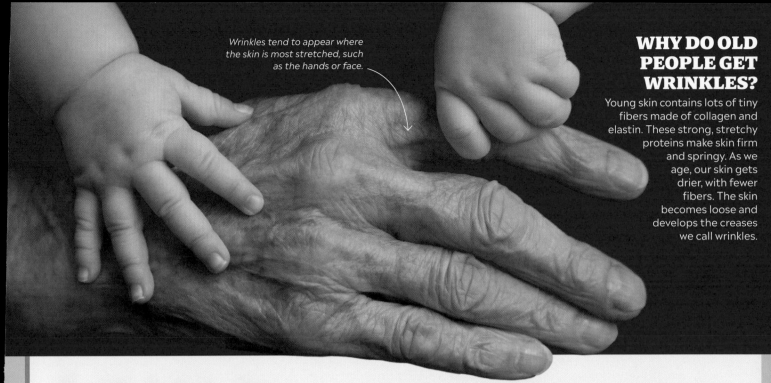

Wrinkles tend to appear where the skin is most stretched, such as the hands or face.

WHY DO OLD PEOPLE GET WRINKLES?

Young skin contains lots of tiny fibers made of collagen and elastin. These strong, stretchy proteins make skin firm and springy. As we age, our skin gets drier, with fewer fibers. The skin becomes loose and develops the creases we call wrinkles.

AGING: The process of growing older, and the changes that happen to our bodies as we move through life

HOW DO OUR BODIES CHANGE WITH AGE?

In childhood, our bodies change rapidly as we grow bigger and stronger. Our bodies are strongest around the age of 25. After this, the body slowly declines. In old age, joints stiffen, muscles weaken, and eyesight and hearing can start to fail.

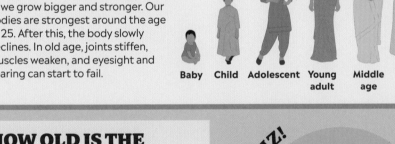

Baby Child Adolescent Young adult Middle age Old age

HOW OLD IS THE OLDEST PERSON?

The oldest recorded person ever was a French woman who lived to the age of 122. But worldwide, more people than ever are reaching the age of 100 and older. Scientists think this is due to better nutrition, more access to healthcare, and life-saving drugs such as antibiotics.

QUICK QUIZ!

IN OLD AGE, YOUR NOSE AND EARS ...?

a: Get bigger

b: Get smaller

c: Stay the same

WHEN DO PEOPLE REACH THEIR PEAK?

We are at the peak of our physical powers between the ages of 20 and 35. However, thinking skills don't reach their maximum until at least the age of 40, as knowledge and experience boost the brain's processing power. Many skills are honed over years of practice!

WHY DO WE DIE?

All living things eventually die. This happens when their cells no longer function well enough for life to continue. Senescence is the term doctors use for this gradual decline. Death happens when the brain is no longer able to send signals to the heart to pump blood or the lungs to function.

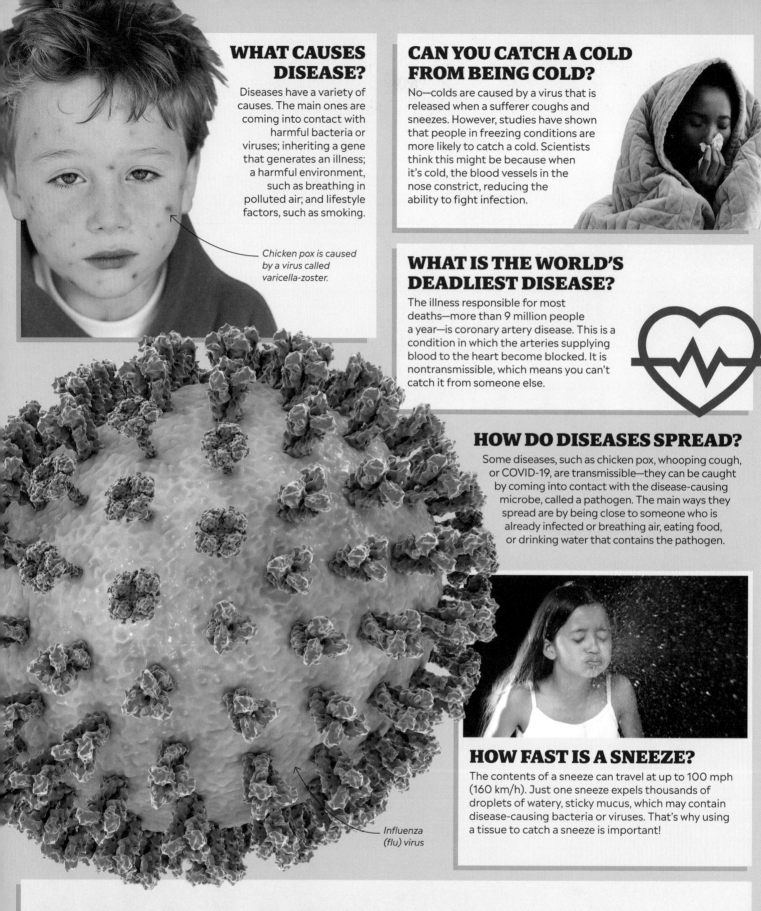

WHAT CAUSES DISEASE?

Diseases have a variety of causes. The main ones are coming into contact with harmful bacteria or viruses; inheriting a gene that generates an illness; a harmful environment, such as breathing in polluted air; and lifestyle factors, such as smoking.

Chicken pox is caused by a virus called varicella-zoster.

CAN YOU CATCH A COLD FROM BEING COLD?

No—colds are caused by a virus that is released when a sufferer coughs and sneezes. However, studies have shown that people in freezing conditions are more likely to catch a cold. Scientists think this might be because when it's cold, the blood vessels in the nose constrict, reducing the ability to fight infection.

WHAT IS THE WORLD'S DEADLIEST DISEASE?

The illness responsible for most deaths—more than 9 million people a year—is coronary artery disease. This is a condition in which the arteries supplying blood to the heart become blocked. It is nontransmissible, which means you can't catch it from someone else.

HOW DO DISEASES SPREAD?

Some diseases, such as chicken pox, whooping cough, or COVID-19, are transmissible—they can be caught by coming into contact with the disease-causing microbe, called a pathogen. The main ways they spread are by being close to someone who is already infected or breathing air, eating food, or drinking water that contains the pathogen.

Influenza (flu) virus

HOW FAST IS A SNEEZE?

The contents of a sneeze can travel at up to 100 mph (160 km/h). Just one sneeze expels thousands of droplets of watery, sticky mucus, which may contain disease-causing bacteria or viruses. That's why using a tissue to catch a sneeze is important!

DISEASE: A condition that impairs or prevents the healthy functioning of the body or mind

BODY DEFENSES:

The ways in which the body protects itself from infection by harmful microbes

WHY DO PEOPLE GET HAY FEVER?

Hay fever is an allergy to pollen, a substance made by plants. When dealing with thousands of threats each day, the immune system sometimes attacks harmless substances, such as pollen, as if they were a germ. In some people, pollen in the air we breathe triggers symptoms such as streaming eyes, sneezes, and coughs.

HOW DO WHITE BLOOD CELLS KILL GERMS?

There are different types of white blood cells to find, identify, attack, and destroy microbes. The type that destroy invaders are called phagocytes. They engulf the germ and digest it, breaking it down using chemicals called enzymes.

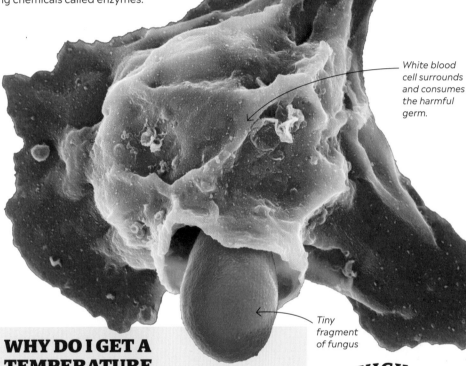

White blood cell surrounds and consumes the harmful germ.

Tiny fragment of fungus

WHY DO WE VOMIT?

If harmful microbes get as far as your stomach, the body tries to get them out of your system before they can do harm. Sensors in the stomach lining trigger strong muscle contractions, which send the stomach contents back up the esophagus and out of the mouth.

WHY DO I GET A TEMPERATURE WHEN I'M ILL?

Fever is a sign that your immune system is fighting germs. The body's thermostat rises to help white blood cells work better. The heat also makes it harder for germs to survive—they prefer to live at the normal body temperature of 98.6°F (37°C).

QUICK QUIZ!

WHERE ARE WHITE BLOOD CELLS MADE?

a: In the heart

b: In bones

c: In muscles

HOW DOES MY BODY PROTECT AGAINST DISEASES?

The body's biggest line of defense against disease-causing microbes is the skin, an all-over suit of armor. In openings not covered by skin, such as the mouth, nose, and eyes, the body puts up different barriers to invaders.

Skin
Skin protects tissue and organs from germs and injury.

Tears
Tears contain a bacteria-busting chemical called lysozyme.

Wax
Earwax traps dust and germs as it slowly flows out of the ear.

Mucus
Sticky mucus in the nose and airways stops microbes from reaching the lungs.

Saliva
Saliva protects the mouth, tongue, and teeth from bacteria.

Acid
Strong acid kills germs that make it as far as the stomach.

Protective clothing prevents contact with hazardous substances.

Pipettes are used to transfer small volumes of liquid for analysis.

Test tubes are used to collect, observe, and compare samples.

WHERE DO MEDICINES COME FROM?

Drugs used to treat illnesses (medicines) are either made from plants and other natural substances or manufactured from chemicals. Scientists experiment with combinations of ingredients when developing new drugs. Before being made available, drugs are tested to make sure they work and are safe to use.

IT'S A MYSTERY!

How can we cure the common cold?
Despite decades of research, scientists still can't cure the common cold. Colds are caused by a virus that changes so often that scientists have not been able to develop a vaccine that works for all colds.

MEDICINE:
The science of treating or preventing illness

HOW DO VACCINES WORK?

Vaccines are medicines that teach the body how to protect itself against infectious disease. The body is injected with a substance that makes the immune system spring into action. It teaches the body to create antibodies—proteins that fight off a specific virus.

The vaccine is injected into a person's body.

Virus is studied in order to produce a vaccine.

White blood cells start to produce antibodies.

Antibodies destroy the virus if it enters the body.

ARE NANOROBOTS REAL?

Not yet, but they are under development in medical research, and the technology is growing fast. Nanorobots are tiny, programmable machines that one day may be injected into the bloodstream (as this artist's impression shows) or taken as a pill in order to take samples for diagnosis, repair damaged organs, or deliver medication precisely where it's needed.

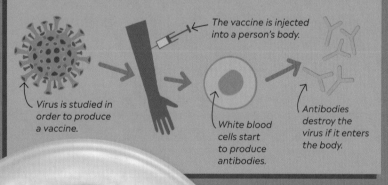

WHICH MEDICINE HAS SAVED THE MOST LIVES?

Penicillin! Before this bacteria-killing antibiotic was discovered by Alexander Fleming in 1928, people often died of minor infections. Penicillin was first used on wounded soldiers in World War II. Since then, an estimated 200 million lives have been saved by antibiotics.

Penicillin is derived from a mold grown in the laboratory.

WHY DO DOCTORS DO BLOOD TESTS?

Blood is packed with valuable clues to your state of health. A small sample can reveal whether you have enough essential minerals such as calcium in your body and shows how well your organs are performing. Blood tests can also detect conditions such as cancer or diabetes.

HOW CAN I KEEP MY BRAIN HEALTHY?

When you are young, learning new things creates many new connections within the brain and increases the brain's processing power. Studies show that continuing to challenge your brain with number puzzles, crosswords, or playing games like chess slows down the decline of the brain's powers as you get older.

HOW MUCH WATER SHOULD I DRINK?

Water is vital to life. It is the main component of your 30 trillion body cells and without water, the body couldn't keep cool, digest food, move joints, or transport essential oxygen. Doctors say we should aim for about 3 pints (1.5 liters) a day. Other drinks count toward the total, but water is the healthiest option!

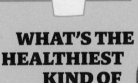
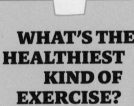

Heart muscle grows larger and stronger with exercise.

WHY ARE SUGARY FOODS SO YUMMY?

All food is broken down by the body into glucose (sugar) for cells to use for energy. When you eat sugar, it doesn't need to be broken down—it can be used right away. The brain, seeing it as a wonder food that the body doesn't have to work at processing, generates feelings of pleasure when you eat sugar, as well as cravings for more.

WHY DO WE SLEEP?

While you sleep, the body is hard at work repairing and renewing cells. Meanwhile, the brain sorts through and stores information as memories, as well as regulating important hormones that control functions such as growth. The immune system also uses sleep time to reset, making you better able to fight off germs and disease.

WHAT'S THE HEALTHIEST KIND OF EXERCISE?

The kind that you like enough to do every day! Staying active is essential to keep the body and mind working well and help prevent illness. You don't have to go to the gym or play competitive sports—anything that makes your heart, lungs, and muscles work harder, such as running, cycling, or skateboarding, is good for you.

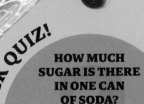

QUICK QUIZ!

HOW MUCH SUGAR IS THERE IN ONE CAN OF SODA?

a: 1 teaspoon

b: 3 teaspoons

c: 9 teaspoons

HEALTH: A state of well-being where the body and the mind are in good working order and free from illness

HISTORY

DID HUMANS EVOLVE FROM MONKEYS?

No, humans did not evolve from monkeys or any of the primate species alive today. We do share a common ancestor with chimpanzees but, from around 7 million years ago, we evolved separately. Our earliest hominin ancestors, such as *Sahelanthropus tchadensis*, still spent a lot of time in trees.

Sahelanthropus **skull**

WHEN AND WHERE DID THE FIRST HOMO SAPIENS LIVE?

Our own human species, *Homo sapiens*, appeared in Africa around 300,000 years ago. Their skulls were shaped to hold a large brain, and they developed many types of new tools as well as skills for hunting and surviving and lived together in big groups.

HOW MANY SPECIES OF HUMANS HAVE EXISTED?

Our closest ancestors all belonged to the genus *Homo*. There have been more than 20 *Homo* species, and in some periods several species existed at the same time. One of the earliest was *Homo habilis*. They emerged 2 million years ago and could use simple tools.

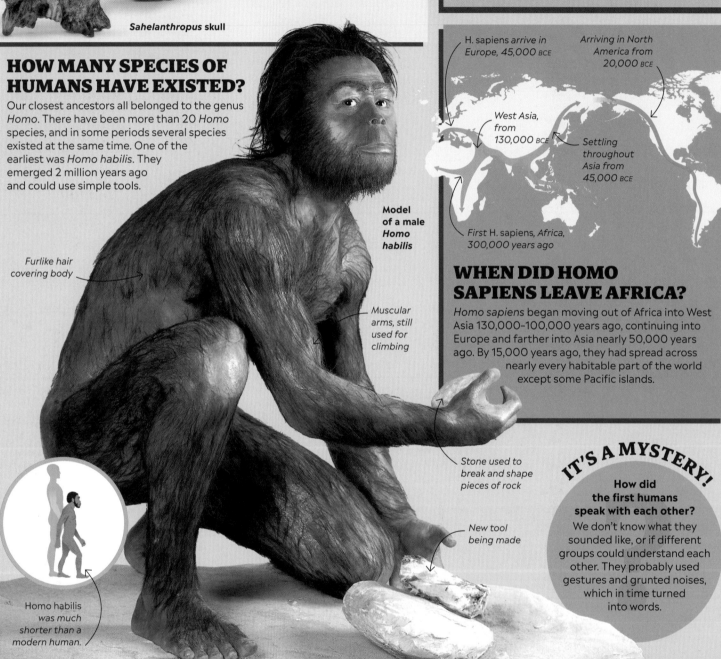

Furlike hair covering body

Model of a male *Homo habilis*

Muscular arms, still used for climbing

Stone used to break and shape pieces of rock

New tool being made

Homo habilis was much shorter than a modern human.

H. sapiens *arrive in Europe, 45,000 BCE*

Arriving in North America from 20,000 BCE

West Asia, from 130,000 BCE

Settling throughout Asia from 45,000 BCE

First H. sapiens, Africa, 300,000 years ago

WHEN DID HOMO SAPIENS LEAVE AFRICA?

Homo sapiens began moving out of Africa into West Asia 130,000–100,000 years ago, continuing into Europe and farther into Asia nearly 50,000 years ago. By 15,000 years ago, they had spread across nearly every habitable part of the world except some Pacific islands.

IT'S A MYSTERY!

How did the first humans speak with each other?

We don't know what they sounded like, or if different groups could understand each other. They probably used gestures and grunted noises, which in time turned into words.

EARLY HUMANS:
Our ancestors, a group of species also known as hominins

COULD ALL HUMAN ANCESTORS WALK UPRIGHT?

Our earliest ancestors moved like chimpanzees and had long arms. Later species developed bones that fitted together in a way that made it easier to walk upright, and their arms got shorter as they were not needed for knuckle walking. *Homo erectus* was the first to walk solely on two legs.

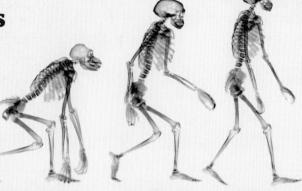
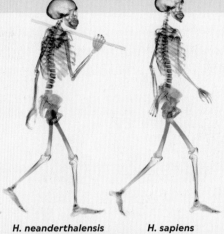

Earliest hominins   **H. habilis**   **H. erectus**   **H. neanderthalensis**   **H. sapiens**

WHAT DID EARLY HUMANS EAT?

Whatever they could find—fruit, berries, nuts, mushrooms, leaves, eggs, seafood, fish, insects, and lizards. Then they began eating meat, which they chewed raw until they learned to make fire.

Meat

Mussels

Mushrooms

Nuts and berries

HOW WERE THE FIRST TOOLS INVENTED?

Small rocks were used to pound fruit and plants. Some people might have picked up a sharp stone or even cut themselves on one and realized it could be used to cut meat off bones. Eventually, they began to use stones to sharpen and shape flint stone into axes, knives, and spear- and arrowheads.

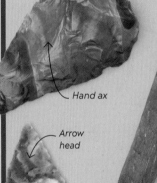

Knife with blade made from flint

Animal sinew kept the blade in place.

Hand ax

Arrow head

Flint could be cut into hard, sharp shapes.

Wooden handle

HOW DID THEY MAKE FIRE?

Early humans would have seen wildfires, caused by lightning strikes, and realized fire produced light and heat. At first, people probably made use of sticks that still smoldered, then learned to create sparks by hitting flint against rock. Later, they made bow drills (right) to ignite kindling.

Using a bow drill

A drill stick is rotated fast to create friction.

Dry moss or straw ignites from the heat caused by friction.

HOW DID THEY MAKE CAVE ART?

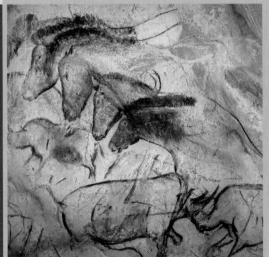

Symbols, hands, and animals were painted using materials with natural pigment—black came from charcoal, red from earth, and white from chalk. Some were made by blowing a paint mix through a tube; others were drawn by using bits of solid minerals like a crayon. This is a reconstruction of art made in a cave in France around 30,000 years ago.

FAST FACTS

Human ancestors learned to use **fire** at least **800,000** years ago.

Needles made from bone were used to make **clothes** from skins and furs.

People used **harpoons** to catch large fish around **90,000 years** ago.

WHAT WAS LIFE LIKE FOR A NEANDERTHAL?

Analysis of Neanderthal skeletons reveals that they lived rather short and harsh lives. But small family groups often lived together in caves and also knew how to build simple shelters. They had tools and could use fire to cook. We also know that they buried their dead, placing their bodies carefully in special pits.

Man arranging the body of a dead person

Neanderthal burial

HOW DO WE KNOW ABOUT THEM?

Scientists have studied fossilized Neanderthal skeletons. For example, analyzing their teeth tells us that they ate a lot of meat. Retrieved DNA shows how closely related to us they were and what they might have looked like.

Teeth absorb elements from the food a person eats.

Lower jaw and teeth from a Neanderthal teenager

DO I HAVE ANY NEANDERTHAL DNA?

Possibly—some people in Europe and Asia have up to 2 percent Neanderthal DNA in their genome. This proves that, at some point, quite a few Neanderthals and *Homo sapiens* met and had children together.

Homo sapiens **skull**　　　**Neanderthal skull**

Why did they disappear?
Neanderthals went extinct 40,000 years ago. Maybe they died out because of a very unstable climate or because they competed for food and space with *Homo sapiens*. Scientists have yet to find out.

HOW WERE NEANDERTHALS DIFFERENT FROM US?

Homo neanderthalensis didn't evolve in Africa like the earliest *Homo sapiens* (see page 176), but in Europe and Asia. They were still the human species most closely related to us, but they were shorter and stockier and adapted to live in a colder climate.

Model of a Neanderthal man

Clothes made of animal skins

Spear with stone tip

DID THEY MAKE ANY ART?

Archaeologists have found symbolic markings in a cave in Spain. Made with red pigment, they date from earlier than when *Homo sapiens* is thought to have lived there. They are likely to have been made by Neanderthals, as are finds of deer bone pieces with carved patterns.

NEANDERTHALS:
A human species that lived in Europe and parts of Asia from 400,000 to 40,000 BCE

WHAT DID ICE AGE PEOPLE DO?

They were skilled hunter-gatherers who built fine shelters, some out of mammoth tusks. They wore warm clothes, often decorated with shells or bones. Many had a rich culture and made mammoth ivory sculptures, such as this head of a young woman.

Ivory head, found in France

WAS ALL OF EARTH COVERED IN ICE AND SNOW?

No, but a large part of North America, Europe, and Northern Asia was iced over. The areas close to the ice sheet edges were cold steppe and tundra. The ice sheets only began to melt some 11,000 years ago.

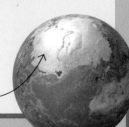

Area permanently under ice during the last ice age

QUICK QUIZ!

HOW TALL WAS THE THICKEST PART OF THE ICE SHEET?

a: 98,400 ft (30,000 m)

b: 9,840 ft (3,000 m)

c: 984 ft (300 m)

DID PEOPLE MOVE AWAY WHEN THE ICE CAME?

Some might have migrated south, away from the ice, while other peoples who had lived in central Europe for thousands of years died out. Those who settled south of the ice sheet survived, and some wandered north once the ice melted.

Warm clothes made from fur

Family moving to warmer lands

DID ICE AGE PEOPLE HAVE DOGS AS PETS?

Wild dogs lived near humans and scavenged on their scraps. Over time, they became domesticated (tamed). They were good to have when hunting, as well as for protection, and pups raised among people became good friends, too.

Ice age dogs looked similar to this one.

ICE AGE: A period of very cold climate, peaking when thick ice sheets covered large parts of the northern hemisphere 26,000–11,000 years ago

Ice sheet edge

Saber-toothed tiger on the hunt

Mother protecting her baby

DID HUMANS HUNT MAMMOTHS?

Yes, people hunted them for meat, fur, and ivory (tusks). There were other predators on the cold steppes (treeless grasslands) where mammoths lived—saber-toothed tigers, brown bears, and wolves also hunted them for food.

WHAT WAS THE FERTILE CRESCENT?

The Fertile Crescent is a name given to an area in West Asia. This was the land where farming first began and where people first built houses and towns. Thousands of years later, the first ancient civilizations formed here, in the area between the rivers Euphrates and Tigris known as Mesopotamia.

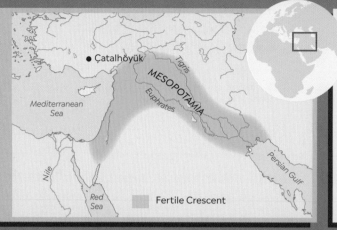

Çatalhöyük

Mediterranean Sea

MESOPOTAMIA

Tigris

Euphrates

Nile

Red Sea

Persian Gulf

▢ Fertile Crescent

WHY DID PEOPLE SETTLE DOWN THERE?

The Neolithic people who arrived in the region found fertile land with lots of water and a good climate. Plants grew easily, providing plenty to eat. This meant people did not have to wander far to forage for food or to hunt prey. They could stay in one place, together with others. As a result, the population began to grow.

THE FIRST TOWNS:

The first large settlements that appeared in West Asia from around 7000 BCE

Emmer, a type of wheat

WHEN DID PEOPLE LEARN TO GROW FOOD?

For a long time, people had lived by hunting and foraging for food. But around 9000 BCE, they began to plant seeds instead of eating them right away, and then harvest the crops. From around 6000 BCE, they invented ways to transfer water from rivers to fields, so crops could grow in the dry season, too. They grew emmer, a form of wheat, and barley, peas, and lentils.

WHAT ANIMALS DID THEY HAVE ON THE FIRST FARMS?

People started to tame and keep species that could produce milk and meat for food and wool and skins for clothing. Goats and sheep were the first animals to be domesticated, around 10,000 years ago. Pigs were added to the menu about a thousand years later. It was not until after 4000 BCE that people tamed oxen and then horses, which were used both for meat and for transport.

Ladders were used to climb onto the roofs.

FAST FACTS

⌂ People settled permanently in the Fertile Crescent **12,000 years** ago.

⌂ The ruins of **Çatalhöyük**, the first known town, are in **Turkey**.

⌂ **Uruk** and **Ur** were two of Mesopotamia's **grandest cities.**

Houses had space for artisans to make pottery or copper objects.

People kept animals in the towns.

WHAT WERE THE FIRST HOUSES LIKE?

Once people stopped moving around, they could build permanent homes instead of temporary shelters. They used bricks of mud, dried in the sun and then stacked on top of each other. Eventually, houses were built in groups to form villages, some of which grew into the first towns.

Rulers had long, curly beards.

One of Mesopotamia's Sumerian rulers

The earliest houses were circular dwellings made of mud-brick.

HOW BIG WERE THE FIRST TOWNS?

As people got better at farming, there was enough food to support lots of people living in one place. Çatalhöyük, the first known town, built over 9,000 years ago, was home to around 8,000 people. There were no streets between the houses, so people would walk from one to another on the roofs.

WHAT WAS MESOPOTAMIA?

It was the part of the Fertile Crescent where some of the earliest ancient civilizations developed. The Sumerians built the first great cities, palaces, and temples in its southern part from 3000 BCE. They were soon joined by the Akkadians, Assyrians, and Babylonians.

WHAT NEW MATERIAL BECAME POPULAR AT THIS TIME?

a: Rubber

b: Bronze

c: Oil paint

QUICK QUIZ!

Open hatches on roofs were used to go in and out of the houses.

WHO INVENTED THE WHEEL?

The wheel evolved in Mesopotamia in the 5th millennium BCE, but we don't know who its inventor was. It was in fact first used horizontally, as a rotating plate for shaping wet clay into pots. Then someone had the idea to turn it upright, and the first wheeled carts appeared. This meant it was quicker and easier to transport cargo, as well as soldiers into battle.

Wheeled war wagon depicted in 2600 BCE

WHY DID PEOPLE LEARN HOW TO WRITE?

People first started writing in Mesopotamia in around 3400 BCE, as a way of counting and recording goods. They wrote with reeds on clay tablets using pictograms that developed into a script known as cuneiform. Later, this was used to write down laws and epic poems.

The writing on this 4,500-year-old object lists the many temples built by the Sumerian king Enannatum I.

181

ARE THERE DIFFERENT KINDS?

Megaliths are placed in different ways. Single, upright standing stones are called menhirs. In some places, menhirs have been placed in a stone circle, which can be round or shaped like a boat. A dolmen consists of several menhirs with a flat capstone placed on top, like a roof.

Menhir

Stone circle

Dolmen

WHEN DID PEOPLE START PUTTING UP MEGALITHS?

The earliest known megaliths were raised in Göbekli Tepe, a Stone Age site in Turkey, around 11,000 years ago. Around 7,000 years ago, people began making them in Spain and France, and then elsewhere in Europe and in Ethiopia.

WHO MADE THEM?

Not much is known about the people who constructed these large monuments. People at this time were farmers who lived in round huts made of clay and sticks. Yet, using various stone tools (they hadn't discovered how to work metal), they were able to quarry these huge stones and also transport them to the sites where the stones were raised.

IT'S A MYSTERY!

How were the stones transported?

Experts can tell from the type of rock that many stones came from faraway quarries. But we don't know if they were floated on rafts or dragged over land.

The capstone shape is rounded on top but completely flat underneath.

This is one of three stones that support the massive capstone.

MEGALITHS:
Very large stones, raised in prehistoric times to stand upright and form a monument

HOW MUCH DO THEY WEIGH?

Megaliths vary in size. At Stonehenge, a stone circle in southern England, UK, the smallest stones weigh 2.2–5.5 tons (2–5 tonnes) each, while the largest are a hefty 27.5 tons (25 tonnes).

ARE MOST MEGALITHS IN EUROPE?

There are lots of megaliths in Europe—as many as 35,000 stand in locations from Scandinavia to the Mediterranean. But people constructed them in Africa and Asia, too. In Korea, for example, there are around 40,000 dolmens. Many of the Korean ones held tombs containing bones and other objects.

Erecting a dolmen

Man using lever to stop the stone from rolling back.

Team of strong workers pull the ropes.

Logs help the stone move forward.

Mound of soil, built by the workers

Standing stones placed in deep holes in the ground

HOW DID PEOPLE PUT STONES IN PLACE?

There are various theories. Even pulling a single stone upright would have been challenging with the tools available at the time. So how were dolmens constructed, with the heavy capstone raised on top? One theory is that they built up a mound of soil around the standing stones and then pulled up the flat-top stone. Once it rested on the standing stones, the soil was dug away again.

The capstone is 16 ft (5 m) long and weighs about 17.6 tons (16 tonnes).

WHAT WERE MEGALITHS FOR?

Dolmens like this one, in Pentre Ifan in Wales, UK, have been thought to mark burial chambers or even been part of burial mounds. But although some have pits underneath, no human bones have been found. European dolmens and stone circles might have had a sacred purpose, including tracking the Sun's path across the sky as its light struck certain stones on certain days, such as at solstices. Or maybe they were simply built as very impressive monuments.

The rock material comes from the nearby Preseli Hills, where it was quarried before being transported here.

ANCIENT EGYPT:

The great civilization that grew around the Nile river and lasted for 3,000 years

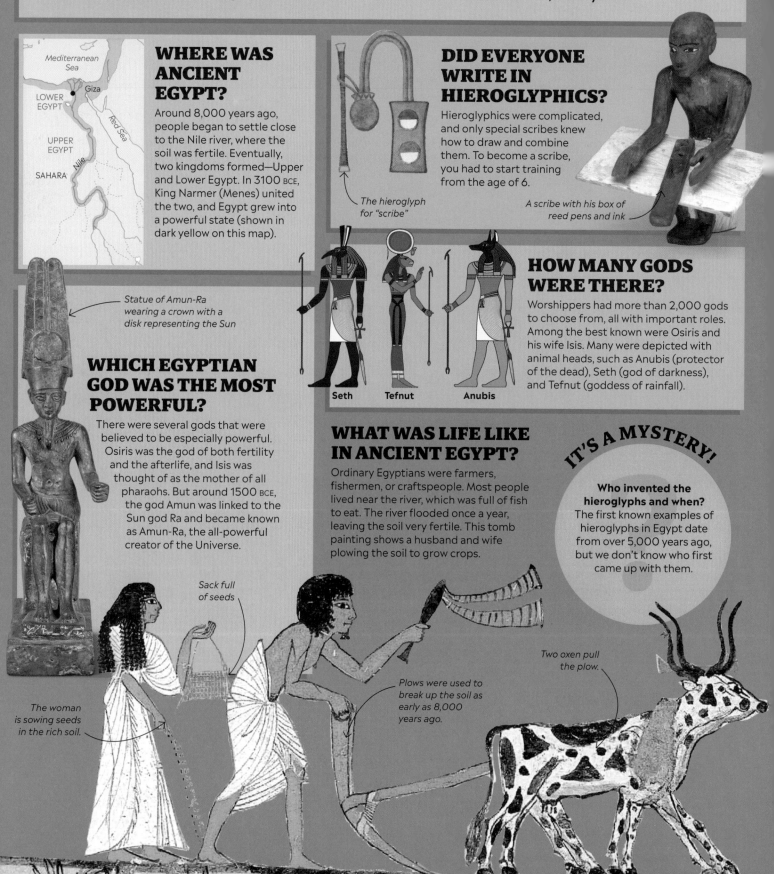

WHERE WAS ANCIENT EGYPT?

Around 8,000 years ago, people began to settle close to the Nile river, where the soil was fertile. Eventually, two kingdoms formed—Upper and Lower Egypt. In 3100 BCE, King Narmer (Menes) united the two, and Egypt grew into a powerful state (shown in dark yellow on this map).

Map labels: Mediterranean Sea · Giza · LOWER EGYPT · UPPER EGYPT · SAHARA · Nile · Red Sea

DID EVERYONE WRITE IN HIEROGLYPHICS?

Hieroglyphics were complicated, and only special scribes knew how to draw and combine them. To become a scribe, you had to start training from the age of 6.

The hieroglyph for "scribe"

A scribe with his box of reed pens and ink

WHICH EGYPTIAN GOD WAS THE MOST POWERFUL?

There were several gods that were believed to be especially powerful. Osiris was the god of both fertility and the afterlife, and Isis was thought of as the mother of all pharaohs. But around 1500 BCE, the god Amun was linked to the Sun god Ra and became known as Amun-Ra, the all-powerful creator of the Universe.

Statue of Amun-Ra wearing a crown with a disk representing the Sun

HOW MANY GODS WERE THERE?

Worshippers had more than 2,000 gods to choose from, all with important roles. Among the best known were Osiris and his wife Isis. Many were depicted with animal heads, such as Anubis (protector of the dead), Seth (god of darkness), and Tefnut (goddess of rainfall).

Seth   Tefnut   Anubis

WHAT WAS LIFE LIKE IN ANCIENT EGYPT?

Ordinary Egyptians were farmers, fishermen, or craftspeople. Most people lived near the river, which was full of fish to eat. The river flooded once a year, leaving the soil very fertile. This tomb painting shows a husband and wife plowing the soil to grow crops.

IT'S A MYSTERY!

Who invented the hieroglyphs and when?
The first known examples of hieroglyphs in Egypt date from over 5,000 years ago, but we don't know who first came up with them.

Sack full of seeds

The woman is sowing seeds in the rich soil.

Plows were used to break up the soil as early as 8,000 years ago.

Two oxen pull the plow.

WHO WAS THE GREATEST PHARAOH?

Thutmose III (1481–1425 BCE) was a military genius who conquered lots of land. But Ramses II, who recaptured many areas that Egypt had lost to other peoples, was greatly celebrated during his long rule (1279–1213 BCE). Ramses made sure to raise lots of giant statues of himself, such as the 65-ft (20-m) tall ones that guard his temple at Abu Simbel (seen here), one of the many massive buildings he constructed.

WHO WAS THE YOUNGEST PHARAOH?

When Tutankhamun became pharaoh in 1332 BCE, he was just 9. He ruled until his death, aged only 19. Experts are not sure whether he died from illness or an accident.

Tutankhamun's golden death mask

A cobra and a vulture, symbolizing Upper and Lower Egypt

Face thought to show the features of Tutankhamun

COULD WOMEN BE PHARAOHS?

There were several influential queens, but only a few women ruled as pharaoh. One of them was Hatshepsut, who set up trade routes and built great temples.

Hatshepsut shown in the form of a sphinx, with a lion body and eagle wings

False beard, like those used by male pharaohs

PHARAOHS: Rulers of ancient Egypt who were worshipped as gods

HOW WAS THE PHARAOH CHOSEN?

The throne usually passed down from father to the oldest son. Before the new pharaoh could be crowned, he had to take part in a long series of ceremonies, which confirmed his link to the gods.

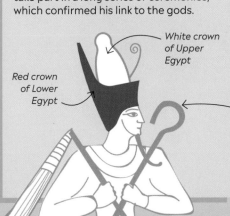

White crown of Upper Egypt

Red crown of Lower Egypt

The crook and flail were symbols of power. Pharaohs were depicted holding them crossed over their chest.

QUICK QUIZ!

WHO WAS THE LAST PHARAOH?

a: Cleopatra VII

b: Tutankhamun

c: Ramses II

WHERE DID THE PHARAOHS LIVE?

Most pharaohs built new palaces for themselves and their families and servants. They were large structures with many halls, gardens, courtyards, and store rooms. But they were built with mud bricks instead of stone, so none stands today.

PYRAMIDS: Giant burial monuments built by the pharaohs in ancient Egypt

WHERE WAS THE FIRST PYRAMID BUILT?

The oldest known pyramid was built in Saqqara, south of Cairo, nearly 5,000 years ago. It was constructed by an architect named Imhotep for the pharaoh Djoser. He came up with the idea to place six traditional flat tombs, known as *mastaba*, on top of each other to form a 204-ft (62-m) tall step pyramid.

WHAT'S INSIDE A PYRAMID?

Most of a pyramid's interior consists of solid stone blocks, just like the outside. A few narrow shafts and passageways might lead to a sealed burial chamber, like in the Great Pyramid in Giza, shown in this cross-section. It was built for Pharaoh Khufu in around 2600 BCE.

Capstone tops the pyramid.

This chamber contains Khufu's stone sarcophagus, but no mummy has been found inside.

Giant stone slabs blocked the chamber entrance.

Original entrance was built 56 ft (17 m) above ground, possibly to stop grave robbers.

Polished white limestone slabs made the surface shine.

Network of passages lead to other empty chambers.

Core of stone blocks, placed in a steplike shape

Stonemasons

HOW WERE THE PYRAMIDS BUILT?

That is still debated, because no descriptions from the time have been found! But it is believed that stone blocks were hauled up along ramps, which were extended as the work went on.

FAST FACTS

🔺 So far, **118** pyramids have been discovered in Egypt.

🔺 An estimated **30,000** workers were needed to build one pyramid.

🔺 A pyramid took around **25 years** to construct.

IT'S A MYSTERY!

What happened to Khufu's mummy? Did looters steal Khufu's mummy in ancient times? Or was he actually buried somewhere else? No one has ever been able to find out.

WHO BUILT THE PYRAMIDS?

Lots of skilled craftspeople and workers were needed to construct the pyramid according to the architect's plan. Stonemasons broke up massive blocks into the correct size, and haulers pulled them into place. Artists and carpenters were also on site. Most lived in camps nearby, provided for by cooks and bakers.

WHY DID THE EGYPTIANS MAKE MUMMIES?

They believed that it was important that a body stayed intact after death so that the spirit of the dead person could return to it in the afterlife. To keep the body from decomposing, it was embalmed, wrapped, and placed inside a sarcophagus.

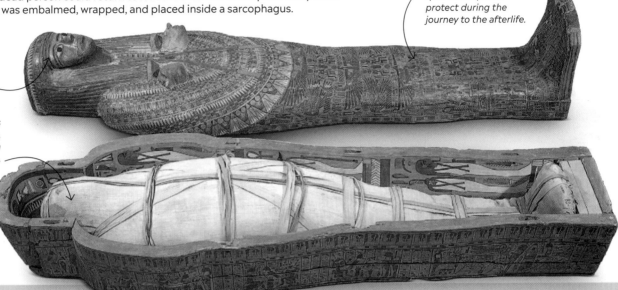

Hieroglyphs forming spells to help and protect during the journey to the afterlife.

The sarcophagus was made from wood, carved and painted with the person's likeness.

The mummy was placed inside, wrapped in linen cloth.

MUMMIES: Bodies of dead humans or animals that have been preserved and wrapped in bandages

WAS THE WHOLE BODY PRESERVED?

The heart was left inside the body, but the other internal organs were removed. The brain was thrown away, but the other organs were dried and placed inside canopic jars for burial alongside the mummy.

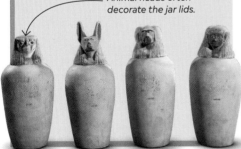

Animal heads often decorate the jar lids.

HOW WERE MUMMIES MADE?

Once the organs had been removed, embalmers covered the body in a saltlike mineral to dry it out. Then priests rubbed the body in scented oils before wrapping it with strips of cloth in many layers. Sacred amulets were placed between the layers, and resin was applied to form a protective coat.

WHO WAS MUMMIFIED?

Mummification wasn't just for pharaohs and their families—anybody who could afford it could have their body preserved. Animals that were thought of as sacred could also be mummified, such as cats and crocodiles.

Mummy of a cat, a loved and revered pet

WERE MUMMIES BURIED WITH TREASURE?

Amulets (charms) and jewelry were placed with the mummy, together with models of things that would be useful in the afterlife. Many tombs were looted not long after the burial, but some treasures were found in modern times.

A sacred scarab (beetle) amulet, found with the mummy of Tutankhamun

QUICK QUIZ!

HOW LONG DID IT TAKE TO MAKE A MUMMY?

a: 7 days

b: 70 days

c: 700 days

ANCIENT GREECE:

A civilization of city-states dominating the Mediterranean in the 8th to 4th centuries BCE

WHY DID ATHENS AND SPARTA FIGHT EACH OTHER?

Ancient Greece was a collection of hundreds of city-states, each with its own army. Two of the most powerful were Athens and Sparta, and they competed for allies among other states. Sparta had superb warriors (see right), but Athens had a large navy. But after decades of conflict, Sparta had acquired better ships, and in 404 BCE, Athens was defeated.

Wooden shield covered in bronze

Brass helmet with a crest of dyed horsehair

Spartan soldier

HOW DID GREEK WARSHIPS WORK?

They were modeled on the ships of the Phoenicians, an earlier naval power in the Mediterranean. They had sails but were also powered by oars, operated by strong oarsmen who sat in tiers—biremes had two tiers, and triremes had three. In sea battles, they would sink enemy ships by ramming them at speed.

Rudder for steering

Ram for sinking ships

Man voting by holding up a hand

Assembly officials

WAS DEMOCRACY INVENTED IN ATHENS?

Yes, Athens was no longer ruled by a king and all its citizens could vote and share opinions about government in the Assembly. Voting was usually by show of hands. However, no women or enslaved people could be citizens of Athens!

FAST FACTS

- The first **Olympic Games** took place in 776 BCE, at Olympia.
- Olympic **athletes** did not win medals—only leafy **wreaths**.
- Greek marble **statues** were painted in **bright colors**.

Alexander the Great

DID THE TROJAN WAR REALLY HAPPEN?

The ancient Greek poet Homer wrote about the Trojan War in his epic poem the *Iliad*. It tells of a long conflict between the Greeks and the city of Troy (a real city whose ruins are in modern-day Turkey). Other versions describe how Greek forces used a wooden horse to defeat Troy. Believing it was an offering, the Trojans took the horse inside their walled city. The soldiers hidden inside jumped out, burnt the town, and killed the king. No one knows whether this took place, but it is one of the most famous stories of all time.

Greek soldiers hid inside the Trojan horse.

WHO WAS THE TOP GREEK RULER?

One of the most powerful Greek rulers was Alexander the Great. He controlled his own kingdom of Macedon, and many city-states, too. In 335 BCE, he set out to conquer foreign lands, and soon ruled over an empire that stretched from Greece into northern India.

DID THE GREEKS WORSHIP THEIR GODS IN TEMPLES?

Yes, they visited temples dedicated to different gods, where priests or priestesses held ceremonies and made sacrifices. Those who wanted to know about their future could go to a sacred site to see an oracle, usually a woman, who could relay answers and messages from the gods.

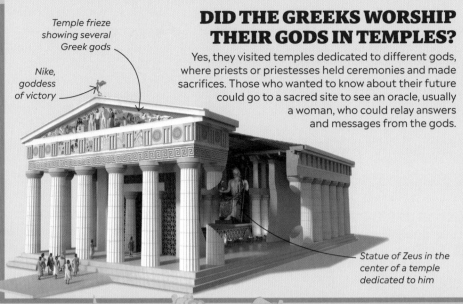

Temple frieze showing several Greek gods

Nike, goddess of victory

Statue of Zeus in the center of a temple dedicated to him

WAS HERCULES A GOD?

The legendary hero Hercules (Heracles in Greek mythology) was a demigod—his father was Zeus but his mother, Alcmene, was a mortal human. He was strong and clever and completed the 12 impossible tasks he was given, including killing a nine-headed hydra. But he did get a little help from other gods, according to the legend.

Hercules killing the hydra

WAS THERE A GOD FOR EVERYTHING?

Yes, there were deities for anything from war to beekeeping, and some had more than one role. The 12 most important gods were known as the Olympians. Five of them are shown here. Other Olympians included Aphrodite, goddess of love; Artemis, goddess of hunting; and Hera, queen of the gods.

Zeus, king of the gods

Ares, god of war

Athena, goddess of wisdom and war

Apollo, god of music, the Sun, and many other things

Poseidon, god of the sea, holding his trident

GREEK GODS:
Deities who were believed to play an active role in wars and daily life

The sky, shown as a sphere

IT'S A MYSTERY!

Was Cerberus, guardian of the Underworld, a dog?
Not a regular one! Some myths say that he was a creature with three dog heads and a serpent's tail, and snakes sliding out of his body. Others say he was a hound with 50 heads.

DID THE GODS LIVE ON EARTH?

Yes, the 12 most important lived on the Greek Mount Olympus, where they feasted, argued, and schemed. People also believed that the gods went out and about among humans and meddled in their lives.

WHO WERE THE TITANS?

In Greek mythology, Titans were the children and grandchildren of Gaia (the Earth) and Uranus (the Sky). They were thought to be ancestors of the Olympian gods but fought them in many battles. When the Titans lost, Zeus made one of them, Atlas, carry the sky on his shoulders.

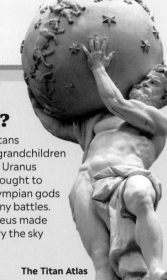

The Titan Atlas

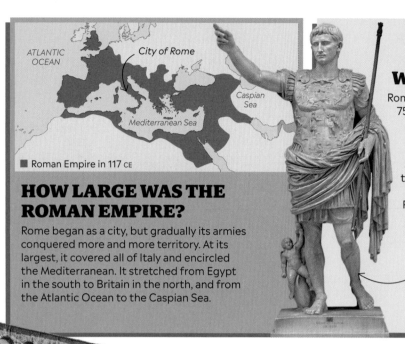

City of Rome

ATLANTIC OCEAN

Caspian Sea

Mediterranean Sea

■ Roman Empire in 117 CE

HOW LARGE WAS THE ROMAN EMPIRE?

Rome began as a city, but gradually its armies conquered more and more territory. At its largest, it covered all of Italy and encircled the Mediterranean. It stretched from Egypt in the south to Britain in the north, and from the Atlantic Ocean to the Caspian Sea.

HOW MANY EMPERORS WERE THERE?

Rome began as a kingdom in 753 BCE. Then, in 509 BCE, it became a republic with elected consuls holding power. But in 27 BCE, a leader named Octavian took sole power, renamed himself Augustus, and Rome became an empire. After him, there were some 70 emperors, the last one dying in 476 CE.

Augustus, the first emperor of Rome, ruled from 27 BCE to 14 CE.

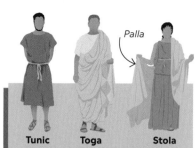

Palla

Tunic   Toga   Stola

DID EVERYONE WEAR TOGAS?

A toga was not very practical—it was a very long piece of fabric that had to be folded carefully to stay in place. Most men, women, and children wore tunics. Women wore a long dress (stola) over the tunic and a shawl called a palla.

HOW COME SO MANY ROMAN BUILDINGS STILL STAND?

Expert architects and engineers were employed to construct all sorts of buildings. They didn't just build with stone, but used concrete, too. Roman concrete was much more durable than modern concrete. Many of their bridges and aqueducts survive, such as the Pont du Gard in southern France, seen here.

ANCIENT ROME:

A civilization founded in the city of Rome, lasting from the 8th century BCE to 476 CE

DID ALL ROADS LEAD TO ROME?

The main ones did! The Romans built a vast network to make it easier for their well-organized armies to move through their huge empire. Messengers used the roads to carry news and orders between Rome and towns and army camps in the conquered provinces.

The paved road surface sloped toward the edges to allow water to drain off it.

Signum with a unit's symbol and medals

Legionaries marched in tight formation.

A centurion leading his unit of 80 legionaries

DID ROMANS EAT SPAGHETTI?

No, it was not yet known in this part of the world, and no Roman had ever seen a tomato either. These foods didn't arrive in Europe until many centuries later: noodles from China and tomatoes from South America.

Army sandals were made of strong leather and had studded soles.

WHAT TYPES OF GLADIATORS WERE THERE?

There were more than 20 kinds, each with a different set of weapons and style of fighting. Some were heavily armored, while others wore almost no protection and had to rely on speed and precision. Here are four of the most popular types, with their Latin names.

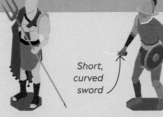

Short, curved sword

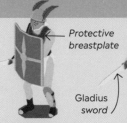
Protective breastplate

Gladius sword

Retiarius, armed with net and trident

Thraex, based on Greek-style soldier

Provocator, styled as a legionary

Murmillo, heavily armed

GLADIATORS:

People who fought each other in violent spectacles staged in ancient Rome

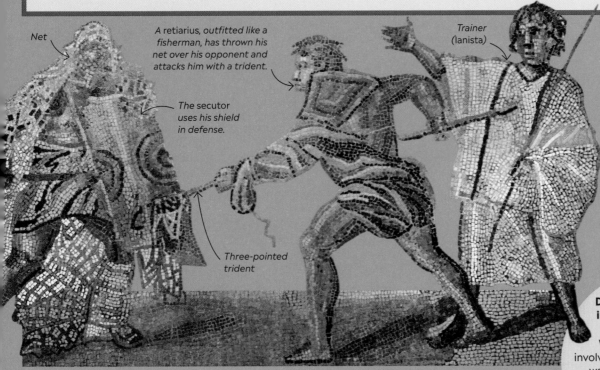

Net

A retiarius, outfitted like a fisherman, has thrown his net over his opponent and attacks him with a trident.

The secutor uses his shield in defense.

Three-pointed trident

Trainer (lanista)

HOW DID THEY LEARN TO FIGHT?

Gladiators lived in gladiator schools (ludi), where they were trained by a lanista in one specific form of combat. There were certain rules, and during fights a referee (summa rudis) was on hand to make sure they were followed.

IT'S A MYSTERY!

Did Roman emperors invent the thumbs-up gesture?

We know a gesture that involved "turning the thumb" was used in gladiatorial spectacles, but we're not sure whether it meant "kill" or "spare" the gladiator.

WHAT WAS A SHOW AT THE COLOSSEUM LIKE?

Spectacles lasted a whole day, with different types of combats taking place in Rome's grand arena. A crowd of up to 80,000 rowdy spectators watched from the tiered seating areas. Below the stage floor, gladiators awaited their turn next to caged animals.

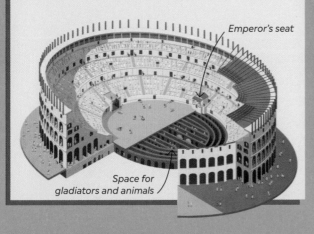

Emperor's seat

Space for gladiators and animals

DID THEY FIGHT ANIMALS?

Animals appeared in hunting shows, but the humans that took part in these were not called gladiators, but bestiarii. Sometimes, wild animals—such as lions or bears—would be used to kill criminals that had been condemned to death.

Roman glass featuring a gladiator

WERE GLADIATORS SUPERSTARS?

Gladiators who won and survived many fights were well known and celebrated for their victories. They were depicted on glasses, vases, and oil lamps. But they were still not fully accepted into Roman society and many, but not all, were enslaved.

MIDDLE AGES:

The period from 500 CE to 1500 CE, when many new empires formed across the world

WHY IS IT CALLED THE MIDDLE AGES?

It describes the period of European history between the fall of the Roman Empire and the start of the Renaissance (an era of new art styles and scientific progress). Anything from this time "in the middle" can be called medieval.

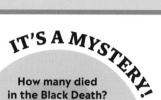

IT'S A MYSTERY!

How many died in the Black Death?

Around 50 million people, half of medieval Europe's population, are thought to have died from the plague in 1347-1353. Many more died in Asia and Africa—we don't know the exact number.

WHO HAD POWER IN EUROPE?

Medieval Europe consisted of many kingdoms. In 800 CE, the largest was that of the Franks, a people ruled by the mighty Charlemagne. The head of the Christian Church, the pope, was also very powerful.

Courtiers look on.

Pope Leo III crowning Charlemagne in 800 CE

WHICH WAS THE GREATEST CITY?

Constantinople (Istanbul) was the splendid capital of the Byzantine Empire (330-1453), which dominated the lands around the Mediterranean. The city was full of churches, such as the Hagia Sophia.

ASIA

Statue of the Byzantine emperor

Hagia Sophia

WHAT WAS THE LARGEST MEDIEVAL EMPIRE?

The Mongol Empire (1250-1450) was founded by Genghis Khan. His grandson, Kublai Khan, expanded it across most of Asia and as far west as eastern Europe. By 1279, it was the area shown in red on this map.

WERE THERE AFRICAN EMPIRES?

Yes, there were many, such as Wagadu (ancient Ghana), formed in 300 CE. In 1226, Sundiata Keita founded the Mali Empire (1226-1670). It grew wealthy on trading gold and salt. A later ruler, Mansa Musa (right) was famous for his riches.

HOW DID ISLAM SPREAD?

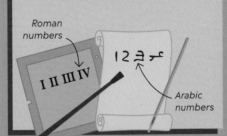

The prophet Muhammad first spread his message from Mecca in 632 CE. As Umayyad and Abbasid rulers conquered more lands, they brought their Islamic faith with them. They built splendid mosques in Arabia, West Asia, North Africa, and Andalusia (in modern-day Spain). Islamic art and crafts also became popular in these regions.

The Islamic world
- Extent in 632
- By 661
- By 750

EUROPE · ASIA · Baghdad · Mecca · AFRICA

DID ISLAMIC SCHOLARS INVENT MATH?

No, but Islamic mathematicians developed geometry, decimal fractions, and the Arabic numbers we use today. They made it much easier to do math than with ancient Roman numerals. An astronomer known as al-Khwarizmi wrote the first book about algebra in 820 CE.

Roman numbers

Arabic numbers

WHAT WAS AN ASTROLABE USED FOR?

It was a scientific instrument that could do many things—from telling the time and identifying stars to measuring the height of a building. It could also give the direction to Mecca, which was important to know when praying. It was invented in ancient Greece, but Islamic scientists perfected it and craftspeople turned it into a desirable status symbol.

Movable plate showing stars and constellations

Outer ring marking hours and minutes

WERE THERE LIBRARIES?

Yes, some of the world's first universities and public libraries opened at this time. Finely illustrated books presented knowledge on many topics, including engineering, medicine, and biology. This book is about horses.

GOLDEN AGE OF ISLAM:
When science, art, and engineering thrived in the Islamic world, in the 8th to 14th centuries

Scholars and scientists debating

Astrolabe

WHY WAS IT A GOLDEN AGE?

The search for knowledge was encouraged by Islam, and people could explore and debate ancient and new ideas. In Baghdad, scientists and thinkers from all over the Islamic world gathered in the House of Wisdom to discuss ideas, translate manuscripts, and exchange knowledge.

QUICK QUIZ!

WHICH OF THESE DRINKS ORIGINATED IN THE MUSLIM WORLD?

a: Hot chocolate

b: Coffee

c: Tea

VIKINGS:

Scandinavian peoples who gained a reputation as fearful warriors in the 8th to 11th centuries

HOW FAR DID VIKINGS SAIL?

Viking ships were built to travel far and handle the open sea. They sailed along the coast of Europe, reached Iceland in the 9th century, then, in 1000 CE, Newfoundland, Canada. In the east, Vikings crossed the Baltic Sea and sailed along rivers all the way down to Constantinople (today's Istanbul).

Sails were made of wool or silk.

QUICK QUIZ!

WHAT ANIMAL DID THE GOD ODIN HAVE?

a: Nine-tailed wolf

b: Eight-legged horse

c: Two-headed cat

WHERE DID THE VIKINGS COME FROM?

Vikings lived in coastal communities in what is now Norway, Denmark, and Sweden (shown in red), and later in Iceland. The red arrows show the routes they took to explore, trade, and raid. Many Vikings settled down in places they had visited or invaded.

Scandinavia

Iceland

Rus

ATLANTIC OCEAN

Newfoundland

Constantinople

Dragon heads decorated some ship bows.

WHICH NORSE GOD WAS MOST POPULAR?

Vikings believed in many gods. Odin ruled supreme, and Frey and Freya looked after harvests, love, and fertility. But it was Thor, the bold god of war and thunder, that ordinary people liked best. Many wore jewelry in the shape of his hammer, Mjölnir.

Holes for oars

The hull was slim but strong, sailing well in all weather.

Valuables, combs, and other personal items stored in wooden chests.

The dead person lies under a shelter, next to her dog.

WHY DID THEY BURY THEIR BOATS?

Boats were highly valued, and people who could afford it were buried in one as a sign of their status. The dead person was surrounded by precious and useful things for the afterlife, such as animals, carts and sleds, jewelry, swords, and precious silk. Then the boat was covered by an earth mound.

Barrel holding weapons and a völva staff

WERE ALL VIKINGS WARRIORS?

Most of the crew on board a ship were also farmers, blacksmiths, craftspeople, or story tellers. They usually set out to sea in spring, while women stayed to run the farms. Some women were *völva*, who predicted the future.

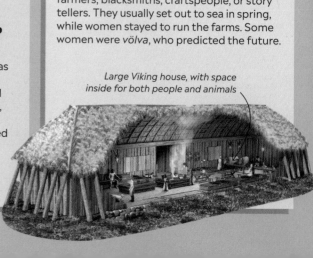

Large Viking house, with space inside for both people and animals

Arab merchants traveling on camels along the Silk Road

Saddle bag for small but valuable goods, such as myrrh

WHY WAS THERE A ROAD JUST FOR SILK?

Silk was one of the most popular exports from China since ancient times, but lots of other goods were transported along the same trade routes. Ideas and inventions spread along the way, too, as merchants told each other and people at home what they had seen and learned. The term "Silk Road" was only invented in the 19th century.

SILK ROAD: A series of trade routes running through Asia between China and Europe from the 2nd century BCE

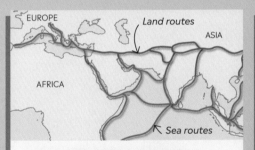

EUROPE

Land routes

ASIA

AFRICA

Sea routes

WAS THERE ONLY ONE TRADE ROUTE?

No, the Silk Road was a series of routes through Asia, but there were also routes across North Africa. A lot of cargo was transported on sea routes along Europe's coast and rivers and across the Indian Ocean between China, India, and Africa.

Chinese bronze coin

DID EVERYONE USE THE SAME MONEY?

No, but coins at this time were made of bronze, silver, and gold, so they could be valued by weight. Some used cowrie shells as payment, while others bartered (swapped) goods.

Tea
Tea leaves were pressed into round bricks to keep their flavor.

Lapis lazuli
This blue stone was used for jewelry or ground to powder for use in paints.

Cinnamon
An aromatic spice, this was popular in the medieval cuisine of many countries.

WHAT THINGS WERE TRADED?

Camel caravans carried porcelain, silk, and tea from China and pearls, gemstones, and spices from Asia. Sugar and horses came from the Islamic world and gold, ivory, and salt from Africa. Wool and furs were exported from Europe.

DID TRADERS STOP ALONG THE WAY?

Carried by a series of caravans, it might take many months for a packet of silk to get from China to Europe. Most merchants would only cover smaller sections, stopping off at trading posts such as this one. Here, they could rest and exchange their goods.

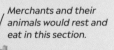

Merchants and their animals would rest and eat in this section.

The gate was locked at night to keep travelers safe.

Caravan arriving, loaded with goods

Marketplace where goods were exchanged

KNIGHTS:
Highly trained fighters who served medieval lords in Europe in the 8th to 15th centuries

WERE THERE DIFFERENT TYPES OF ARMOR?

Armor was expensive, and most knights probably just had one set. But those who could afford it might have a plain but strong one for battle; a highly protective one for jousting; and a fancier one, with ornaments etched into the metal, for parades.

Battle helmet
A visor could be raised for a better view and lowered to protect the face in battle.

Visor

Jousting helmet
The shielded slit meant that a knight had to drop his head to see his opponent coming toward him.

Shielded, narrow slit

HOW DID THEY GET ALL THEIR ARMOR ON?

A knight needed help from his squire to get dressed. First, underlayers of leather or chainmail went on, then the different plates of armor, which were tied together by leather straps. There were lots of different parts to fit, but it usually didn't take more than 10 minutes.

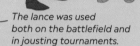

A squire puts the breastplate in place.

Lance made of strong wood with a metal tip, blunted for jousting

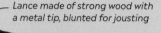

QUICK QUIZ!

HOW MUCH DID A FULL SUIT OF ARMOR WEIGH?

a: Up to 155 lb (70 kg)

b: Up to 66 lb (30 kg)

c: Up to 11 lb (5 kg)

The lance was used both on the battlefield and in jousting tournaments.

WHO COULD BE A KNIGHT?

Usually, it was sons of knights, who began training as children. At the age of 7, they started as pages, living in a lord's castle; doing chores; and learning fighting, reading, and writing. At 14, they became squires, training as the apprentice of a knight. At 21, they could be dubbed a knight.

A decorative covering called the caparison is in the colors of the knight's coat of arms.

WHAT DID A KNIGHT DO APART FROM FIGHTING?

Knights were expected to know how to write poetry, dance, read and write in Latin, play chess, and hunt. These were essential skills needed for spending time at court when not at war. In reality, many probably didn't have all those skills.

A knight singing to a lady

WHAT DO THE IMAGES ON THEIR SHIELDS MEAN?

Shield decoration was a way to show who was who in battle or at a tournament, when faces were covered by armor. A knight would be awarded the right to use certain colors and patterns on his coat of arms, according to rules called the heraldic code. Animals or mythical creatures could also be added. Some were family motifs and would be passed down through generations of knights.

WHAT WERE THE DIFFERENT PARTS OF A CASTLE?

All castles were different, but in the late Middle Ages, most had one or more sets of thick walls that connected defensive towers. The entrance was the weak point, so it could have a drawbridge and a fortified gatehouse with an iron portcullis (gate) that could be lowered into position. In the center stood the keep, or stronghold.

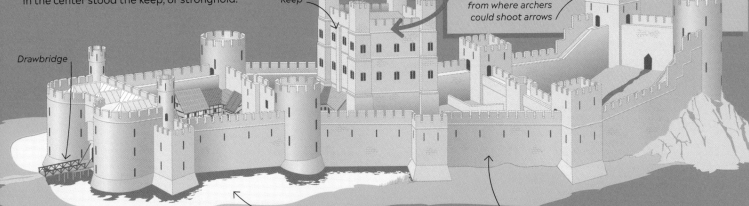

Great hall, where the lord feasted

Guards hall for knights and servants

Keep

Drawbridge

Moat

WHO LIVED IN A CASTLE?

The local lord and his family lived in the well-protected central keep. But the castle was also full of knights, ladies-in-waiting, pages, servants, blacksmiths, stable boys, gardeners, and cooks. Medieval kings and queens often had several castles.

Crenellated towers from where archers could shoot arrows

Curtain walls, topped by sheltered battlements

CASTLES: Large strongholds with thick walls, built to defend the surrounding area and its people in turbulent medieval times

HOW COULD AN ENEMY ARMY TAKE A CASTLE?

Medieval armies used machines, such as trebuchets, to hurl rocks at the walls; battering rams to break through; and ladders and siege towers. But attackers were met by archers' arrows and hot oils tipped on them from the battlements. Instead of trying to break a castle's defenses, an enemy army would besiege the castle. No one could get in or out and supplies were cut off, so those inside ran out of food and water and usually gave up.

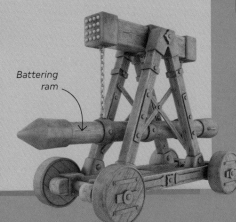

Battering ram

Curved roof of a Japanese castle

WHICH COUNTRIES HAD CASTLES?

Most European countries had lots of castles. Many kingdoms in Africa and Asia also built castles at this time, including in modern-day Morocco, Syria, India, and Japan. Those in Japan looked different from walled castles elsewhere but had the same function.

FAST FACTS

🏰 The **largest** castle in the world is **Malbork Castle** in Poland.

🏰 **Wales** has **more castles** per square mile (km) than any other nation.

🏰 The **siege** of Harlech Castle in Wales lasted for **7 years.**

DID CASTLES HAVE TOILETS?

Toilets were often built in the castle wall, but they were just a hole emptying out into the moat below. Night potties would be emptied out of windows, so people had to look out.

The contents of the toilet would fall down through a hole.

WHO WERE THE TERRACOTTA WARRIORS?

This is the name given to the statues that stand in the tomb of the first emperor of China, Qin Shi Huang. They represent the armies he used to conquer rival kingdoms and create a first united empire in 221 BCE.

Each one of the 8,000 soldier statues looks slightly different.

WHO WAS THE MOST FAMOUS EMPEROR?

It is hard to pick one from the more than 500 emperors who have ruled China! But the Yongle Emperor (1402–1424) of the Ming Dynasty made Beijing capital and built a palace there, known as the Forbidden City. He also sent out his admiral Zheng He on voyages of exploration and trade to India and Africa.

IMPERIAL CHINA:

When ancient China was ruled by a long series of dynasties (ruling families)

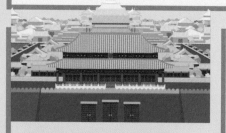

WHY WERE DRAGONS IMPORTANT SYMBOLS?

Chinese dragons were seen as powerful and life-giving and a symbol of luck. They appear on and inside palaces and temples, on vases, and on fabrics. Those in the Imperial Palace (such as the one shown here) have five claws, while dragons featured elsewhere could only have four.

HOW BIG IS THE FORBIDDEN CITY?

The walled grounds contain 980 buildings and nearly 9,000 rooms. The emperor and his family lived in the Inner Court, but he held audiences in an Outer Court hall, sitting on his Dragon Throne. The the grounds teemed with servants and officials.

Guards lived in the towers.

Gunpowder, weapons, and food supplies were stored.

WHY WAS THE GREAT WALL OF CHINA BUILT?

Several emperors built walls to defend their realm from invaders. The earliest sections date from 200 BCE and were made from soil. The wall was later extended and reinforced. During the Ming Dynasty (1368–1644), its solid brick guard towers were added.

Guard tower

QUICK QUIZ!

WHICH OF THESE WAS USED TO MAKE THE WALL?

a: Sticky tree sap

b: Steamed rice

c: Concrete

WHERE WAS THE BENIN KINGDOM?

It was (and still is) in modern-day Nigeria. Settlements founded by the Edo people grew into a kingdom around 1000 CE. It was ruled by kings known as Ogisos, but then a new dynasty of rulers known as Obas took over. In the 15th century, it expanded into an empire.

Benin City

Benin Kingdom heartland

AFRICA

→ Expansion

Modern-day Nigeria

The Oba's crown was made of coral beads.

WHO RULED THE KINGDOM?

It was the mighty Oba, who lived in a grand palace in the large Benin City. This brass plaque, one of many that decorated the royal palace, shows an Oba surrounded by courtiers, warriors, and officials. He is joined by chiefs from important clans. Other chiefs were appointed to be in charge of towns.

WHAT KIND OF JOBS DID PEOPLE DO?

Many were highly skilled artisans, supplying precious art and objects for the royal palace. Metalworkers made brass plaques and other items. Others were ivory carvers, instrument makers, and basket weavers. There were also soldiers, hunters, priests, and musicians.

Court musician playing a horn made from an elephant tusk

Royal staff, jointly held by the Oba and a chief

FAST FACTS

🐆 **Oba Ewuare** (1440–1473) was the empire's greatest ruler.

🐆 The **capital** had wide streets and was surrounded by a fortified **wall**.

🐆 The **British** army invaded in 1879, **plundering** the palace.

BENIN KINGDOM:

An African kingdom founded in the 10th century that grew into a wealthy empire

Portuguese traders offering brass bracelets

HOW DID THE OBA GET SO RICH?

The kingdom exported ivory, pepper, palm oil, and cloth. At first, it traded with other African kingdoms and with Arabic states. Then, in the 1470s, Portuguese merchants arrived. They paid with brass bracelets, which were melted down to make precious objects and panels for the palace.

DID THE OBA REALLY HAVE TAME LEOPARDS?

Yes, a pair of leopards were kept in the palace. The leopard symbolized power, beauty, and intelligence, so it also often appears in palace artifacts, shown next to Obas on plaques, or as figurines. This grinning leopard head was made in brass by a skilled Edo artisan in the 17th century.

AZTECS:

A people, also known as the Mexica, who conquered and ruled large parts of central Mexico in the 14th to 16th centuries

NORTH AMERICA

DID THE AZTECS HAVE LOTS OF GOLD?

Yes, gold was extracted from rivers and also collected from conquered peoples. Skilled gold workers created sacred objects and ceremonial jewelry such as this snake. It was worn as a lip piercing by an Aztec ruler, symbolizing his power.

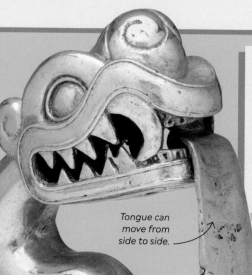

The end of the snake ornament is inserted through a piercing below the lower lip.

Tongue can move from side to side.

WHERE DID THE AZTECS LIVE?

They lived in what is now Mexico. They built their glorious capital Tenochtitlan on an island in a lake in 1325 and went on to control many of the surrounding lands and people (Aztec land shown in red on the map).

The Great Temple stood in the capital's center.

FAST FACTS

💀 The Great Temple at Tenochtitlan was a **196-ft (60-m)** tall step pyramid.

💀 Aztec astronomers used two complex **calendars** to keep track of time and key events.

💀 In **1519–1521**, Spanish invaders destroyed the Aztec Empire.

IT'S A MYSTERY!

Who built the ancient city of Teotihuacan?
This large city, full of huge temples, had long been in ruins when the Aztecs found it. It may have been built as early as 150 BCE, but no one knows which ancient people constructed it.

DID ALL AZTEC KIDS GO TO SCHOOL?

Yes, there were different schools, including one type where they taught sciences and religion and one type for military training. All children were taught to be respectful. They also learned useful things from their parents, such as fishing, farming, and weaving.

A girl learns to weave from her mother.

DID THEY PLAY SOCCER?

They did play an ancient ballgame—but it was nothing like soccer! The players had to keep the ball in motion without using their hands or feet. It was played as part of a religious ceremony instead of for fun and could be followed by ritual sacrifice of prisoners captured in battle.

High stone walls with circular markers lined custom-built courts.

The ball, made from hard rubber, could be up to 10 in (25 cm) in diameter.

DID THEY USE COINS?

No, they paid for goods using copper ax blades or cocoa beans. Peoples conquered by the Aztecs paid tribute in the form of cocoa beans, cloth, turquoise gems, and other items.

Cocoa beans

Turquoise

Several layers of leather offered some protection from the hard ball.

WHAT ANIMALS DID THE INCA KEEP?

Llamas (right) and alpacas were adapted to breathe and live at high altitude, so they were highly valued. They carried cargo along the paved mountain paths, their wool was used for weaving warm clothes and blankets, and they provided milk and meat. But people didn't ride on them!

HOW DID PEOPLE TRAVEL?

The Inca were expert road and bridge builders, but didn't use wheeled carriages. Nobles were carried in chairs, but ordinary people had to walk. Messages were sent by relay teams of swift *chaski* runners.

Chaski runner

Khipu, a system of knotted strings that represent messages

Blowing the shell alerts the next runner.

WHERE WAS THE INCA EMPIRE?

The Inca, who believed they were created by the Sun god Inti, first lived around Cuzco (in today's Peru) from the early 15th century. They expanded their realm under their leader Pachacuti Inca Yupanqui, and it quickly grew into what, at the time, was the world's largest empire.

SOUTH AMERICA

The Inca Empire at its height in 1525

Maize was a staple food prepared and cooked in many different ways.

WHAT FOOD DID THEY GROW?

The Inca were skilled farmers. They constructed terraces on the mountain sides and built water cisterns and canals to keep crops watered. They grew grain crops, such as maize and quinoa, and hundreds of different types of potatoes.

Terraces were built up with stones shaped to stay put without mortar.

QUICK QUIZ!

WHICH OF THESE DID THE INCA INVENT?

a: Freeze-dried food

b: Potato chips

c: Ice cream

INCA:
A people who ruled the largest empire in the Americas in the 15th to 16th centuries

WHAT WAS MACHU PICCHU?

This was a mountaintop city with expertly constructed palaces, temples, and houses. Their straw roofs are gone, but the stone walls have survived both time and earthquakes. It was not the Inca capital—that was Cuzco, located even higher up in the Andes.

The main temple was for worship of Inti, the Sun god.

Workshops and warehouses (colcas)

Terraces for growing vegetables and other crops

EXPLORATION:

When people set out on long journeys to lands unknown to them

QUICK QUIZ!

WHEN COLUMBUS REACHED LAND IN 1492, WHERE DID HE THINK HE HAD LANDED?

a: Canary Islands

b: Caribbean

c: India

WHO WERE THE FIRST EXPLORERS?

People have always been explorers. Since the first humans left Africa (see page 176), people all over the world have set out to find new places to live. The Polynesians were some of the earliest seafaring explorers. They settled islands in the Pacific Ocean from 2500 BCE, reaching Hawaii in around 900 CE.

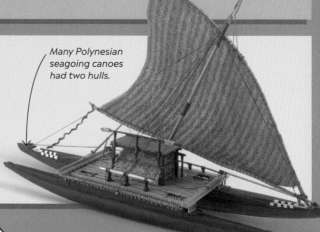

Many Polynesian seagoing canoes had two hulls.

DID EARLY EXPLORERS USE MAPS?

Early seafarers looked at wind and wave patterns and the Sun or stars to help them find their way. Later, navigational aids, such as the compass and sextant, helped orientation. Travelers began mapping out what they saw, which gave others a better idea of islands and coastlines. This map of Africa was made in Spain in 1500.

WHO DISCOVERED AMERICA?

The first people to arrive in North America did so more than 15,000 years ago. Over time, their descendants explored and settled across all of the Americas. Peoples like the Maya founded great civilizations and rich cultures thousands of years before the Europeans arrived.

Dug-out canoe

Early Indigenous American explorers

WHY WERE THERE SO MANY EUROPEAN EXPLORERS?

From the late 14th century, European explorers set out to forge new trade routes, especially sea routes. They wanted to trade in precious goods directly from Africa and Asia. Once they knew of the Americas, after Columbus's 1492 voyage, that continent became their new main destination.

Italian explorer Marco Polo arriving in Hormuz, in the Persian Gulf

WHO TRAVELED THE FARTHEST?

Ibn Battuta, who was born in 1304 in what is now Morocco, traveled all across the Islamic world. He made his first trip when he was 21, and in total went on to cover around 75,000 miles (120,000 km). He wrote a book about his travels, too.

WHAT IS A COLONY?

It's a piece of land taken over by a country by force without considering and respecting the people who already live there. The aim was to claim land and resources before another colonizing power did.

French colonizers arriving in Florida, 1564

WHAT HAPPENED TO THE INDIGENOUS PEOPLES?

Colonization was devastating for Indigenous people who lived in the lands that Europeans were claiming. Most peoples, including the Aztecs (see page 200), put up resistance, but European invaders had guns and made alliances with other peoples who were rivals or enemies. European illnesses, new to people in the Americas, spread quickly and killed millions.

Spanish soldiers   Aztec warriors

WAS THE US A COLONY?

Colonizers built forts, with soldiers standing by in case of attack.

Spain, Britain, France, and the Netherlands all colonized parts of North America, including what is today the United States. The Spanish were in the south and southwest, the French south and north, and the British and Dutch along the east coast.

COLONIZATION:

When a country takes control over foreign land and the people who live there

Gold objects, such as this one made by the Muisca people in Colombia, were stolen and shipped back to Europe.

WHY DO THEY SPEAK PORTUGUESE IN BRAZIL?

The Portuguese arrived in Brazil in 1500 CE. They claimed this region as a colony, while Spain invaded other parts of the Americas. As a legacy of colonization, their languages are still spoken alongside Indigenous ones.

Brazil

Spanish-speaking areas in the Americas

WHY DID COLONIZERS WANT LAND SO FAR AWAY FROM HOME?

European colonizers wanted to get their hands on the riches and raw materials that explorers had described were abundant in faraway lands, such as gold in South America. From the 16th to the late 19th centuries, many European nations aimed to expand to become empires, and colonies were a way to have military and civilian presence in places all over the world.

FAST FACTS

⚫ European **colonization** went on from the late 15th century to the early 20th century—more than **500 years**.

⚫ Spain, Portugal, France, Britain, and the Netherlands had the **most colonies**.

⚫ By **1932**, there were still **94 colonies** in the world.

TRANSATLANTIC SLAVERY:

The system used to traffic millions of Black Africans to enslaved labor in the Americas

HOW LONG DID THE SLAVE TRADE GO ON FOR?

From its beginnings in the late 15th century, it went on for 400 years. Even after the slave trade from Africa became illegal in the early 19th century, people were still being bought and sold in the Americas, and slavery itself didn't become illegal until many decades later. It destroyed the lives of those who were uprooted and their enslaved descendants. This modern statue, erected in their memory, also symbolizes the liberation from slavery.

Broken chains symbolizing freedom

The "Liberation from Slavery" statue stands on Gorée Island, Senegal, once one of the main slave trade centers in West Africa.

HOW DID IT START?

The Portuguese, who were trading in Africa in the late 15th century, were first to acquire enslaved people there. Soon, they and many other European nations were trafficking millions of people from Africa across the Atlantic to work on plantations and in mines in their colonies (see page 203) in the Americas.

Enslaved African men being taken to the ships

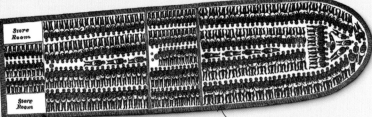

People were chained and stored as if they were cargo.

HOW LONG WERE PEOPLE ON THE SHIPS?

The Atlantic crossing could take up to two months, depending on the winds. But ships often first spent many months sailing between trading stations along the coast of Africa to take on board further groups of enslaved people, until the ship couldn't fit any more.

FAST FACTS

○ Around **12.5 million** Africans were trafficked across the Atlantic.

○ Denmark was first to **ban** the slave trade (but not slavery) in **1803**.

○ In the US, slavery only became illegal in **1865**, after the American Civil War.

HOW COULD PEOPLE SURVIVE BEING ENSLAVED?

Millions didn't. Many died on the long, horrific journey across the Atlantic from illness that spread quickly on board or from the despair of being separated from their families. Others died from the extremely hard work they were forced to do on the plantations or the violent punishments if they tried to escape.

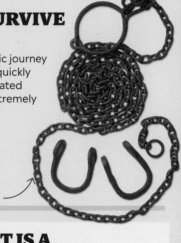

An iron chain was used to connect the shackles, a degrading punishment that totally restricted movement.

WHAT IS A PLANTATION?

Plantations were farms in the Americas that relied on enslaved labor to grow produce for export to Europe and, later, across North America. The main crops were sugar, cotton, or tobacco, all sold at great profit. This painting shows unpaid, enslaved workers on a sugar plantation in Antigua in the Caribbean, then a British colony.

WHAT WAS LIFE LIKE ON PLANTATIONS?

Enslaved men, women, and children were forced to work very long hours in harsh conditions. Many labored in the fields, others in factories processing the cotton or sugar. Some worked in the "master's" house as servants, cooks, or nannies. Abuse from overseers and the plantation owners and their families added to their hardship.

Enslaved laborers cutting sugar cane

WERE THERE SLAVE REVOLTS?

Uprisings on plantations were common. Many newly enslaved rebelled on the ships, too, but it was difficult because they were chained. But in 1839, a revolt on the ship *Amistad,* and the court case that followed, led to its captives eventually making it back to Sierra Leone in West Africa.

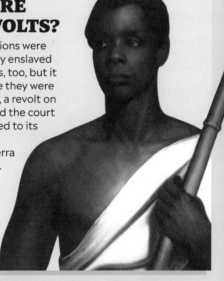

Sengbe Pieh, revolt leader on board the ship Amistad →

HOW DID IT END?

While enslaved people rebelled, Black and white abolitionists campaigned to make the public understand how wrong slavery was and influence politicians to outlaw it. From the early 19th century, countries began to make the slave trade, and eventually slavery itself, illegal.

Olaudah Equiano
In 1789, Equiano published a book on his experiences of being enslaved.

Frederick Douglass
An influential abolitionist speaker, Douglass toured the US, Britain, and Ireland.

Sojourner Truth
Truth campaigned against slavery and later for women's suffrage and fairer laws.

Harriet Tubman
After escaping from slavery, Tubman helped many others flee to freedom.

REVOLUTIONS:

When people rise up to demand a change to how they are governed

WHY DO REVOLUTIONS HAPPEN?

Revolutions can happen when people are unhappy with the way they are being governed or the conditions they are living under. Some revolutions are not caused by uprisings, but are major changes to the way people live, such as the Industrial Revolution (see pages 208-209).

WHAT WAS THE AMERICAN REVOLUTION?

In the 18th century, British colonies in North America were ruled by and paying taxes to the British king. Thirteen of these colonies wanted independence. After years of fighting, the United States of America was formed in 1776. Its first constitution, with laws on people's rights and how the country should be run, was signed in 1787.

The American Constitution

Toussaint Louverture, a formerly enslaved man, was a leader in the Haitian revolution.

QUICK QUIZ!

WHAT YEAR WAS THE RUSSIAN REVOLUTION?

a: 1666

b: 1848

c: 1917

People gave soldiers carnations to place in their guns to celebrate victory.

ARE ALL REVOLUTIONS BLOODY AND VIOLENT?

Most revolutions have involved bloodshed, but some have been peaceful. In the 1974 revolution in Portugal, its people and part of the military ousted the ruling dictator without a war. It became known as the Carnation Revolution.

1848 uprising in Prague, Czech Republic

DID ANY SLAVE REBELLIONS SUCCEED?

In 1791, the Caribbean island of Haiti was a French colony. But enslaved and formerly enslaved people rose up against local white slave owners, the French army, and then Britain and Spain, too. They won, and the island became an independent republic in 1804.

DO REVOLUTIONS ALWAYS LEAD TO CHANGE?

No—in 1848, for example, there were a number of revolutions across Europe. People in many nations demanded more rights or different forms of government. Some succeeded, but most were quashed within a year, and things went back to how they were. But it was a sign that the power of the people was on the rise.

WHAT STARTED THE FRENCH REVOLUTION?

Thinkers like Rousseau and Voltaire had begun to question rules and introduce new ideas about freedom. Their followers, and people who were poor and starving, came together to demand more rights for themselves and less power for the king and the aristocracy.

Red cap with a cockade in blue, white, and red, worn by many revolutionaries

DID QUEEN MARIE-ANTOINETTE REALLY SAY "LET THEM EAT CAKE"?

The queen was rumored to have exclaimed this upon being told that the people had no bread. She probably never did, but the quote has been used to demonstrate her ignorance of how and why people suffered. In October 1789, women marched to the royal palace at Versailles to demand reforms.

WHAT HAPPENED TO THE KING AND QUEEN?

At first, King Louis XVI was just forced to give up some of his power and approve a new constitution. But after trying to flee the country in 1791, the whole royal family was put under arrest. In 1793, Louis was taken to the guillotine, and a few months later, Queen Marie-Antoinette was executed, too.

FAST FACTS

⚑ **July 14**, France's national day, commemorates the revolution.

⚑ In **1793**, a new calendar renamed the months and introduced 10-day weeks.

⚑ France had **three** more revolutions, in 1830, 1848, and 1871.

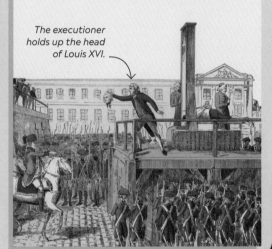

The executioner holds up the head of Louis XVI.

Sharp blade fell fast to sever the head from the neck.

Device fitted around the victim's neck to hold them still.

WHY WERE PEOPLE SENT TO THE GUILLOTINE?

Anybody who was deemed to be an enemy of the revolution was condemned to death. Not all of them were royals and aristocrats. From 1793, revolutionaries who didn't agree with how things were done were also executed. An estimated 17,000 men and women lost their heads this way.

DID IT HELP THE FRENCH PEOPLE?

The slogan of the revolution was "Liberty, Equality, and Brotherhood," and a few things improved for people. All male citizens got the right to vote and women got more rights, too, although not the vote. Freedom of speech and religion was introduced. But there was still a lot of poverty and inequality.

FRENCH REVOLUTION:

The events from 1789 to 1799, when the French people got rid of the monarchy

DID THINGS CHANGE EVERYWHERE?

Yes, but not at the same time. Industrialization began in Britain in the 18th century. At this time, there were cottage industries—people working from home to produce anything from pots to clothing for sale. But thanks to new inventions, production moved into factories, and transportation was transformed. It soon caught on in Europe and North America, and eventually in parts of South America, Africa, and Asia. In the 1860s, Japan was the first Asian country to introduce European-style industrialization.

Steam railroad in Tokyo, Japan, 1871

HOW DID FACTORIES TRANSPORT GOODS BEFORE THERE WERE TRUCKS?

The first factories were powered by water mills and built near waterways. In Britain, a vast canal network was constructed so that barges could carry goods between factories, warehouses, and ports. Soon, barges also carried coal for steam-powered factory engines.

INDUSTRIAL REVOLUTION:
A period of great change to the way people lived and worked in the 18th and 19th centuries

Blast furnaces, where iron was smelted from ores

Main factory building of Wentworth Works, Sheffield, UK, which produced steel

WHY IS IT CALLED A REVOLUTION?

The Industrial Revolution completely changed people's lives. Things previously made by hand were made by machines, and farmers and craftspeople became factory workers. It changed how and where they lived, too, as people moved from the countryside into the new towns that sprang up around factories and railroads. Steam-powered ships, trains, and cars gradually replaced sail ships and horse wagons.

WENTWORTH WORKS

HOW DOES A STEAM ENGINE WORK?

It burns coal to heat water in a boiler, which produces steam. The pressure of the steam moves a piston, which, through a system of other moving parts, makes a wheel turn. The motion of the wheel can then be used to make other machines move. This is Watt's engine, made for use in factories from 1776.

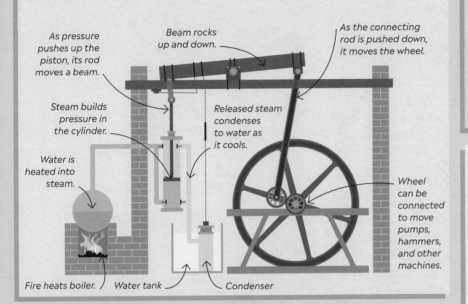

As pressure pushes up the piston, its rod moves a beam.

Beam rocks up and down.

As the connecting rod is pushed down, it moves the wheel.

Steam builds pressure in the cylinder.

Released steam condenses to water as it cools.

Water is heated into steam.

Wheel can be connected to move pumps, hammers, and other machines.

Fire heats boiler.   Water tank   Condenser

DID COTTON GROW IN BRITAIN?

No, cotton—key to the successful textile industries—came from India, and from Britain's Caribbean colonies and the US, where it was grown by enslaved laborers. Much of the money invested in factories and railroads came from wealth made from the slave trade and products produced as a result of it, such as sugar and tobacco.

Cotton fiber

IS IT TRUE THAT CHILDREN WORKED IN FACTORIES?

Yes. At the time, it was common for children to do farm work, but when mines and factories needed lots of workers, children were hired to work long hours for little pay. In Britain, laws to improve things came in from 1833. Children under the age of 9 could no longer work in factories, but children aged 9 to 13 could still be employed to work nine-hour days.

Children hauling coal in a coal mine shaft

WHAT DID THEY MAKE IN THE FIRST FACTORIES?

At first, the top products were cotton fabrics and porcelain—popular items that were expensive to import from abroad and too pricey for most people. Mass production in factories meant that more people could afford them. Soon, other products, too, were factory-made, such as shoes and kitchen goods.

Factory-made bowl showing a lady in early 19th-century fashion

HOW FAST DID THE FIRST TRAIN GO?

a: 50 mph (80 km/h)

b: 25 mph (40 km/h)

c: 5 mph (8 km/h)

QUICK QUIZ!

WAS THE FIRST STEAM ENGINE USED IN A TRAIN?

No, steam-powered machines were first used to pump water out of coal mines. Soon, they powered all machines needed in cotton fabric production, which was becoming Britain's top industry. The first steam locomotive was used to haul iron in 1804, but the first one to pull passenger wagons was George & Robert Stephenson's Locomotion No. 1 in 1825.

Chimney released exhausts.

A boiler, inside the barrel, powers two pistons. They push rods that make the wheels move.

Rod

Piston

Container holding water for the boiler; coal was carried in the wagon behind.

Wheels made from cast iron

WORLD WAR I:
A global conflict that took place between 1914 and 1918

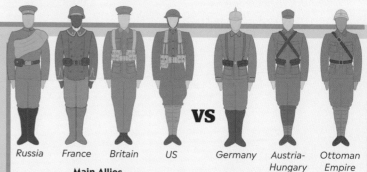

Russia	France	Britain	US		Germany	Austria-Hungary	Ottoman Empire
Main Allies (the Entente)				**VS**	**Central Powers**		

WHY DID WORLD WAR I START?

At the beginning of the 20th century, the main rival powers in Europe were Britain, France, Germany, Austria-Hungary, Russia, and the Ottoman Empire (ruled from Turkey). They all competed in who had the most colonies and best equipped armies. But many also formed alliances. This meant that in 1914, when a Bosnian Serb rebel shot the archduke of Austria-Hungary, it triggered a chain reaction as nations honored their alliances, taking sides and declaring war.

WHAT WERE THE TRENCHES LIKE?

The trenches were a main feature in the war. They were constructed to provide shelter from artillery fire and allowed soldiers to keep any gained ground by staying close to enemy lines instead of retreating. Deep ditches dug into the soil, they were enforced with sandbags, wooden planks, and barbed wire. On the Western Front (in France and Belgium), they were often mud-filled; in Gallipoli (Turkey) and North Africa, they were boiling hot. Soldiers would spend days in a trench, trying to stay brave while waiting for the order to attack.

WHO WAS FIGHTING WHOM?

There were two opposing sides: the Allies (or Entente) and the Central Powers. At first, the main Allies were Serbia, Russia, France, and Britain. Japan joined them, and then Italy (1915) and the US (1917). On the other side were the Central Powers: Germany, Austria-Hungary, and the Ottoman Empire. At different points, other nations joined and left the conflict.

Sandbags protecting from artillery impact

Barbed wire to prevent enemy soldiers entering

Shelter for sleeping, eating, and resting

Medic helping a wounded soldier

Gas mask

Rifle with a sharp blade, known as a bayonet, attached

Soldiers going "over the top," the terrifying maneuver that meant leaving the relative shelter of the trench to fight the enemy at close range.

Leather boots couldn't keep the mud and wet out, which often led to "trench foot," causing swelling and pain.

Rats were plentiful, scurrying around the men looking for food.

WHY IS IT CALLED A WORLD WAR?

The war impacted every continent. By 1918, over 30 countries were involved. Men from regions of Africa, Asia, Oceania, and the Caribbean that were part of the British and French empires also fought. Battles raged in Europe, Africa, and Asia.

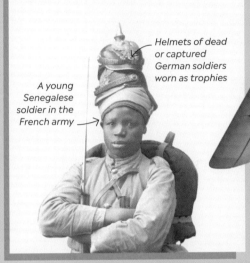

A young Senegalese soldier in the French army

Helmets of dead or captured German soldiers worn as trophies

Triple wings

The pilot sits in an open cockpit.

DID THEY HAVE FIGHTER PLANES?

Yes, planes were a new invention, first flown successfully in 1903. New models were tried out as the war went on. Early planes were used for surveying enemy positions. Later, enemy planes circled each other in "dog fights," aiming to shoot the other down.

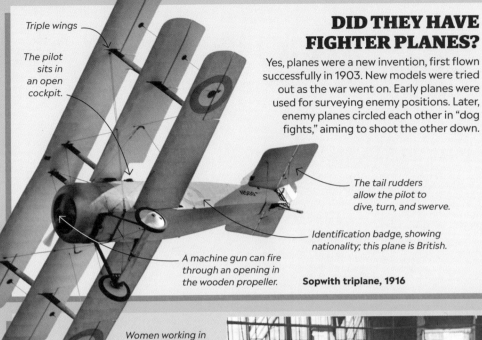

The tail rudders allow the pilot to dive, turn, and swerve.

Identification badge, showing nationality; this plane is British.

A machine gun can fire through an opening in the wooden propeller.

Sopwith triplane, 1916

QUICK QUIZ!

WHICH OF THESE WAS A NEW FEATURE FOR UNIFORMS?

a: Waterproof pants

b: Camouflage fabric

c: Padded knees

Women working in a factory making ammunition

WHAT WAS IT LIKE AT HOME?

Most men and teenage boys were away fighting. So women, including those who had never worked outside the home before or at all, went to work in factories and on farms. Many enrolled as nurses or ambulance drivers at home and near frontlines abroad. Their effort would contribute to women's suffrage (see page 212).

WHAT WAS NO MAN'S LAND?

This was the muddy wasteland between the trenches on the Western Front, dotted with craters made by heavy artillery shelling. Soldiers from either side could be commanded to storm across it to capture an enemy trench. These expeditions always saw huge casualties because there was no shelter for soldiers running into enemy fire.

WHAT KIND OF WEAPONS DID SOLDIERS FIGHT WITH?

Soldiers had rifles, grenades, and cannons such as mortars and field guns. The machine gun, a new deadly invention, could fire more than 600 rounds per minute. Another new weapon was poison gas. Tanks, huge armed vehicles that could roll across trenches and withstand machine gun fire, were used for the first time.

British Mark V tank

Gun is operated from inside the tank.

ME9828

211

WOMEN'S SUFFRAGE:

Women's right to vote, long fought for and achieved at different times in different countries

WHY COULDN'T WOMEN VOTE?

In the late 1800s, many believed that women shouldn't preoccupy themselves with politics, but focus on the home. Usually, a girl's father (or male guardian) made decisions about her life and then, once she got married, her husband took over that role. Women often couldn't inherit property or control their own money.

This medal was given to suffragettes who continued their protest by going on hunger strike while in prison.

Suffragette medal

WHICH COUNTRY WAS FIRST TO LET WOMEN VOTE?

It was New Zealand/Aotearoa, in 1893. After years of campaigning by Pākehā (white) and Māori women, such as Meri Te Tai Mangakāhia (left), a law came into place that said that all adults—men and women, Pākehā and Māori, over the age of 21—could vote.

WHY WAS GETTING THE VOTE SO SLOW?

Most politicians were unwilling to change the law or actively opposed female suffrage. But many women who had been active in the abolitionist movement (see page 205) went on to focus on suffrage. By the early 19th century, campaigns were gaining ground, with organized marches aimed at changing opinions.

WHAT IS A SUFFRAGETTE?

Suffragists used peaceful means of protest to get the right to vote, but the women known as suffragettes believed nothing could be achieved without attracting attention through (at times violent) action. They were often imprisoned, but continued once they were let out again.

Suffragettes newly released from prison

CAN ALL WOMEN VOTE NOW?

All nations except Vatican City now have universal suffrage rights, but in some countries, it is still difficult for women to vote and to run for parliament. In many countries, it has taken much longer for women who are of ethnic minorities in that country to get the vote.

Women marching for female suffrage in London, UK, in 1908

WHAT WAS THE ECONOMIC BOOM?

Once World War I was over, people began investing lots of money in new industries, such as car factories, and the stock market flourished, with the value of shares going up and up. A construction boom saw skyscrapers springing up in American cities, such as the Chrysler Building in New York, shown here.

HOW DID PEOPLE LISTEN TO MUSIC AT HOME?

The gramophone, which was first invented in the 1880s, became popular. A record had space for about four minutes of music on each side, then you had to turn it over before the next dance.

1920s record player

WHY IS IT CALLED THE JAZZ AGE?

The new popular music of the time was jazz, an African-American music style. It was fast and had a very different rhythm to the dance music that white people were used to. Dance halls and shows introduced it to an ever-widening audience.

King Oliver's Creole Jazz Band, 1923

King Oliver

Louis Armstrong

Lil Hardin

QUICK QUIZ!

WHICH WAS A 1920s DANCE CRAZE?

a: The Turkey Trot

b: The Mamba Slide

c: The Frog Hop

JAZZ AGE: The 1920s, also known as the Roaring Twenties, when jazz music filled dance floors in the US and the economy boomed

WHY DID FASHION CHANGE SO MUCH?

Many women, including those who had been out to work while men were away in the war, wanted the freedom of comfortable clothes. Designers like Coco Chanel created fabulous outfits that were easy to dance in, play sports, or just move freely without a restraining corset.

Tight corsets restricted movement.

Loose-fitting clothes for sports

Short dresses made for dancing

1900

1920s

WHAT WAS THE WALL STREET CRASH?

Wall Street is another name for the New York Stock Exchange, where shares are bought and sold. But shares had been overvalued, and when the stock market crashed in 1929, investors lost a lot of money. This led to the Great Depression of the 1930s, when many businesses went bust and people lost their jobs.

WHY WAS THERE ANOTHER WORLD WAR?

Germany was unhappy with the treaty agreed to after World War I, especially its loss of land. Then, in the 1930s, Germany and Italy were ruled by fascist dictators who began to expand their territories. In Asia, Japan had invaded China and planned to take over European colonies. As tensions rose, attempts to keep the peace failed.

WHO STARTED IT?

Germany was ruled by Adolf Hitler (left), a fascist dictator and leader of the Nazi party. Aiming to unite all German-speaking people and create a Greater Germany by force, he first made Austria and part of the Czech Republic part of his German Reich (empire). When he invaded Poland on September 1, 1939, France and Britain declared war. Soon, other countries also joined in.

WORLD WAR II:

A conflict raging from 1939 to 1945, affecting countries and people around the world

WHY WERE CITIES BOMBED?

Both sides—the Allied and the Axis powers—targeted each other's industries, ports, and railroad stations, but buildings and homes nearby also got hit. Later in the war, whole cities were targeted to make civilians lose hope and resistance. Many were damaged during the Allied liberation of Europe.

One of the few houses left standing in the French city of Saint-Lô in 1944

Two boys watching Allied soldiers driving though their ruined hometown

QUICK QUIZ!

WHAT FOODSTUFF MADE AMERICAN SOLDIERS POPULAR IN EUROPE?

a: Hamburgers

b: Noodle soup

c: Chocolate

Flags of the Allied nations forming a "V" for "victory"

Allied British forces included soldiers from India, Africa, the Caribbean, Australia, New Zealand, and Canada.

Other Allied forces, including the USSR, the US, and China

WHO WERE THE ALLIES?

The Allied forces were led by Britain, the USSR, and the US (from 1941). They included people of many nationalities and ethnicities from around the globe, as shown in this poster from 1942. They fought against the fascist Axis powers, led by Germany, Italy, and Japan.

A T-34 tank, used by the Soviet army throughout the war

An American B-17 bomber, or "Flying Fortress"

WHAT WERE THE DEADLIEST WAR MACHINES?

Tanks had evolved since World War I, and dominated the battlefields. Submarines targeted military, merchant, and passenger ships across the oceans. But it was the bomber planes that caused most deaths overall.

The German U-48 submarine sank more than 50 Allied ships.

WHY DID JAPAN ATTACK THE US?

Japan aimed to expand its empire throughout China and Southeast Asia. It attacked the US Pacific fleet, based at Pearl Harbor, Hawaii (right), to incapacitate it and force the US to negotiate. But after the devastating attack on December 7, 1941, the US joined the war on the Allied side.

FAST FACTS

By **1944**, Hitler had occupied **18 countries**, including France.

Up to **85 million** people are estimated to have been killed in the war.

China and the **Soviet Union** lost more people than any other country.

WHY WAS FOOD RATIONED?

There was a lack of food (and textiles and fuel) because it became hard to import goods. Trains, ships, roads, and railroads were attacked, and farms struggled to produce enough. In Britain, this was a week's average allowance of certain foods for one adult.

Cheese 1.8 oz (50 g)

1 egg

Sugar 8 oz (225 g)

Bacon 3.5 oz (100 g)

Margarine 3.5 oz (100 g)

WHAT HAPPENED TO CHILDREN?

Some children were evacuated from cities and industrial towns that were targeted by bombs to stay in the countryside. Others were sent abroad to countries not directly affected by the war. For those who stayed, life also changed, with food shortages, bombed homes and schools, and sleeping in bomb shelters.

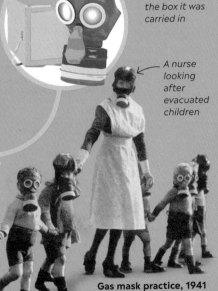

Children's gas mask, next to the box it was carried in

A nurse looking after evacuated children

Gas mask practice, 1941

HOW DID IT END?

From 1944, the Allies were making progress in Nazi-occupied Europe, marching into Germany in 1945. Germany surrendered on May 8, 1945. In the Pacific, the war ended after the US dropped atomic bombs on the Japanese towns of Hiroshima and Nagasaki. Japan surrendered on September 2, 1945.

HOLOCAUST:

The organized murder of 6 million Jewish men, women, and children, carried out by Nazi Germany and its collaborators during World War II

WHAT DOES THE WORD HOLOCAUST MEAN?

It comes from the ancient Greek words for "completely" (*holos*) and "burnt" (*kaustos*). It is used to describe the murder of Jewish people in Nazi Germany and Nazi-occupied territories during World War II, although many prefer to use the Hebrew term for it, *Shoah*, which means "catastrophe."

HOW DID IT BEGIN?

When Adolf Hitler took power in Germany in 1933, he introduced antisemitic laws that encouraged prejudice and hatred toward Jews. Antisemitism grew, and in a night of violence in 1938, known as *Kristallnacht* (night of broken glass), Jewish stores and homes were attacked. Soon, Jews were forced out of their homes and into ghettos and camps.

Cardboard tag showing the child's name and where they were from

WHY DID THE NAZIS TARGET JEWISH PEOPLE?

The Nazis unjustly blamed Jewish people for the problems that Germany faced after World War I, from its defeat to its poor economy. They spread propaganda based on their belief that the German ("Aryan") race was superior and that Jews were inferior. From 1941, the Nazi's "final solution" was a plan to kill all Jews.

All Jews were forced to wear a yellow star on their clothes.

Rescue organizers in Britain, many Jewish themselves, met children at the train stations to take them to foster homes.

This child is among the younger of this group, but many were no more than toddlers when they left their parents behind.

DID ANYONE ESCAPE THE HOLOCAUST?

As discrimination and persecution increased in Nazi Germany and Austria, many Jewish families began thinking about emigrating. Many left, but once the war began, it became very difficult to get out. Some people in Nazi-occupied Europe hid Jewish people in their homes, while others organized passports and exit visas or escape routes. In 1938-1940, around 10,000 Jewish children were sent to Britain in a program called the Kindertransport. This photo shows some of them arriving in London in 1939.

WHAT WAS LIFE LIKE IN A GHETTO?

From 1939, Jews were forced to move into ghettos. The first were located in Poland, after the Nazi invasion. They were separate, often walled parts of towns, and space was cramped. People tried to continue to live their lives, but nobody could leave without permission, illness spread quickly, and food shortages were very common.

WERE THERE UPRISINGS?

Jewish men and women put up resistance in any way they could, both in ghettos and in camps. But it was difficult to get a hold of weapons. Most uprisings resulted in people being deported from ghettos to camps or executed right away. But one major revolt, in the Sobibór extermination camp in Poland in 1943, led to the escape of up to 300 detainees.

WHAT IS A CONCENTRATION CAMP?

The Nazi regime used different types of camps. People held in concentration camps had to carry out hard labor, and often died as a result of it. Extermination camps were places where people were sent to be killed in gas chambers, most of them directly after arriving.

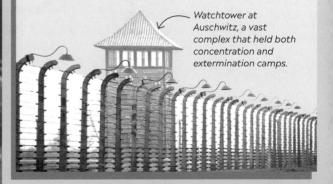

Watchtower at Auschwitz, a vast complex that held both concentration and extermination camps.

WHO GOT TAKEN TO CAMPS?

At first, concentration camps held political prisoners, taken there without any court trials. Soon, anyone that the Nazis thought of as inferior was sent there, too: homosexual men; Roma; and, from 1938, Jews. From 1941, as the Nazis started their organized mass murder of Jews, millions of men, women, and children were sent to the six extermination camps built in Poland.

DID ANYONE SURVIVE THE CAMPS?

Allied forces liberated any survivors found in the camps at the end of the war. But Europe's Jewish population had shrunk to 3.5 million, compared to 1933, when it was 9.5 million. Many survivors went on to talk about their experiences to combat ignorance and prejudice and to prevent it from ever happening again.

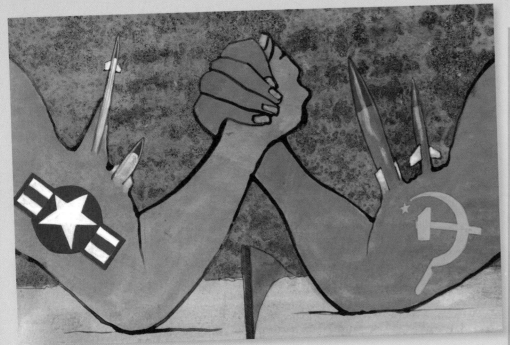

Cartoon showing the conflict as an arm wrestling match between the US (left) and USSR (right)

WHAT DEVICES DID SPIES USE?

Both sides used spies to find out what the opposite side was doing. They came up with all sorts of tools to intercept radar signals or listen in on secret conversations. Some devices were weirder than others!

Spy camera hidden inside a coat, with lens made to look like a button

This device operates the camera shutter.

WHY IS IT CALLED THE "COLD" WAR?

This conflict between the US and the USSR began after World War II. Both nations started an arms race, competing to stockpile the most weapons. But they never used these weapons against each other. The "war" was fought with propaganda, spies, and the threat of a nuclear attack from either side.

WHAT WAS THE CONFLICT ABOUT?

It was a battle about political influence and power. The US and its Western Bloc allies stood for capitalism and democracy, while the USSR and its allies in the Eastern (Soviet) Bloc were communist. Both superpowers wanted to convince other countries that their system was the best.

COLD WAR: The era of high tension between the US and the Soviet Union (USSR) that lasted from 1945 to 1991

WERE THERE ANY BATTLES?

The US and the USSR did not fight each other directly in battles. But there were several conflicts, known as proxy wars, where the US supported one side with weapons and personnel, and the USSR the other. For example, US soldiers fought for South Vietnam against the communist North Vietnam in the Vietnam War (1955–1975), seen above.

Flag of the USSR

US flag

President Gorbachev

President Reagan signing the treaty

HOW DID IT END?

In 1987, President Gorbachev of the USSR and US President Ronald Reagan signed a treaty to destroy their missiles. In 1989, many European countries that were under Soviet influence or rule began breaking away and, in 1991, the USSR itself was dissolved.

IT'S A MYSTERY!

How many spies did each side have?

There were thousands of spies, some working for the US, and some for the USSR, or their allies. Some spies were actually working for both sides, and because it was all very secret, it's hard to know!

SPACE RACE:

The competition between the US and the USSR to be first to send a person to the Moon

WHY DID THEY COMPETE INSTEAD OF WORKING TOGETHER?

The space race took place in the 1950s and 1960s, when the US and the Soviet Union (USSR) were at the height of the Cold War. They were rivals in everything, from sports to political influence in other countries. They were suspicious about the other's plans for military presence in space, and both were determined to be first to go there.

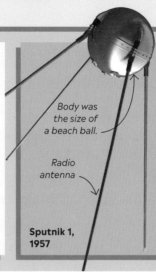

Body was the size of a beach ball.

Radio antenna

Sputnik 1, 1957

WHO MADE THE FIRST OBJECT TO FLY IN SPACE?

On October 4, 1957, the USSR launched Sputnik 1. Other objects, such as rockets, had been launched already in the 1940s, but this satellite was the first object to successfully orbit Earth. Its signal could be picked up around the world.

Laika in her space cabin, 1957

IS IT TRUE THAT A DOG WAS FIRST IN SPACE?

Both the US and the USSR made tests with animals before trying with human astronauts. The first animal to go up was a monkey, launched by the US in 1948. But the first animal to orbit Earth was a dog named Laika, in Sputnik 2, on November 3, 1957.

WHO WAS THE FIRST PERSON IN SPACE?

Valentina Tereshkova

Yuri Gagarin

It was the Soviet astronaut Yuri Gagarin on April 12, 1961. He orbited Earth on board Vostok 1. The USSR launched the first woman into space, too. Valentina Tereshkova orbited Earth 48 times in three days in June 1963.

WHO WON THE RACE?

In July 1969, the US Apollo 11 mission successfully landed on the Moon. Neil Armstrong and Buzz Aldrin were the first people ever to walk on its surface, while Michael Collins orbited above aboard the spacecraft. The event was broadcast to 600 million people on Earth.

The Eagle, Apollo 11's lunar landing module

FAST FACTS

🚀 There were **140** crewed space flights from **1961** to **1990**.

🚀 The first **photo** of **MARS** was taken by US spacecraft Mariner 4 in 1965.

🚀 In 1975, the **crews** of Apollo (US) and Soyuz (USSR) **shook hands in space.**

Pilot Buzz Aldrin checks that everything is in order.

QUICK QUIZ!

HOW MANY PEOPLE HAVE WALKED ON THE MOON?

a: Seventeen

b: Twelve

c: Three

CIVIL RIGHTS MOVEMENT:

The push for equal rights for Black people in the US, which gained new ground from the 1950s

WHEN DID CAMPAIGNING START?

The struggle for civil rights began as soon as it became clear that the legal end of slavery in the US, in 1865, did not mean equal rights for Black people. Early activists, such as Ida B. Wells, spoke out against racism and lynchings (illegal executions). But change was very slow. From the 1950s, however, the movement had more impact as increasingly more people joined and stood up for equal rights.

Ida B. Wells (1862-1931)

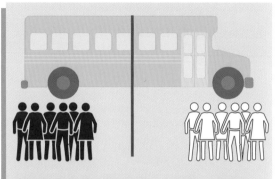

WHY COULD BLACK AND WHITE PEOPLE NOT USE THE SAME SPACES?

Known as segregation, this racist practice was still legal in the southern states of the US in the 1950s. It meant that Black people were not allowed to use the same spaces as white people, including on buses, in restaurants and movie theaters, in waiting rooms, and in schools. If they did, they could be arrested, abused, or assaulted.

WHAT DID PEOPLE DO TO PROTEST AGAINST RACISM?

In the US, many joined civil rights organizations such as the NAACP. These worked for change by launching court cases and organizing marches to demand equality, voting rights, and the end of segregation. This photo shows the 1963 March on Washington, in which more than 200,000 people from all over the US traveled to the capital.

Banners with slogans demanding better housing, schools for all, and an end to racism

Marchers filled the avenue leading to the US State Capitol.

WHO WAS MARTIN LUTHER KING JR.?

As a preacher, Martin Luther King Jr. was an excellent speaker who could rally and unite supporters and convince many others. He believed that strong but peaceful activism was the only way to achieve equality, voting rights, and the end of segregation. The whole world was shocked when he was assassinated on April 4, 1968.

Dr. King speaking to a crowd in Mississippi in 1966

WHO HELPED SPREAD THE MESSAGE?

Famous sports stars such as baseball player Jackie Robinson and boxer Muhammad Ali were outspoken civil rights campaigners. Popular singers like Harry Belafonte, Aretha Franklin, Sam Cooke, Nina Simone, and Sammy Davis Jr. raised money and recorded songs that became civil rights anthems.

Poster for a concert raising money for the cause

WHAT OTHER ACTIVISTS WERE THERE?

Many people were brave enough to stand up against prejudice and hatred. Among the best known are Rosa Parks and Mamie Till-Mobley, who became famous for speaking out, while Bayard Rustin and John Lewis were organizers close to Martin Luther King.

Mamie Till-Mobley
The mother of murdered teenager Emmett Till called out racist violence in 1955.

Bayard Rustin
Campaigning since the 1930s, Rustin organized protests and marches.

Rosa Parks
In 1955, Parks became a leading figure in the fight to end bus segregation.

John Lewis
One of the key leaders of the 1960s protests, Lewis later became a US congressman.

WHAT IS A SIT-IN?

Students would organize protests against segregated diners and lunch counters by sitting in white-only seats or on the floor to block access. This drew attention to their cause in a new way, when photographs of these events spread via newspapers that both Black and white people read.

WHAT WAS THE BLACK POWER MOVEMENT?

Peaceful protest and legal action had achieved a lot. But many felt that things were moving too slowly and that racism was preventing them from living equal lives. Groups like the Black Panthers, influenced by Malcolm X, promoted armed self-defense and pride in Black culture, education, and society.

POWER TO THE PEOPLE

Black Panther Party badge

WHEN DID SCHOOL SEGREGATION END?

Black parents challenged a law that said that their children could only attend Black schools, even if there were other schools closer to their home. In 1954, segregation became illegal in public (state) schools, but not in private schools. Black children were often not made welcome by white staff and parents, and some even needed military protection to enter their new schools.

Students of Little Rock School, escorted by soldiers

1957 Little Rock Nine   37 USA

FAST FACTS

✊ The Civil Rights Act of **1964** made many forms of **discrimination illegal** in the US.

✊ Many activists were **assassinated** while trying to achieve their **goal**.

✊ **Black civil rights** campaigns are still going on across the **world**.

HOW MUCH OF THE WORLD WAS COLONIZED?

It has varied since colonization began (see page 203). By 1914, the only fully independent countries in Africa were Ethiopia and Liberia. European nations and the US had colonies in the Caribbean and in Asia, too, where Britain controlled what is now India, Pakistan, Bangladesh, Sri Lanka, and Myanmar.

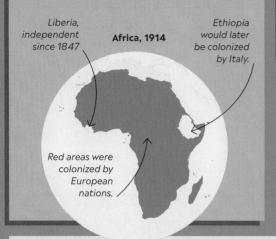

Africa, 1914

Liberia, independent since 1847

Ethiopia would later be colonized by Italy.

Red areas were colonized by European nations.

WHICH COLONY WAS THE FIRST TO ACHIEVE INDEPENDENCE?

The US declared independence from Britain in 1776, and Spanish and Portuguese colonies in the Americas became independent in the 19th century. But most colonies did not gain their freedom until the 20th century—a few around the end of World War I, but most only in the decades following World War II.

(see page 203)

QUICK QUIZ!

WHICH OF THESE ISLANDS IS NOT AN INDEPENDENT COUNTRY?

a: Madagascar

b: Greenland

c: Malta

Nelson Mandela campaigning to be president of South Africa, 1994

FAST FACTS

★ India's and Pakistan's independence in 1947 ended **200 years** of British rule.

★ Algeria fought an **8-year-long war** to become free from French rule in **1962**.

★ **80** former colonies have achieved independence **since 1945**.

HOW DID DECOLONIZATION START?

Countries worked for independence in many ways. Political organizations were formed. Many colonial soldiers who had fought in the two world wars began campaigning for more rights. Independence was sometimes achieved through negotiations, but often fought for through war, such as in Angola.

Demonstration before Angola's liberation war 1961–1974

A star later featured on Angola's first flag.

People celebrating 50 years of independence in Ghana in 2007

WHEN DID COUNTRIES IN AFRICA BECOME INDEPENDENT?

Several countries in North Africa achieved independence in the early 1950s, such as Libya (1951), Egypt (1952), and Morocco and Tunisia (1956). In 1957, Ghana declared independence from Britain, led by Kwame Nkrumah. Other nations colonized by France and Britain soon followed, many of them in 1960. Nearly all former Portuguese colonies had achieved freedom by 1975.

DECOLONIZATION:
When people and lands that were colonized by other nations achieve independence

DID MANDELA MAKE SOUTH AFRICA INDEPENDENT?

No, South Africa gained self-government from Britain in 1931. However, it was ruled by a white government, which used a system called Apartheid to segregate, abuse, and oppress the nation's majority Black population. Nelson Mandela led their resistance movement, even while in prison. He was released in 1990, and by 1994, Apartheid was illegal and Mandela was elected president.

HOW LONG DID IT TAKE FOR INDIA TO BE FREE?

Over 60 years! Organized campaigns for freedom from British rule began in 1885, when the Indian National Progress Party formed. From the 1910s, leaders such as Mahatma Gandhi and Sarojini Naidu (above) put increased pressure on Britain through nonviolent protest. In 1947, two new independent nations emerged: India and Pakistan.

WHY IS THERE SOMETIMES VIOLENCE AFTER INDEPENDENCE?

Violent struggles have been part of many nations' road to independence, as many colonizing nations refused to let go. But sometimes violence continues afterward, too. This can happen when different groups fight for power and when elections to decide which party will rule the new nation are not yet free and fair.

Weapons such as the AK-47 were used in many wars of liberation.

Paint splashed on the statue in 2020

Toppled statue of slave trader Edward Colston, now in a museum in Bristol, UK

CAN YOU DECOLONIZE OTHER THINGS THAN COUNTRIES?

Yes, the term can be used to describe a change in how we think about the effect of colonization, slavery, and racism and how these are described in books and education. It can involve debate about a country's past. For example, statues representing people who profited from the slave trade may be removed, or streets named in their honor renamed.

ARE THERE STILL COLONIES?

The Union Jack on the flag of Montserrat in the Caribbean

Yes, even now, there are still around 2 million people in 17 territories that do not have full self-government. Most are islands in the Caribbean and the Pacific Ocean, and several are campaigning for increased or total self-rule.

Flag of Turks and Caicos, a British Overseas Territory in the Caribbean

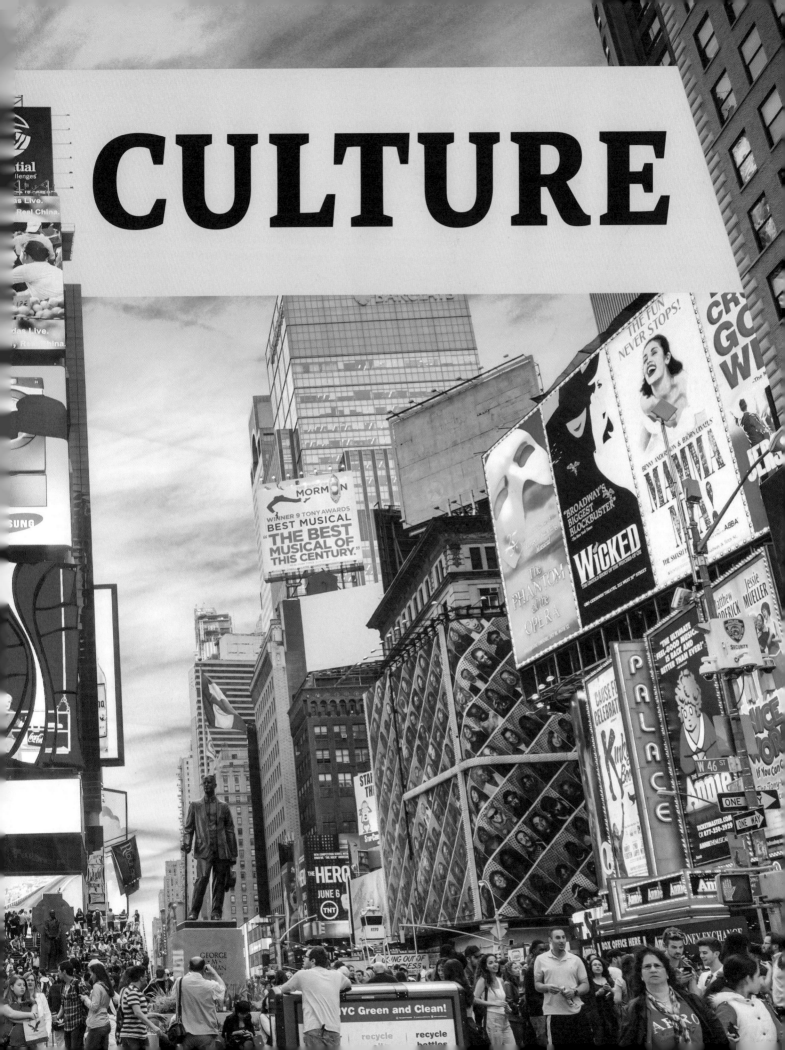

CULTURE

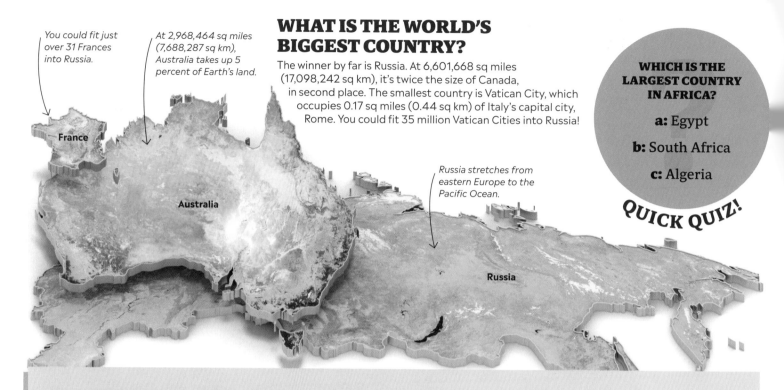

WHAT IS THE WORLD'S BIGGEST COUNTRY?

The winner by far is Russia. At 6,601,668 sq miles (17,098,242 sq km), it's twice the size of Canada, in second place. The smallest country is Vatican City, which occupies 0.17 sq miles (0.44 sq km) of Italy's capital city, Rome. You could fit 35 million Vatican Cities into Russia!

You could fit just over 31 Frances into Russia.

At 2,968,464 sq miles (7,688,287 sq km), Australia takes up 5 percent of Earth's land.

France

Australia

Russia stretches from eastern Europe to the Pacific Ocean.

Russia

WHICH IS THE LARGEST COUNTRY IN AFRICA?

a: Egypt

b: South Africa

c: Algeria

QUICK QUIZ!

COUNTRIES: An area of land ruled by a single government, with its own land boundaries, called borders

South Sudan

In 2011, South Sudan became Earth's newest country.

HOW MANY COUNTRIES ARE THERE?

It depends who you ask! Currently, the United Nations (UN) recognizes 193 countries as full-member states, but conflicts and border disputes mean new nations frequently emerge and claim their right to exist.

WHY DO WE NEED PASSPORTS TO TRAVEL?

A passport is a document, issued by a country's government, confirming that the holder is a citizen of that country and has the right to protection by their government while they are abroad. It also proves that travelers are allowed back into their country when they return.

Each country's passport has a different design.

IS ANYWHERE NOT PART OF A COUNTRY?

Only one place on Earth is not divided into countries: the vast, icy landmass of Antarctica. It is jointly managed but not owned by the 50 countries that signed up to the Antarctic Treaty. This states that Antarctica can only be used for peaceful purposes, such as scientific research.

FAST FACTS

🌍 Africa contains **54 countries**, more than any other continent.

🌍 **China and Russia** each border 14 other countries.

🌍 Canada has the **longest coastline** in the world.

WHY ARE SOME COUNTRIES' BORDERS SO WIGGLY?

Many countries have borders defined by nature, which doesn't do straight lines! Natural borders include rivers, mountain ranges, lakes, and coastlines. The Rio Grande river (left) forms part of the border between Mexico and the United States.

226

HOW DO WE COMMUNICATE WITH FLAGS?

Colorful and easily recognizable, flags can send a visual signal. In auto racing, they are used to communicate with drivers on the track. The black-and-white checkered flag signifies that a car has crossed the finish line.

QUICK QUIZ!

THE STUDY OF FLAGS IS CALLED …?

a: Pennology

b: Vexillology

c: Bannerology

DID PIRATE SHIPS REALLY FLY THE JOLLY ROGER FLAG?

Yes, they did, but there wasn't just one Jolly Roger design—pirate captains had their own individual flags. These were often black and white, but red was also used. Skulls, bones, and swords all featured heavily. Bloodthirsty designs sent a clear message: "Surrender—or else!"

WHY DOES A RED FLAG MEAN DANGER?

Red warning flags have signaled danger and conflict for centuries—possibly because red is the color of fire and blood and symbolizes strong emotions. Today, a red flag on the beach warns of rough, dangerous seas; in a forest, it means wildfires.

Flag of India

The charge is the flag's emblem.

The staff is the pole a flag hangs from.

The fly is the farthest part from the staff.

The flag's background is called the field.

The house is the part closest to the staff.

WHAT MAKES A FLAG A FLAG?

Flags may have different designs, but they all have some features in common. They have one or more prominent colors that often have symbolic meanings. Most flags are rectangular, but they can also be square, triangular, or swallowtail (rectangular with a "V" cut into it).

WHY DO COUNTRIES HAVE NATIONAL FLAGS?

A flag symbolizes a country. It can be used formally by governments to assert their authority, and informally by a country's people as a sign of pride. The design of a national flag reflects that country's history, culture, and values.

Lithuania

Yellow for the Sun; green for the land; red for bloodshed for freedom

Brazil

Grenada

Stars represent the country's parishes.

Kenya

Stars for the 50 states

US

Stripes stand for the 13 original colonies.

Charge shows stars in night sky above Rio de Janeiro, one star for each of the Brazilian states.

Masai shield refers to the fight for independence.

FLAGS: A piece of material, often rectangular, decorated with a special, symbolic design and displayed on a pole

WHAT MAKES A CITY A CITY AND NOT A TOWN?

There's no set rule, but cities are home to lots of people and act as centers for healthcare, education, and transportation. A capital city usually houses a country's government. Cities have lots of shopping and entertainment areas, like Times Square in New York (left).

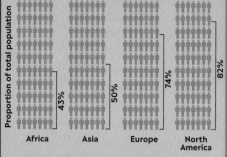

Proportion of total population

Africa 43% Asia 50% Europe 74% North America 82%

DO MORE PEOPLE LIVE IN CITIES OR IN THE COUNTRYSIDE?

It varies depending on where you are in the world. More than three quarters of North Americans are city dwellers. In Africa, more people live in the country than in cities. The charts above show the proportion of people living in cities in yellow compared to the country in green.

A temple called a ziggurat stood in the center of Uruk.

WHY DO CITIES GET SO BIG?

As people move to a city, it expands, as long as there is space. Sometimes, cities spread and merge into other cities. In the US, the cities of San José, Oakland, and San Francisco form a vast urban sprawl of 10,000 sq miles (26,000 sq km) called the Bay Area.

WHERE WAS THE FIRST EVER CITY?

The first cities grew from the first farms—which became villages, then towns—in a region called Mesopotamia, now in Iraq (see pages 180–181). Around 4000 BCE, villages gradually merged to make Uruk, the first city mentioned in history.

WHAT IS THE BIGGEST CITY?

With 37.7 million people, Tokyo in Japan is the world's biggest city. It has held this position for over 60 years, but its population is shrinking, and other cities are growing fast. By 2050, Mumbai in India is expected to take first place, with Tokyo slipping to seventh.

At 2,080 ft (634 m), Tokyo Skytree is the world's tallest tower.

The cone-shaped Mount Fuji can be seen on a clear day.

QUICK QUIZ!

BRAZIL'S CAPITAL, BRASILIA, WAS BUILT IN 1960 IN THE SHAPE OF ...?

a: A square

b: An airplane

c: A circle

CITIES: Large towns that are centers of business, government, and culture for people in a region

HOW MANY CHILDREN ARE THERE?

There are 2.4 billion under-18s in the world—30 percent of the population. These Indian children are in good company: with more than 400 million under-18s, India is home to nearly one-fifth of all the world's young people.

IT'S A MYSTERY!

How many people are alive right now?

We don't know precisely how many people there are, as it's impossible to count every single person—and the figure changes by the second! Statisticians' calculations could be wrong by up to 2 percent.

POPULATION:

All the people living in a place such as a country, town, or village

HOW MANY BABIES ARE BORN EVERY YEAR?

Worldwide, about 134 million babies are born each year. This baby was born in Niger, the country with the highest birth rate, where more than 46 babies are born for every 1,000 people in the country. In Japan and Italy, the birth rate is less than 7.

HOW MANY PEOPLE ARE THERE IN THE WORLD?

There are currently about 8.1 billion people on the planet. Global population is rising by 0.9 percent, which means every year there are about 73 million more people on Earth. Statisticians expect population growth to slow toward the end of the century.

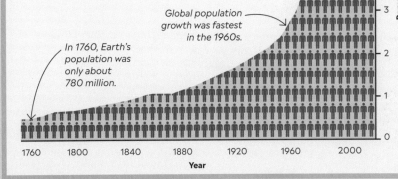

In 1760, Earth's population was only about 780 million.

Global population growth was fastest in the 1960s.

Population (billions)

Year

WHICH CONTINENT HAS THE MOST PEOPLE?

Almost 60 percent of the global population lives in Asia, with 4.8 billion of Earth's 8.1 billion people. Africa has the fastest-growing population at over 2 percent a year. Europe is the only continent with a falling population.

Asia 59%
Africa 18.4%
Europe 9%
N. America 7.5%
S. America 5.5%
Australia/Oceania 0.6%

ARE THERE MORE BIRTHS OR DEATHS?

In 2023, there were 134 million births and only 61 million deaths worldwide—so the babies tip the scales! This is why the population is growing each year. But the birth rate is slowing down, and if that trend continues, by 2100 there will be more deaths than births and the number of people will shrink.

RELIGION:

A set of beliefs, teachings, and practices about the nature of existence, the purpose of life, and how to behave

WHEN DID PEOPLE FIRST START BELIEVING IN GODS?

Before written records, it's hard to know exactly what early humans believed. Nature was the most powerful force in people's lives, and it is very likely that the first rituals and beliefs centered around pleasing spirits or gods associated with things like weather and the availability of food. As societies evolved around 5,000 years ago, organized religions emerged. These created a structure around belief, with a set of shared stories about the gods' origins and deeds, and priests who dedicated their lives to the religion.

WAS THE BUDDHA A REAL PERSON?

Yes! Siddhartha Gautama was born in what is now Nepal in the 5th century BCE. He came from a wealthy family, but gave up his riches to seek meaning in his life. His example still inspires the millions of Buddhists around the world today, and he is commemorated with statues like this one.

Flamelike headdress symbolizes the light of knowledge.

Long ears to hear the suffering of the world with compassion

QUICK QUIZ!

IN JUDAISM, WHAT IS *SHABBAT*?

a: A man's head covering

b: A weekly day of rest and worship

c: A prayer

DO ALL RELIGIONS HAVE A HOLY BOOK?

Most—but not all—major religions have writings that believers regard as sources of divine guidance and wisdom. These holy books may describe the lives of a religion's major figures or set out rules for how followers should practice their faith and live a good life.

A pointer called a yad (meaning "hand" in Hebrew) is used to protect the delicate parchment and handwritten text.

The Torah is the most sacred scripture in Judaism.

HOW MANY PEOPLE DON'T BELONG TO ANY RELIGION?

A recent study found that 1.1 billion people don't follow any religion. But just because a person isn't a member of a religion doesn't mean they don't have spiritual beliefs. Some may not be sure what they believe, or they simply haven't thought about it very much! Atheists are people who think that there are no gods or divine beings.

The wheel is an important Buddhist symbol.

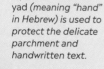

HOW IS THE POPE CHOSEN?

The head of the Roman Catholic Church is elected by a conclave, which is a group of top-ranking priests, called cardinals. After each vote, the ballots are burned and the results appear as a smoke signal: black smoke means "we're still deciding," while white means that a new Pope has been elected.

WHAT IS THE BIGGEST RELIGIOUS SITE IN THE WORLD?

The complex of Angkor Wat, a Buddhist site in Cambodia, spreads over a vast 402 acres (162.6 hectares). It was originally built in the 12th century for King Suryavarman II as a Hindu temple. However, as the religion in the region gradually shifted, Angkor Wat came to be used a Buddhist site.

WHAT ARE THE MAIN WORLD RELIGIONS?

This list shows five of the world's major religions. These have the most followers worldwide, and some of them are among the planet's oldest faiths.

Followers of all faiths are welcome at Sikh holy buildings, called gurdwaras.

Muslims typically attend mosque on Friday.

Christianity
There are 2.4 billion Christians. They follow the teachings of Jesus Christ, who lived in the Middle East around 2,000 years ago.

Islam
Founded by Muhammad in what is now Saudi Arabia, Islam is around 1,400 years old and has 1.9 billion followers around the world.

Hinduism
Developing more than 4,000 years ago in India, Hinduism is a blend of many different beliefs and practices. Today, there are 1.1 billion Hindus.

Sikhism
Founded by Guru Nanak in the Punjab (now India and Pakistan) around 500 years ago, today Sikhism has 25 million followers.

Judaism
Tracing their origins back 4,000 years, the world's 14 million Jewish people follow the laws inscribed in their holy book, the Torah.

DO ALL RELIGIONS HAVE MONKS AND NUNS?

Monks and nuns are men and women who devote their lives to studying and following the teachings of their faith. Not all religions have monks and nuns, but they are important figures in Christianity, Hinduism, and Buddhism.

Hindu sādhu, or wandering monk

FAST FACTS

◗ **Shinto** is Japan's native religion. The name means "way of the gods."

◗ **Bahá'í** is one of the world's youngest religions. It was founded in **1853** in Persia (now Iran).

◗ The Christian Bible is the biggest- selling book of all time—**5 billion** copies have been printed.

WHY DO RELIGIOUS PEOPLE GO ON PILGRIMAGES?

Pilgrimages are journeys that believers make to holy sites. This could be to prove their faith, to thank their god, to seek a cure for illness, or to ask for answers to a problem. Islam requires followers to make at least one pilgrimage to the holy city of Mecca in Saudi Arabia (above) in their lives.

CELEBRATIONS:
Activities, ceremonies, or rituals that mark a special day, an important occasion, or the anniversary of a historical event

WHY ARE THERE DIFFERENT NEW YEAR'S CELEBRATIONS AROUND THE WORLD?

Different countries and cultures base the start of their New Year on different things. Some celebrate New Year on a fixed date according to their religion's calendar; others use the cycles of the Moon or Sun, or a combination of the two. These changing cycles mean that in some places, the date of New Year differs from year to year.

Gregorian New Year
JAN 1ST
Many countries follow the Gregorian calendar and celebrate New Year with fireworks on January 1st.

Orthodox New Year
JAN 13TH
People in Russia and Serbia may give gifts on a date based on the calendar of the Orthodox Church.

Lunar New Year
EARLY FEB
In China and many Asian countries, New Year is marked with parades and dragon banners.

Aluth Avurudda
APRIL 13/14TH
People share special snacks called *kokis* to celebrate the traditional Sri Lankan New Year.

Rosh Hashanah
SEPT/OCT
At Jewish New Year, people eat apples dipped in honey.

WHERE IS THE WORLD'S BIGGEST FESTIVAL?

The Hindu festival of *Kumbh Mela* (Festival of the Sacred Pitcher) is described by the United Nations as "the largest peaceful congregation on Earth." Every four years, millions of pilgrims gather to bathe in the waters at one of India's four most sacred river sites. In 2019, the festival attracted more than 200 million people, with 50 million gathering on the busiest day.

ARE FESTIVALS ALWAYS RELIGIOUS?

No! People hold festivals for many reasons. Farmers may celebrate harvest time or the changing seasons, and countries often mark the date they gained independence or the birthday of a national hero. Festivals are also an important way of keeping old traditions alive and bringing communities together.

Playing music and dancing reflects the belief that death can be celebrated.

WHAT IS A FESTIVAL?

A festival is a time when a group of people come together to celebrate something special to them. It may involve music and dancing, such as at Mardi Gras in New Orleans, Louisiana; or special foods, like the mooncakes eaten in China during the Mid-Autumn Moon Festival. Some festivals are giant street parties—at the Day of the Dead festival in Mexico, thousands of people dress up in costumes representing the dead and parade through the streets!

WHO INVENTED FIREWORKS?

More than 1,200 years ago, Chinese inventors created gunpowder from sulfur, charcoal, and a compound called saltpeter. They packed this explosive mix into hollow bamboo stalks or paper tubes to make the first-ever fireworks, which they used to scare off evil spirits or to mark celebrations such as weddings.

Skull masks and colorful costumes are worn to honor the dead.

WHAT'S THE WORLD'S OLDEST FESTIVAL?

Zoroastrianism is one of the world's most ancient religions, and *Nowruz*, the traditional Persian festival of Spring, dates back more than 3,500 years. People mark the new season by lighting bonfires and jumping over them—a ceremony said to bring luck. A festive table of seven foods is set out; these include garlic to symbolize good health, vinegar for patience and wisdom, and apples for prosperity.

ARE BIRTHDAYS THE SAME AROUND THE WORLD?

Birthday celebrations differ around the world. In some faiths, such as Islam, birthdays are not marked in a special way. In Denmark, you might receive a *Kagemand* (cake man)—and you get to eat his head! In Jamaica, you might have flour flung over you. The Mexican tradition of *piñata*—smashing open a papier-mâché model full of candy—is so much fun that it has spread all around the world!

The piñata is hung up and attacked with sticks by children wearing blindfolds.

QUICK QUIZ!

WHERE DID THE HANAMI FLOWER FESTIVAL ORIGINATE?

a: Japan

b: Brazil

c: Greenland

HOW MANY MUSICIANS ARE IN AN ORCHESTRA?

An orchestra consists of up to a hundred musicians, split into different sections, under the direction of a conductor. Each musician or section plays a different tune or rhythm, which combine to create a single sound for the audience to enjoy.

Percussion section at the back may include cymbals, glockenspiels, drums, and a gong.

WHAT WAS THE FIRST MUSICAL INSTRUMENT?

The oldest instruments we know about are flutes made 40,000 years ago, from bone or ivory. There may have been earlier instruments, such as drums, but they were likely made from wood or animal skin—materials that usually don't last for a very long time.

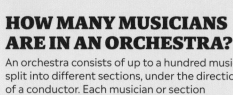

Strings section usually includes violins, violas, cellos, and double basses.

The lead musician is always a violinist, who sits in the "first seat" to the conductor's left.

Conductor

Woodwind section behind the strings may include flutes, clarinets, oboes, and bassoons.

Brass section behind the woodwind can include French horns, trumpets, and a tuba.

MUSIC: Sounds made by voices or instruments, often grouped together to create an effect or express an emotion or idea

WHY DO WE ENJOY MUSIC?

Music stimulates the brain to produce the chemical dopamine, which generates strong feelings of happiness. Music also evokes joyful memories, and moving to music is also a proven mood booster.

WHICH MUSICIAN HAS SOLD THE MOST RECORDS EVER?

Recorded music formats have changed a lot over time, from vinyl discs, to tapes, to CDs, and now digital streaming. This can make it complicated to keep count. But these three very different musical maestros stand out as super successful:

Most recorded musician
The music of 18th-century classical composer Wolfgang Amadeus Mozart has been recorded by thousands of musicians over the years.

Most streamed artist
By the end of 2023, Taylor Swift had amassed more than 26 billion streams on the Spotify platform.

Most records sold
The Beatles have sold more than 600 million records since their first hit in 1962.

WHAT MAKES SOMETHING MUSIC AND NOT JUST SOUNDS?

In music, sounds are not random but are organized by people in some way. This includes arranging notes into a melody (tune), by playing them in a rhythm, or by playing different notes at once to make a harmonious sound.

FAST FACTS

♪ Studies show that **cows** produce more **milk** when they hear soothing music.

♪ The **youngest** artist to have a US **no. 1** hit record is Stevie Wonder. He was just 13!

♪ Taylor Swift's 2023 tour sold **2.4 million** tickets in **one day**!

DANCE:

Moving the body in a series of rhythmic movements, usually accompanied by music

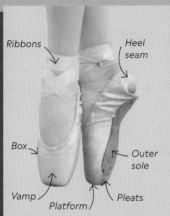

Ribbons
Heel seam
Box
Outer sole
Vamp
Platform
Pleats

HOW DO BALLERINAS DANCE ON TIPTOES?

Pointe shoes have reinforced platforms in the toes made from cardstock, paper, and fabric. These, as well as stiff soles, help dancers support their weight on their toes—although the technique still requires a lot of practice!

IN WHICH US STATE DID HULA DANCE ORIGINATE?

a: Alaska

b: Florida

c: Hawaii

QUICK QUIZ!

WHY DOES DANCING MAKE YOU FEEL GOOD?

People of all ages love dancing—babies often start to dance before they can walk properly! Exercise, including dancing, releases endorphins in your brain—these "happy hormones" trigger feelings of comfort, relaxation, and happiness.

Energetic, acrobatic moves are performed in the dance.

A tall, decorated gold crown is worn by dancers playing royalty or gods.

Painted masks are worn by dancers playing male demons and animals.

IS DANCING A SPORT OR A HOBBY?

You can dance for fun or competitively. Breaking, or breakdancing, is an urban dance style that became an Olympic medal sport in 2024. Dancers are graded on technique, musicality, and creativity.

CAN DANCE TELL A STORY?

In many cultures, dance is a powerful way to keep traditional or sacred stories and legends alive. Khon (left) is an ancient Thai dance form that depicts dramatic episodes from the life of Rama, the human incarnation of the Hindu god Vishnu.

THEATER:
A form of entertainment where actors perform in front of a live audience

Actors wore masks that represented different emotions.

WHO WROTE THE FIRST PLAYS?

The earliest surviving plays were written in Greece in the 5th century BCE. Performed in open-air theaters, plays were either comedies, which were often very rude, or tragedies, where characters came to a sticky end (usually because they had angered the gods in some way).

WHERE IS THE OLDEST THEATER?

The oldest indoor theater still in use is Teatro Olimpico in Vicenza, Italy. It opened way back in 1585. To protect the building's fragile wooden structures, there is no heating or air conditioning.

DO ALL ACTORS LEARN LINES?

Not all dramas are played out in words. In Japanese Noh theater, actors speak very little. They tell stories using masks, facial expressions, or body language, while live musicians play.

Fans are carried by most Noh performers.

HOW DO PEOPLE FLY ON STAGE?

Specialist "flying crews" devise and operate the complex rigging systems that enable actors wearing harnesses and hanging from wires to "fly" onstage, like these actors in a production of *Peter Pan*. Speaking or singing in midair can be tricky, so actors receive training in how to breathe and deliver lines while in the harness.

WHAT'S THE MOST SUCCESSFUL PLAY?

Singing, dancing, puppetry, and Disney—that's the recipe for the biggest theatrical blockbuster ever: *The Lion King*. Since it opened in 1997, the stage show version of the popular movie has taken a whopping $8.2 billion in ticket sales worldwide.

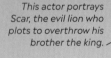

This actor portrays Scar, the evil lion who plots to overthrow his brother the king.

The actors wear masks to represent the animal characters in the musical.

WHAT IS FASHION?

Fashion is any style that becomes popular with a group of people or at a particular place or time. All kinds of things can be fashionable: hairstyles, music, toys, furniture—even food! But it's most often used to describe the clothes people wear and the industry that makes them.

Designer fashion is displayed by models at a show.

Fashion shows often attract journalists and celebrities.

QUICK QUIZ!

WHEN WERE SUNGLASSES INVENTED?

a: The 1750s

b: The 1850s

c: The 1950s

FASHION:

Styles of clothing and accessories that are popular at a particular time

WHO INVENTED ATHLETIC SHOES?

Rubber-soled athletic shoes were created more than 150 years ago in England by the Liverpool Rubber Company. The first factory-made athletic shoes were made by the USA Rubber Company in 1916. People called them "sneakers" because they could sneak around in them!

Women's Keds athletic shoes dating from 1916

IS FASHION BAD FOR THE PLANET?

We are buying more clothes than ever, and manufacturing clothes uses billions of gallons of water and emits harmful greenhouse gases. We also throw out clothes, which often end up in huge dumps that pollute the environment. These discarded clothes have washed up on the beach in Accra, Ghana.

WHY DO THINGS GO OUT OF FASHION?

Tastes change as we are influenced by new music, movies, or even political ideas. Brands use advertising to encourage us to like—and buy—new things. We start to wear new things, which then become the new fashion.

WHO WORE THE FIRST JEANS?

Denim jeans were first made in 1875 by a German immigrant to the US named Levi Strauss. Called "waist overalls," the thick, hard-wearing pants were originally made for cowboys and gold miners. Today, more than 3 billion pairs of jeans are made and sold every year.

ART:

A piece of work that expresses the emotions, thoughts, or ideas of the creator, usually intended to be seen or experienced by others

The bright yellow of this pigment comes from the metal cadmium.

Model of a prehistoric paintbrush

WHAT IS PAINT MADE OF?

Paint is a mixture of pigment (which gives color) and a medium (liquid substance), such as water, oil, acrylic resin, or egg yolk. The medium (also known as a binder) makes the powdery pigment sticky enough to be applied to surfaces. Natural pigments are obtained from rock, earth, or plants, while synthetic pigments are manufactured from chemicals.

Who was the subject of the *Mona Lisa*?
Some experts believe the painting is of Lisa del Giocondo, the wife of a rich merchant. Others claim it portrays the mother of the artist, Leonardo da Vinci, or even that it is a self-portrait!

IT'S A MYSTERY!

WHAT IS ART?

People don't always agree on what art is, but most artists try to make people feel an emotion. Art includes drawing, painting, sculpture, photography, printing, and animation.

Flowers That Bloom Tomorrow (2010), Yayoi Kusama

WHAT'S THE OLDEST ARTWORK IN THE WORLD?

The oldest-known work of figurative art (showing a subject from real life) is this 45,500-year-old cave painting of a wild pig, discovered on the Indonesian island of Sulawesi in 2017. The pig was painted using a red ocher pigment, ground from the surrounding rocks and soil.

CAN ANYONE BE AN ARTIST?

Yes! As well as being a career for professional artists, designers, and illustrators, art can be a fun hobby, as well as a way of bringing communities together. Local street art projects brighten up neighborhoods and allow everyone to explore their creativity.

WHAT'S THE MOST EXPENSIVE PAINTING IN THE WORLD?

In 2017, *Salvator Mundi* ("Saviour of the World") by Leonardo da Vinci was auctioned in New York and sold to a Saudi Arabian prince for more than $400 million. However, some scholars have cast doubts that Leonardo was the artist—they say it is more likely that it was painted by others at Leonardo's studio.

$450.3 million

WHAT IS THE BIGGEST ART MUSEUM?

The Louvre in Paris, France, is the world's largest gallery, with more than 753,470 sq ft (70,000 sq m) of exhibition space. However, its collection of 500,000 objects is eclipsed by the Hermitage Museum (pictured above) in Saint Petersburg, Russia, which is home to more than 3 million artworks!

DOES ART HAVE TO BE REALISTIC?

No! Abstract works of art don't depict recognizable people, animals, or objects. Instead, abstract artists use color, lines, and shapes in unusual, unexpected, or seemingly random ways. They make works that express how they felt while they were making the artwork, to create an atmosphere, or to explore ideas about the world around them.

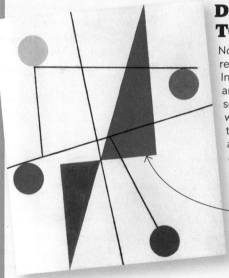

The balance of geometric shapes and color creates a joyful effect.

Untitled (1932)
Sophie Taeuber-Arp

WHAT IS AN INSTALLATION?

Installations are works of art created for a specific place. Often set in a large space, they are usually designed so that people can interact with them in some way. Digital art gallery teamLab Borderless has turned a maze of rooms in Tokyo into an immersive, constantly changing wonderland of dazzling imagery.

IS GRAFFITI REALLY ART?

While "tagging"—writing on buildings, walls, or trains—is often considered vandalism, street art is a vibrant art form that is inclusive and challenging and that helps people take pride in their environment. Australian street artist Fintan Magee has created large-scale artworks in cities around the world. This one, named *The Migration*, is in the Australian city of Perth.

LANGUAGE:

A set of words, gestures, or symbols used by people to communicate with each other

HOW MANY LANGUAGES ARE THERE?

Around 7,000 languages are spoken around the world. However, this number is steadily falling as languages die out. Experts say that by 2050, there will be only 4,500. Almost a third of languages are in Africa. South Africa has 11 official languages—its National Court building (above) displays its name in all of them.

WHY ARE THERE DIFFERENT LANGUAGES?

Most early humans didn't travel far from home and developed their own languages within their communities. When people began to move to new places, words evolved and changed to describe new environments and activities, meaning new languages formed.

WHO INVENTED SIGN LANGUAGE?

Signing has been used by deaf people since ancient times, but the first book setting out a finger alphabet and hand gestures was written in 1620, by a Spanish priest named Juan Pablo Bonet. Today, there are over 300 different sign languages worldwide.

DO LANGUAGES DIE OUT?

Yes, languages can disappear if a community is broken up by wars or invaded by another country. Other languages die out because so many speakers choose to use a second, more widespread language. But some languages evolve into new forms. For example, Ancient Greek is no longer spoken, but it changed into the modern Greek language people speak today.

IT'S A MYSTERY!

What was the first-ever language?
It's very likely that in Africa, early humans developed different spoken languages more than 100,000 years ago. But with no written evidence, we will never know for sure.

WHICH LANGUAGE IS SPOKEN BY MOST PEOPLE?

The language with the most native speakers (meaning it is their first language) is Mandarin Chinese. However, the most spoken language in the world is English—because so many people speak it as their second language. English is now the unofficial international language of business, science, and academia.

hello
Heh-low, **ENGLISH**

bonjour
boh-zhoo, **FRENCH**

नमस्ते
nuh-muh-stay, **HINDI**

hola
o-la, **SPANISH**

您好
nee-how, **MANDARIN**

مرحبا
marr-hah-bah, **ARABIC**

Standard Arabic	**French**	**Spanish**	**Hindi**	**Mandarin Chinese**	**English**
274 million speakers	309.8 million speakers	559.1 million speakers	609.5 million speakers	1.1 billion speakers	1.5 billion speakers

HOW MANY BOOKS ARE PUBLISHED EVERY YEAR?

About 4 million new books come out every year. That's just the number of new titles—the number of books printed is in the hundreds of millions! Roughly a quarter are released by traditional publishers. The rest are self-published, which means that authors sell the books themselves, usually online.

WHO WAS THE FIRST AUTHOR?

The authors of the oldest surviving written works are unknown. The first author whose name we know is Enheduanna, a high priestess in Sumeria, now Iraq. Around 2300 BCE, she wrote poetry about her life and in praise of Inanna, the goddess of both love and war.

Enheduanna is depicted on this small 4,000-year-old plaster disk.

A worker arranges books at the Frankfurt Book Fair in Germany, a yearly trade fair for publishers.

LITERATURE:

Creative writing, stories, or poetry that are valued by people and communities

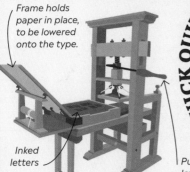

Frame holds paper in place, to be lowered onto the type.

Inked letters

Pulling the handle lowers the press onto the paper.

QUICK QUIZ!

THE STORY OF SOMEONE'S LIFE IS A ...?

a: Biography

b: Biopic

c: Biovolume

WHAT'S THE BEST-SELLING BOOK EVER?

The Christian Bible, with over 5 billion copies sold worldwide so far, is the world's biggest bestseller. However, the record for the fastest-selling book goes to *Harry Potter and the Deathly Hallows*, by JK Rowling. When it was first published, it sold 8.3 million copies in one day in the US!

HOW DID BOOK PRINTING WORK BEFORE WE HAD MODERN TECHNOLOGY?

Before printing, books had to be copied by hand. This was very time-consuming and meant books were only for the wealthy. Then in 1440, Johannes Gutenberg made his printing press. Moveable metal letters – first invented in Korea in the 1230s – were covered in ink, then pressed onto paper. Pages were quick to print and books became available for many more people to enjoy.

DO ALL COUNTRIES HAVE THE SAME FOLK TALES?

Folk tales are traditional stories passed down through generations. In different countries, tales may have different settings but very similar themes. Cinderella stories, where a young girl's fortunes suddenly change, are told all over the world but with key differences. In Russia, the girl's guardian is a magic doll. In China, she is helped by a magical fish. In Iceland, the wicked stepmother turns into a giant troll!

WHAT IS THE MOST POPULAR SPORT?

Soccer is the planet's most popular sport. Almost every nation has a soccer team, and international matches are viewed by fans worldwide. The 2022 Men's World Cup Final in Qatar was seen by 1.5 billion people—the most-watched World Cup final ever. It is also the most-played sport, with some taking part professionally while others play for fun.

WHO INVENTED TENNIS?

Modern tennis developed from the indoor game Jeu de Paume. Invented in the 12th century by French monks, it was played with a wooden racquet and a leather ball. The word "tennis" comes from *Tenez*, a phrase players would shout, meaning "Take this!"

FAST FACTS

⚽ Since 1896, **Olympic Games** have been held in **23** countries.

⚽ In 1971, **golf** became the first sport played on the **Moon**.

SPORTS:
A game or competition, requiring physical effort and skill, that is played according to an agreed-upon set of rules

WHO HAS WON THE MOST OLYMPIC AND PARALYMPIC MEDALS?

US swimmer Trischa Zorn (left) has the most Paralympic medals, winning a total of 55—41 of which are gold! The Paralympics, for athletes with a disability, are held every four years in the same host city as the Summer Olympics. Swimmer Michael Phelps is the top Olympic Games medalist, with 28 medals, 23 of which are gold.

IS CHESS A SPORT?

Most agree that sports involve physical effort. Chess is very competitive and requires a lot of skill, but it doesn't involve physical effort. The International Olympic Committee (IOC) classifies chess as a sport, but other sporting bodies do not.

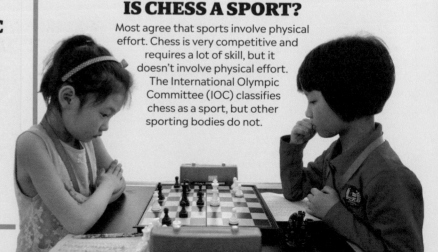

The players' hands, or any part of their arms, must not touch the ball.

Soccer cleats have studs underneath to provide grip.

The modern ball is flight accurate, reducing its wobble as it is passed between players.

Chalk stops climber's hands from slipping.

Akiyo Noguchi, 2020 Olympic bronze medallist

HOW ARE SPORTS CHOSEN FOR THE OLYMPICS?

The International Olympic Committee (IOC) decides which sports to include, taking into account the popularity of the sport and the cost of putting it on. Sports that rely on machines, such as auto racing, are excluded, and the line-up of sports is constantly changing as some are dropped and new ones are added. Climbing is one of the newest, having been introduced at the Tokyo Summer 2020 Olympics.

WHO IS THE HIGHEST-PAID SPORTS STAR?

The biggest sports earner is US basketball star Michael Jordan, who has made a massive $3.75 billion. Most of this is due to the Air Jordan shoe brand, made by Nike and named after him. Launched in 1985, the shoes sell approximately 60 million pairs every year. In 2024, a set of sneakers that Jordan wore during championship games, including the Air Jordan 11 (above), sold for $8 million.

WHO IS THE FASTEST HUMAN EVER?

In 2009, Jamaican Usain Bolt ran the fastest 100 m ever, in 9.58 seconds. The quickest woman is US athlete Florence Griffith-Joyner. Her record of 100 m in 10.49 seconds has stood for more than 30 years. This image shows their top speeds, reached for only a few seconds, compared to those of some of the fastest land animals.

Who stole the original World Cup trophy?
Soccer's first World Cup, the Jules Rimet trophy, was stolen from Brazil's soccer HQ in 1983. The thieves were never caught and the trophy is still missing!

IT'S A MYSTERY!

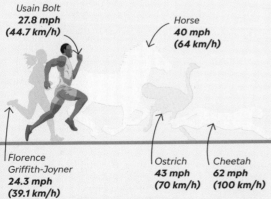

Usain Bolt
27.8 mph (44.7 km/h)

Horse
40 mph (64 km/h)

Florence Griffith-Joyner
24.3 mph (39.1 km/h)

Ostrich
43 mph (70 km/h)

Cheetah
62 mph (100 km/h)

WHAT IS THE MOST DANGEROUS SPORT?

Sports such as mountain climbing and elite road cycling carry a high risk of injury, but many consider base jumping to be the most dangerous. It involves jumping off a tall building or mountainside, then operating a parachute. The danger is that if the parachute fails, there may not be enough time to release a back-up parachute before the jumper hits the ground.

GLOSSARY

ABBASID DYNASTY
Dynasty that dominated the Islamic world, including North Africa and Spain, in 750–1258 CE, a period in which science, art, and culture flourished.

ABDOMEN
The part of an animal's body that contains most of its vital organs.

ALGAE
Simple organisms that photosynthesize.

AMERICAS, THE
Describes North, Central, and South America, and the Caribbean.

AMOEBAS
Microscopic, shape-shifting one-celled organisms.

ANTHER
The part of a flower's stamen that produces pollen.

ANTISEMITISM
Prejudice against or hatred of Jews.

ADAPTATION
The process of evolution by which organisms become suited to their environment.

ANTHROPOIDS
Monkeys, apes, and humans.

ARACHNIDS
Eight-legged arthropods, including spiders.

ARCHAEA
Bacteria-like one-celled organisms that live in extreme places.

ARTHROPODS
The largest group of animals on Earth, including insects, arachnids, and crustaceans.

BACTERIA
One-celled, microscopic organisms without a nucleus.

BACTERIOPHAGE
Virus that infects bacteria.

BALEEN
Sievelike structure in the mouth of some whales used to filter food from sea water.

BIODIVERSITY
The variety of life on Earth.

BRACHIATION
A way of swinging from branch to branch by the arms.

BREED
Subgroup of animals of the same species, such as different dog breeds.

BYZANTINE EMPIRE
Empire that evolved from the eastern part of the Roman Empire and was ruled from Constantinople (Istanbul). It lasted from 395 to 1453 CE.

CARBON DIOXIDE
A chemical compound consisting of carbon and oxygen that is needed for photosynthesis.

CARNIVORE
Meat-eating animal, plant, or other organism.

CARPEL
Female reproductive organ of a flower, consisting of the stigma, style, and ovary.

CARTILAGE
Strong, flexible tissue found in human nose and ears and a shark's skeleton.

CHLOROPHYLL
Green substance in plants that helps them absorb energy from sunlight during photosynthesis.

CIVILIZATION
A society where people have created a culture, beliefs, and an organized way of living together. Early civilizations include Mesopotamia and Ancient Egypt.

DEMOCRACY
A system by which people choose their ruler through voting in elections, or a nation that follows this system.

DENSITY
The mass (amount of matter) of a substance per unit of volume.

DIATOMS
Tiny algae with silica skeletons.

DNA
Deoxyribonucleic acid—the molecule that carries an organism's genetic information.

DYNASTY
A series of rulers from the same family, or a period in history in which a country is ruled by that dynasty, such as the Ming Dynasty in China.

ECHINODERMS
A group of marine invertebrates, many of which have star-like symmetry, including sea stars.

EMPIRE
A group of nations or peoples ruled by another nation that invaded and occupied them—for example, the Roman Empire. In the 16th to 20th centuries, several European countries created empires by invading and occupying territories overseas and making them their colonies.

EXOSKELETON
A hard external covering that supports and protects the body of some invertebrates.

FASCISM
A far-right political system, usually enforced by a dictator, that promotes nationalism and racism.

FILAMENT
The part of a flower that supports the stamen.

FLAGELLUM
The whiplike tail of some bacteria and other organisms that helps them move.

FLUID
A substance that can flow—usually a liquid, but sometimes a gas.

GILLS
Organs that fish and other aquatic animals use to breathe.

HOMININS
A group that includes our own species *Homo sapiens* and all species of human ancestors.

HORMONE
A chemical messenger that travels through the blood stream to control certain life processes, such as puberty.

HYPHAE
Branching, threadlike strands of a fungus that make up its mycelium.

INVERTEBRATE
Animal without a backbone.

KERATIN
Substance found in human fingernails and hair and in reptile scales.

KINGDOM (OF LIFE)
One of seven main groups used to classify life.

LARVA
Immature form of an insect and some other animals that undergo metamorphosis.

LIGHT-YEAR
A unit of distance, based on how far light travels in a year.

LUNGS
Organs that land-living animals use to breathe.

MARSUPIALS
Mammals, such as kangaroos, that give birth to undeveloped young that usually develop in their mother's pouch.

MICROBE
A tiny living organism that can only be seen through a microscope.

MOLECULE
Two or more atoms that are bound together.

MOLLUSK
Invertebrate with a soft body and often hard shell, such as a snail or an octopus.

MONARCHY
A nation ruled by a king or queen, who is usually part of the same family as the king or queen that ruled before them.

MONOTREME
Mammal that lays eggs.

MUTATION
A change in the genetic make-up of an organism.

MYCELIUM
A network of hyphae (thin threads) that make up the main part of fungi.

NAZISM
The far-right ideology of the German Nazi Party in the 1920s, enforced during Adolf Hitler's rule (1933–1945).

NEOLITHIC
Describes something that existed in the later Stone Age, when people had started to farm but still used tools made of stone, from around 10,000 BCE to 2,000 BCE (depending on location).

NUTRIENT
A food substance needed by an organism to thrive.

OMMATIDIA
Units that make up the compound eyes of insects.

ORBIT
The path one object takes around a heavier one due to gravity.

ORGANISM
A living thing.

OTTOMAN EMPIRE
An empire, also known as the Ottoman Sultanate, founded in 1299. At its greatest extent in 1683, it included land in southeast Europe, West Asia, and North Africa. The empire fell in 1922, and its heartland became modern-day Turkey.

OVARY
Egg-producing female reproductive organ, in the flower of a plant or in the body of an animal.

OXYGEN
A chemical element, present in Earth's atmosphere and necessary for life.

PARTICLE
Can refer to any extremely small piece of matter. It can mean a speck of dust or, in science, a part of an atom, such as an electron.

PHOTOSYNTHESIS
Process by which plants and algae use water, carbon dioxide, and light energy to make food, such as sugar.

POISON
A toxic substance made by some plants and animals that is harmful if absorbed through the skin, eaten, or inhaled.

PREDATOR
Living organism that hunts and kills other organisms.

PREHISTORIC
Something that happened or existed before historic events began to be recorded.

PROSIMIANS
Primates that are not monkeys or apes.

PROTEINS
One of a group of food substances essential for life, and used by organisms to grow and thrive.

PROTOZOANS
Single-celled organisms, including amoeba.

PUPA
Life stage of some insects between larva and adult, which takes place in a cocoon.

RENAISSANCE
The period in European history when art and science flourished, beginning in the late 15th century, marking the end of the Middle Ages.

REPUBLIC
A country ruled by a leader elected by the people—for example, a president instead of a king or queen.

ROOM TEMPERATURE
A standard scientific term for a temperature that's neither hot nor cold, usually around 68°F (20°C).

SAUROPOD
A type of often very large, plant-eating dinosaur.

SCAVENGER
Animal that feeds on dead plants and animals.

SEDIMENT
Small bits of rock, sand, or mud that settles in layers, usually underwater.

SPECIES
Group of animals or other organisms that share common characteristics and can breed with each other.

STAMEN
Male reproductive organ of a flower, made up of the anther and filament.

STIGMA
The part of a flower's female reproductive organ that collects pollen.

STYLE
Stalk that supports the stigma and connects it to the ovary of a flower.

THEROPOD
Group of two-legged mainly meat-eating dinosaurs that included the ancestors of birds.

THORAX
The middle section of an insect's body to which its legs and wings are attached.

TISSUE
In the body of animals and humans, a group of similar cells that carry out the same function, such as muscle tissue or skin tissue.

TREBUCHET
A type of weapon that could hurl large stones, used in medieval warfare to attack a castle.

UMAYYAD DYNASTY
A dynasty that dominated the Islamic world, including North Africa and Spain, in 661–750 CE.

US CIVIL WAR
A war fought in the US from 1861 to 1865 between the northern Union states, who wanted to make slavery illegal throughout the nation, and the southern Confederate states, who wanted to keep it.

USSR
Abbreviation for the Soviet Union, the state consisting of 15 socialist republics led by Russia from 1922 until its break-up in 1991.

VENOM
Toxin that enters a body through a wound made by fangs, claws, or a sting.

VIRUS
A microbe, generally regarded as nonliving, that causes infectious diseases.

QUIZ ANSWERS

SPACE

page 9: The universe

b: 13.8 billion years old

The universe sprang into existence 13.8 billion years ago, in a single huge explosion known as the Big Bang.

page 11: Milky Way

c: 1610

Italian astronomer Galileo first saw the Milky Way through his telescope in 1610.

page 12: Stars

c: Red dwarfs

Small, dim red dwarfs are the most common and also the longest-living type of star in the universe.

page 14: Supernovas

b: 11 light-years wide

The Crab Nebula was formed in 1054 CE and has been expanding ever since. Astronomers estimate that it is about 11 light-years wide.

page 21: The Moon

b: Saturn

Out of all the planets in our Solar System, Saturn has the most moons—with over 140 in its orbit.

page 23: Comets

a: Long-haired stars

The word "comet" derives from the Greek *aster kometes*, which means "long-haired star."

page 25: Space telescopes

a: $10 billion

Over the course of 30 years, the James Webb Space telescope cost $10 billion to build.

page 27: Space station

b: 16 times

The International Space Station takes 90 minutes to circle the Earth, completing 16 orbits every day.

page 28: Astronauts

a: Yuri Gagarin

Soviet Yuri Gagarin was the first person to go into space, in April 1961.

page 31: Spacecraft

b: Marina 2

This spacecraft flew by Venus on 14 December 1962, becoming the first successful mission to another planet.

EARTH

page 34: Planet Earth

c: 4.54 billion years

Earth was created from a cloud of dust and gas 4.54 billion years ago.

page 42: Erosion

b: 70 million years old

Some sections of the canyon formed 70 million years ago and joined with other sections that are between 5 and 6 million years old.

page 44: Mountains

b: Mars

Olympus Mons on Mars is around 16 miles (25 km) tall—about three times the height of Mount Everest.

page 48: Ice

c: 68%

Much of the world's fresh water is stored in ice sheets and glaciers.

page 50: Atmosphere

b: Oxygen

Oxygen is needed for living things as it allows them to breathe. It helps the cells in our body get energy from food.

page 52: Storms

c: 253 mph (407 km/h)

Winds of 253 mph (407 km/h) were recorded in Australia during Tropical Cyclone Olivia, in April 1996.

page 54: Climate change

b: 12%

Due to warmer temperatures, Arctic sea ice is shrinking by about 12 percent every decade.

LIFE

page 66: Fungi

c: 3.9 sq miles (10 sq km)

A humongous honey fungus in Oregon weighs 440 tons (400 tonnes) and covers a vast area.

page 67: Trees

b: 375

There are around 3.04 trillion trees on Earth and about 8.1 billion people.

page 74: Insects

c: 190

A bee's wings beat 190 times a second—that's 11,400 times a minute!

page 77: Crabs

c: Near hot, deep-sea volcanic vents

Little yeti crabs are found in the hot waters near hydrothermal vents on the Pacific seafloor.

page 78: Fish

c: 300,000,000

Ocean sunfish can release as many as 300 million eggs at a time and spawn several times throughout their lifetimes. However, many of the eggs do not survive.

page 83: Turtles

a: Green body fat

Adult green turtles eat mainly algae and seagrass, which is thought to give them their greenish-colored fat.

page 89: Raptors

c: Stomps on snakes

The secretary bird is a large, eaglelike bird of prey with long, cranelike legs. It kills snakes by stomping on them, sometimes dropping them from a height, too.

page 90: Mammals

a: Giant anteater

Anteaters are one of the few mammals that have no teeth. Their long tongues are covered in tiny spines and sticky saliva, which can lap up termites.

page 93: Rodents

b: Capybara

The capybara is a social rodent that lives in herds in South America. About the size of a pig, it can weigh up to 143 lb (65 kg).

page 95: Primates

c: Hot baths

Japanese snow monkeys (macaques) are the most northerly primate apart from humans. They have thick coats to survive the winter and take hot baths in natural thermal springs to stay warm.

page 97: Bears

a: 1–3

Bears usually have between one and three cubs (with twins being common) once a year, in winter. The cubs stay with their mother for around two and a half years.

page 100: Giraffes

c: Up to 20 ft (6 m)

Giraffes are the tallest land mammals. Males can be as tall as 20 ft (6 m), while females may reach 16 ft (5 m).

page 103: Hippos

a: Whales

Hippos and whales are each others' closest living relatives. They shared a common ancestor about 55 million years ago.

SCIENCE

page 112: Forces

a: Newtons

This measurement is named after English scientist Isaac Newton, who came up with rules to explain how motion works.

page 115: Rocket science

a: 1926

American scientist Robert Goddard flew the first liquid propellant rocket on March 16, 1926. It only climbed 41 ft (12.5 m).

page 117: Time

b: 24

There are 24 time zones, with an hour's distance between each. There are 11 time zones across Russia alone!

page 118: Floating

c: Archimedes

Greek mathematician Archimedes (c. 287-212 BCE) was the first to notice that floating objects are supported by an upward force, or buoyancy, that equals the weight of the fluid they displace.

page 120: Materials

a: Toothbrush bristles

In 1938, nylon was first used commercially in nylon-bristled toothbrushes. Nylon stockings became available the following year.

page 123: Heat

b: -459.4°F (-273°C)

On a special temperature scale used by scientists called the Kelvin scale, this is zero Kelvin.

page 124: Electricity

b: 1859

Many people had invented different types of batteries in previous years, but it was French physicist Gaston Planté who designed a rechargeable one.

page 130: Color

c: Bees

Bees see colors very differently from humans—they can see ultraviolet light, but not the color red!

page 133: Engines

a: 1832

The first electric cars were designed as early as the 1830s. But there was no way to charge the batteries back then, and they didn't become popular until much later.

page 137: Tunnels

b: Thames Tunnel, UK

Built under the River Thames in London, this tunnel was completed in 1843 and was used by pedestrians.

page 139 Transportation

a: 12 seconds

The plane, flown by Orville Wright in 1903, traveled only 120 ft (36.5 m) and reached a top speed of 6.8 mph (10.9 km/h).

page 141: Satellites

b: Sputnik 1

On October 4, 1957, the Soviet Union successfully launched Sputnik 1—the first satellite—into orbit.

page 143: AI

c: Alan Turing

In 1950, British scientist Alan Turing came up with a method known as the Turing Test.

HUMAN BODY

page 147: Genes

a: Genome

The human genome is made up of 23 pairs of chromosomes. You have a copy of your complete genome in nearly every cell of your body.

page 148: Cells

c: 70%

Human body cells are mostly made of water.

page 150: Skin

b: 11 lb (5 kg)

The average adult's skin weighs 11 lb (5 kg)—that's about the same mass as an average-sized cat!

page 153: Bones

a: 15%

Your bones are big but lightweight. They only account for 15 percent of your total body weight.

page 154: Muscles

b: 8

The tongue is made up of 4 pairs of muscles, so 8 in total.

page 158: Heart

c: 2.5 billion times

Your heart beats about 100,000 times in one day, so that's 2.5 billion beats over the average lifetime.

page 162: Breathing

b: About 22,000

That's about 15 breaths per minute. Children tend to breathe faster than adults.

page 165: Senses

a: Brain

The brain itself doesn't have any pain receptors. When you get a headache, it is the tissues around the brain that are sensing pain.

page 167: Reproduction

c: 100 million

In fact, there can be more than 100 million sperm racing to reach the single egg cell and be the first to burrow through its outer coating.

page 169: Aging

a: Get bigger

Our nose and ears get bigger as we age due to the effect of gravity on the cartilage and the skin tissue becoming more elastic.

page 171: Body defenses

b: In bones

White blood cells are made in bone marrow and account for less than 1 percent of blood.

page 173: Health

c: 9 teaspoons

That's about 1.3 oz (36 g) of sugar in just one 11.6 fl oz (330 ml) can of soda. That's more than an adult's recommended daily intake.

HISTORY

page 179: Ice Age

b: 9,840 ft (3,000 m)

The height of the ice wasn't the same everywhere. In the far north, where it was thickest, it weighed down the land. As it moved across the land, it shaped the landscape, creating deep holes that became lakes and polishing or grating rocks and cliffs.

page 181: The first towns

b: Bronze

At first, metal workers in Mesopotamia used copper, which is soft. But around 5,500 years ago, they began adding another metal, tin, so they could make a harder metal, bronze. It was soon used for everything from weapons to jewelry.

page 185: Pharaohs

a: Cleopatra VII

Reigning from 51–30 BCE, she was the last pharaoh to actively rule ancient Egypt. Her son Caesarion only ruled independently for 18 days before he was killed, aged 17.

page 187: Mummies

b: 70 days

It was the embalming process that took so long—around 30 days were needed just to dry out the body.

page 190: Ancient Rome

a: Fermented fish

The Romans splashed it on dishes in the same way we use soy, ketchup, or chili sauce.

page 193: Golden Age of Islam

b: Coffee

Although the beans grew in Ethiopia, they were imported by Yemeni merchants in the Arabian Peninsula, where coffee drinking took off. From there, it spread to Europe.

page 194: Vikings

b: Eight-legged horse

Odin's impressive horse was named Sleipner, and was the child of god Loki and a horse named Svaðilfari.

page 195: Silk Road

a: Gunpowder

A 9th-century Chinese alchemist discovered gunpowder while

experimenting. First used as fireworks, it was developed to use in warfare, and the knowledge spread to Europe.

page 196: Knights

b: Up to 66 lb (30 kg)

Armor wasn't actually that heavy, and because of the many small plates, it was quite flexible to move in.

page 198: Imperial China

b: Steamed rice

The sticky rice was mixed with slaked lime and used as mortar between the bricks to help them stay together.

page 201: Inca

a: Freeze-dried food

To always have a good supply of food, the Inca would leave potatoes and meat to dry out in the cold mountain air, which reached freezing temperature at night. Food could then be kept in their storehouses until it was needed.

page 202: Exploration

c: India

Columbus was looking for a westward sea route to India. Europeans didn't yet know that two large continents (North and South America) lay in the way, so when he landed on a Caribbean island he assumed he had arrived in the "West Indies."

page 206: Revolutions

c: 1917

In 1917, the February and the October revolutions, followed by a civil war lasting until 1923, led to the end of the Russian Empire and the formation of the Soviet Union (USSR).

page 209: Industrial Revolution

c: 5 mph (8 km/h)

This was the speed of Trevithick's 1804 locomotive, hauling iron on a 10-mile (16-km) journey—just slightly faster than walking pace!

page 211: World War I

b: Camouflage fabric

WWI was the first conflict where camouflage became widespread. In most earlier wars, European soldiers wore brightly colored coats, and officers often had tall feather plumes on top of their shiny helmets.

page 213: Jazz Age

a: The Turkey Trot

That's just one of the many dances to go with the popular jazz music, most based on African dances adapted in America, such as the Charleston.

page 214: World War II

c: Chocolate

Chocolate was one of the many foods that was hard to get in Europe during the war. American soldiers were given it as part of their army rations and would sometimes share with people in Britain and the countries they helped free from Nazi occupation.

page 219: Space Race

b: Twelve

These were all US astronauts, on the six lunar landings that took place between 1969 and 1972 (Apollo 11, 12, 14, 15, 16, and 17).

page 222: Decolonization

b: Greenland

The huge island of Greenland, lying just east of Canada in the Arctic Ocean, is still part of the kingdom of Denmark, although its population can decide in local government issues.

CULTURE

page 226: Countries

c: Algeria

At 919,595 sq miles (2,381,740 sq km), Algeria is the largest country by area in Africa.

page 227: Flags

b: Vexillology

The word comes from the Latin word *vexillum*, which means a kind of square flag carried by the Roman cavalry.

page 228: Cities

b: An airplane

Designed in the shape of a cross, Brasilia is often compared to an airplane, a bird, or a dragonfly.

page 230: Religion

b: A weekly day of rest and worship

Shabbat, or the Sabbath, marks the day when God is said to have rested after creating the world. It starts at sunset on Friday and ends at sunset on Saturday.

page 233: Celebrations

a: Japan

Hanami, a major Japanese festival which celebrates the appearance of pink cherry blossom in spring, is now celebrated in many parts of the world.

page 235: Dance

c: Hawaii

A hula dance is a form of storytelling through wavy body movements and gestures.

page 237: Fashion

a: The 1750s

Tinted glasses to protect the eyes from the Sun first appeared in the 1750s, but it wasn't until the 1900s that they became a fashion item.

page 241: Literature

a: Biography

The word "biography" is made up of two parts: *bio*, from a Greek word meaning "life," and *graphy*, meaning "written."

INDEX

ACKNOWLEDGMENTS

DK would like to thank all the children who submitted their questions, without whom this book would not have been possible, including:

Aarav; Abdullah; Adar; Adrián; Akshita; Andy; Anubhuti; Anushka; Avantika; Blessy; Charlie; Ella; Emilia; Enyi; Etelia; Eva; Faiz; Finnegan; Frankie; Harry; Heling; Hunter; Ilayda; Isla; Isla-Rose; Jake; Jiajie; Kezia; Kuankuan; Leo; Martín; Max; Mengyue; Milo; Minghang; Nicholas; Niklas; Noah; Oliver; Olivia; Oluwatomi; Paul; Peach; Peiyu; Priyansh; Rayaan; Rebecca; Riddhima; Rouven; Ruize; Shunhan; Shuojun; Sumika; Yiyi; Yujun; Zijin; Zitong; Zixuan.

Thanks to the following school classes and their teachers:

Senior Secondary school, New Delhi, India; Secondary school class, Simmern, Germany; Secondary school class, Wittlich, Germany; Secondary school class, Vancouver, Canada; Primary school class, Bexleyheath, UK; Primary school class, Walthamstow, UK.

And thanks to Hanba and all the parents and children who submitted questions through their channels.

DK WOULD LIKE TO THANK:

Chris Barker for reviewing the dinosaur pages; Keira Fitzgerald for reviewing the Holocaust pages; Sam Kennedy and Fleur Star for editorial help; Samantha Richiardi for design help; Simon Mumford for maps; Sarah Hopper for additional picture research; Hazel Beynon for proofreading; Elizabeth Wise for the index; Maria Hademer for her help in sourcing the children's questions.

Thank you to the DK Delhi team: Vijay Kandwal and Mohammad Rizwan for hi-res; Balwant Singh and Anita Yadav for CTS.

The publisher would like to thank the following for their kind permission to reproduce their photographs:

(Key: a-above; b-below/bottom; c-center; f-far; l-left; r-right; t-top)

1 Getty Images / iStock: Hakule. **2 Alamy Stock Photo:** SOPA Images Limited (br). **Getty Images / iStock:** Henk Bogaard (ca). **3 Alamy Stock Photo:** imageBROKER.com GmbH & Co. KG / Ronald Wittek (br). Tony Bela: (clb). **4 Alamy Stock Photo:** Nature Picture Library / Chris Mattison (tr). **Depositphotos Inc:** Lifeonwhite (br). **Dreamstime.com:** Scisettialfio / Alfio Scisetti (bl). **Getty Images:** Photodisc / Siede Preis (c). **5 Alamy Stock Photo:** Jon Arnold Images Ltd / Jon Arnold (crb). **Dorling Kindersley:** Cairo Museum / Alistair Duncan (tr); University of Pennsylvania Museum of Archaeology and Anthropology / Gary Ombler (bl). **6-7 Science Photo Library:** Robert Gendler. **8 ESA:** Image by AOES Medialab (crb). **9 Science Photo Library:** Detlev Van Ravenswaay (br). **10 NASA:** ESA CSA STScI (tc). **Science Photo Library:** Robert Gendler (c). **11 Getty Images / iStock:** Mat Raven (r). **NASA:** JPL-Caltech / R. Hurt (SSC / Caltech) (c). **12 ESA / Hubble:** NASA (cr). **Getty Images / iStock:** Hakule (bl). **NASA:** ESA and D. A. Gouliermis (MPIA) (t). **Science Photo Library:** Lynette Cook (cl). **13 Science Photo Library:** NASA / SDO (br). **14 123RF.com:** Leonello Calvetti (tr). **NASA:** ESA, NRAO / AUI / NSF and G. Dubner (University of Buenos Aires) (t). **Science Photo Library:** Marc Ward (bc). **14-15 Getty Images / iStock:** E+ / Soubrette (bc). **15**

ESA: NASA, HEIC and The Hubble Heritage Team (STScI / AURA) (cla); NASA / M. Livio & Hubble 20th Anniversary Team (STScI) (b). **ESO:** (ca/X2). **18 123RF.com:** Forplayday (cra). **Dreamstime.com:** Scol22 (crb). **NASA:** Ames / JPL-Caltech (br); Johns Hopkins University Applied Physics Laboratory / Southwest Research Institute (crb/Pluto). **Science Photo Library:** Julian Baum (clb). **19 ESA:** DLR / FU Berlin (tr). **NASA:** JPL / MSSS (tl); Pat Rawlings, SAIC (ca); JPL-Caltech (cr); JPL-Caltech / MSSS (b). **20 ESA:** P. Carril (cl). **NASA:** (r). **21 Dreamstime.com:** (tl); Vjanez (bl); Diego Barucco (bl/Neptune moons and Earth moon, clb, bc). **Getty Images / iStock:** GettyTim82 (tr). **NASA:** JPL / Space Science Institute (c). **Science Photo Library:** Ron Miller (crb). **22 Alamy Stock Photo:** NASA Image Collection (c). **Getty Images / iStock:** Adventtr (cr). **NASA:** JPL-Caltech (tr). **23 Bridgeman Images:** © Novapix / A.Fujii / David Malin Images (bl). **Getty Images / iStock:** Bjdlzx (crb). **24 Alamy Stock Photo:** Mint Images Limited (c); Panoramic Images (tr); Xinhua (b). **25 ESA:** NASA and J. Kastner (RIT); CC BY 4.0 (tr). **ESA / Hubble:** NASA / ESA (br). **NASA:** (tl). **Shutterstock.com:** Paul Fleet (bl); Dotted Yeti (c). **26-27 ESA:** NASA / Roscosmos. **28 Alamy Stock Photo:** © First Run Features / Courtesy Everett Collection (cr); Artsiom Petrushenka (clb). **NASA:** (t). **29 Dreamstime.com:** Ralwel (tr). **photo Nicolas Escurat:** (tl). **Getty Images:** Gallo Images ROOTS RF collection / Danita Delimont (b). **NASA:** JPL-Caltech (clb). **Science Photo Library:** Claus Lunau (c). **30 Alamy Stock Photo:** Stocktrek Images, Inc. (tr). **NASA:** ESA, and J. Zachary and S. Redfield (Wesleyan University); (cla). **31 Tony Bela:** (ca). **Getty Images:** Handout (br). **Science Photo Library:** Detlev Van Ravenswaay (cb); Spacex (tr). **32-33 Alamy Stock Photo:** imageBROKER.com GmbH & Co. KG / Michael Weber. **34 Depositphotos Inc:** Imagesbykenny (cl). **Dreamstime.com:** Ralf Lehmann (bl). **36 Alamy Stock Photo:** Associated Press / Etnawalk; Giuseppe Di Stefano (t); Robertharding / Roberto Moiola (br). **Dorling Kindersley:** Museo Archeologico Nazionale di Napoli / James Stevenson (cr). **Getty Images:** AFP / Halldor Kolbeins (bl). **37 Alamy Stock Photo:** ITPhoto (cra). **Getty Images:** AFP / Jiji Press (cr); AFP / Ted Aljibe (b). **38 Dreamstime.com:** Rixie (c/

Rock). **Science Photo Library:** Susumu Nishinaga (c). **39 Alamy Stock Photo:** GRANGER - Historical Picture Archive (cb). **Dreamstime.com:** David Tadevosian (tl). **Getty Images / iStock:** E+ / Malerapaso (t). **40-41 Alamy Stock Photo:** Universal Images Group North America LLC / De Agostini Picture Library (b). **42 Alamy Stock Photo:** imageBROKER.com GmbH & Co. KG. / Michael Weber (b); PA Images / Owen Humphreys (tr). **Getty Images / iStock:** E+ / Nico_Blue (cl). **43 Alamy Stock Photo:** R.M. Nunes (clb); Dinal Samarasinghe (tr). **Dreamstime.com:** Ssstocker (cr, br). **Getty Images / iStock:** Rvika (bc). **44 Dreamstime.com:** Daniel Prudek (br); Wim Wyloeck (bl). **45 Alamy Stock Photo:** Suzanne Long (bl); Quebecfoto (cl). **Getty Images / iStock:** Passakorn_14 (tr). **46 Dreamstime.com:** Mxwphoto (c). **Getty Images:** Moment / Mark Fox (crb). Petra Kaczensky: (cra). **Shutterstock.com:** Cheng Yuan (Background). **47 Shutterstock.com:** GuilhermeMesquita (clb); Longjourneys (bc). **48 Dreamstime.com:** Sergey Kichigin / Kichigin (b). **Getty Images / iStock:** Markus-Barthel (tr); Photofex (cl). **49 Alamy Stock Photo:** Blickwinkel / A. Rose (tr). **Dreamstime.com:** Panaceadoll (tc). **Getty Images / iStock:** IPGGutenbergUKLtd (cla). **Science Photo Library:** Dr Juerg Alean (c); NASA's Scientific Visualization Studio / GSFC / Jaxa (tl, cla). **50 Dreamstime.com:** Romolo Tavani (tr). **NASA:** (bl). **51 Alamy Stock Photo:** USFS Photo (br). **Dreamstime.com:** Stefano Garau (tl); Constantin Opris (clb). **Getty Images / iStock:** Milehightraveler (tr). **52-53 NASA:** JSC (b). **54 Alamy Stock Photo:** Arctic Images / Ragnar Th Sigurdsson (bl). **Shutterstock.com:** TR STOK (t); Vikks (br). **55 Getty Images:** Ed Wray / Stringer (tc). **naturepl.com:** Juergen Freund (bl); Oceanwide / Gary Bell (cl). **56-57 Getty Images / iStock:** br3kkancs. **58 Alamy Stock Photo:** Minden Pictures / Michael & Patricia Fogden (c). **BluePlanetArchive.com:** Alvaro E. Migotto (tc). **Science Photo Library:** John Durham (tr); Eye of Science (cr, crb). **59 Dreamstime.com:** Auntspray / William Roberts (cla); Burgstedt (tl); Mala Navet (cla/Bacteria); Yun Gao (clb). **Science Photo Library:** Wim Van Egmond (tr); Eye of Science (ca). **Shutterstock.com:** Ekky Ilham (ca/Diatom). **60 naturepl.com:** Alex Hyde (cla). **Science Photo Library:** Chase Studio (b). **Shutterstock.com:** Anton Rodionov (cra). **61 Getty Images:** AFP / Bay Ismoyo / Stringer (cb). **naturepl.com:** Lucas Bustamante (br). **Science Photo Library:** Mauricio Anton (t); Dirk Wiersma (cl); Ron Miller (bl). **63 Alamy Stock Photo:** Science Photo Library / Mark Garlick (crb). **Dorling Kindersley:** James Kuether (bl, br). **Dreamstime.com:** Yevgeniy Steshkin (tr). **Getty Images:** The Image Bank Unreleased. / Layne Kennedy (c). **64 Dreamstime.com:** Leonello Calvetti (c). **64-65 Dreamstime.com:** Marciomauro. **66 Dreamstime.com:** Mchudo (cla). **naturepl.com:** Alex Hyde (ca). **67 Alamy Stock Photo:** Science Photo Library (tl). **Dorling Kindersley:** Batsford Arboretum and Garden Centre / Gary Ombler (bl). **Getty Images:** Cavan / Patrick Orton (r). **68 Alamy Stock Photo:** Roman Stetsyk (bl/Conifers). **Dorling Kindersley:** David Fenwick (clb). **Dreamstime.com:** Feherlofia (cb); Febrika Nurmalasari (clb/Funaria); Rcpixel (bc). **Shutterstock.com:** Hank Erdmann (bl). **68-69 Dreamstime.com:** Verastuchelova (c). **69**

Dreamstime.com: Scisettialfio / Alfio Scisetti (tr). naturepl.com: Nick Hawkins (clb). Shutterstock.com: LuchschenF (bc). 70 Alamy Stock Photo: All Canada Photos / Roberta Olenick (cb). Dreamstime.com: Nostone (bl). Minden Pictures: Mitsuhiko Imamori (cra). Marco Todesco, University of British Columbia: (br). 71 Alamy Stock Photo: Myrleen Pearson (tr). Dreamstime.com: Icefront (bl/Peach); Artem Samokhvalov (bl). 72 Alamy Stock Photo: Stocktrek Images, Inc. / Terry Moore (tr); WaterFrame_Fur (b). Dreamstime.com: Xunbin Pan /Defun (ca/Worms); Sarah2 (ca). 73 Alamy Stock Photo: Reinhard Dirscherl (br). Getty Images: Stone / Microdon (cla). naturepl.com: Fred Bavendam (cb); David Fleetham (tr). 74 Dreamstime.com: Gary Webber (cla). Getty Images / iStock: br3kkancs (bl). Shutterstock.com: Digital Images Studio (br). 75 Alamy Stock Photo: Redmond Durrell (b); Anton Sorokin (cl). Science Photo Library: Susumu Nishinaga (c). 76 Alamy Stock Photo: ISF Photography (br). Dreamstime.com: PeterWaters (bc). Andreas Kay: (cra). Science Photo Library: Dr Morley Read (t). 77 Alamy Stock Photo: Buiten-Beeld / Seraf van der Putten (b). Minden Pictures: Birgitte Wilms (tl). naturepl.com: Doug Perrine (r). 78 Alamy Stock Photo: Nature Picture Library / Tony Wu (tr); Martin Strmiska (cla). Getty Images: The Image Bank / Stephen Frink (b). 79 Alamy Stock Photo: Nature Picture Library / Chris Mattison (tr). Dreamstime.com: Isselee (ca). Getty Images / iStock: GlobalP (cl). 80-81 copyright Martin Strmiska: (b). 82 Alamy Stock Photo: Joe Blossom (tc); Vicki Wagner (tr); Anuranjan Kumar (cra); RooM The Agency / Lessydoang (bl); Minden Pictures / Ch'ien Lee (cb). Shutterstock.com: Kurit Afshen (c). 83 BluePlanetArchive.com: Doug Perrine (b). Dorling Kindersley: Natural History Museum / Colin Keates (tl). Getty Images: AFP / Rodrigo Buendia / Stringer (bl). Getty Images / iStock: Searsie (bc). 84 BluePlanetArchive.com: imageBROKER / Clement Carbillet (b). Dreamstime.com: Thawats (tr). Shutterstock.com: Rich Carey (tl). 85 Getty Images / iStock: LeoMercon (ca). Shutterstock.com: Bournemouth News / Ricardo Castillo (b); Marc Pletcher (tl). 86 Alamy Stock Photo: imageBROKER.com GmbH & Co. KG / Thomas Hinsche (tl). Dreamstime.com: Hpbfotos (cb); Isselee (bc). Shutterstock.com: Vishnevskiy Vasily (cl). 86-87 Getty Images / iStock: Henk Bogaard (c). 87 Alamy Stock Photo: Robertharding / Lizzie Shepherd (tr). naturepl.com: Tim Laman (tl). 88 Alamy Stock Photo: Justin Hofman (cra); Robertharding / Thorsten Milse (tl); Nature Picture Library / Fred Olivier (cr). Dreamstime.com: Slew11 (cl). 89 Alamy Stock Photo: Evan James (bl); USDA Photo (cl). Dreamstime.com: Sander Meertins (c). Mark Smith: (cra). 90 Alamy Stock Photo: Simon Phillpotts Photography (crb). naturepl.com: Doug Perrine (bl); Mark Taylor (c/1, ca, c, cr). Science Photo Library: Merlintuttle.org (tl). 91 Alamy Stock Photo: Minden Pictures / D. Parer & E. Parer-Cook (tr); Dave Watts (cla). naturepl.com: Steven David Miller (crb); D. Parer & E. Parer-Cook (cb). 92 Dreamstime.com: Izanbar (l); Valentyn Shevchenko (tr). 93 Alamy Stock Photo: Blickwinkel / S. Meyers (br). Dreamstime.com: Rudmer Zwerver (tr). Getty Images / iStock: Stefonlinton (cla). naturepl.com: Photo Ark / Joel Sartore (bl). 94 Alamy Stock Photo: F30 / Juniors Bildarchiv (tr). Depositphotos Inc: Lifeonwhite (tl). Getty Images / iStock: Georgeclerk (br). 95 Alamy Stock Photo: imageBROKER.com GmbH & Co. KG / Peter Davey / FLPA (cr). Getty Images / iStock: E+ / Freder (br). Getty Images: Moment / Seng Chye Teo (br/1). 96 123RF.com: Andrei Samkov / Satirus (bc). Alamy Stock Photo: imageBROKER.com GmbH & Co. KG / Ronald Wittek (crb).

Dreamstime.com: Jim Cumming (t). 97 Alamy Stock Photo: Cheryl Schneider (tl). naturepl.com: Nature Production (tr). 98 Getty Images / iStock: Webguzs (tl). naturepl.com: Shin Yoshino (bl). Shutterstock.com: Howard Darby (tr). 99 Dreamstime.com: Appfind (cb/Leopard); Denisa Prouzová (cb); Waldemar Manfred Seehagen (cb/Jaguar fur). Getty Images: San Francisco Chronicle / Hearst Newspapers (tl); The Image Bank / Ibrahim Suha Derbent (r). Shutterstock.com: hamhaful (tl). 100 Alamy Stock Photo: Panoramic Images (tl); Tierfotoagentur / D. M. Sheldon (tc). Dreamstime.com: Mollynz (br); Oleksandra Tsvid (cr). 101 Alamy Stock Photo: Garry Bowden (tr); CTK Photo / Michal Krumphanzl (tl). Guinness World Records Limited: (b). 102 Alamy Stock Photo: Blue Planet Archive EP-TMI (cra); Minden Pictures / Flip Nicklin (cla). Dreamstime.com: Bhalchandra Pujari (bl). Shutterstock.com: Level 1 Studio (bl/Water Splash). 103 Dreamstime.com: David Da Costa (cl); Lenaivanova2311 (tc); Isselee (b). Shutterstock.com: Nimit Virdi (tl). 104 Alamy Stock Photo: Minden Pictures / Michael & Patricia Fogden (tr). Shutterstock.com: Dmitri Gomon (tl). 104-105 Alamy Stock Photo: Michael Patrick O'Neill (Background). 105 123RF.com: Pandavector (ca/Habitat change). Alamy Stock Photo: IanDagnall Computing (br); Christian Loader (ca). Dreamstime.com: Matthijs Kuijpers (tr); Miceking (c). naturepl.com: Laurie Campbell (cl). Shutterstock.com: Loc Thanh Pham (cb); RedlineVector (cb/Climate change). 106-107 Science Photo Library: Giphotostock. 108 Dreamstime.com: Photoolga (crb). Dzulfikri: (cl). 109 Alamy Stock Photo: dpa picture alliance archive (tr). Dorling Kindersley: RGB Research Limited / Ruth Jenkinson (cla, bl). NASA: X-ray - NASA, CXC, SAO; Optical - NASA,STScI (bc). 110 Alamy Stock Photo: Associated Press / Joel Bissell (b); Duc Giap (tl/Honey). Dreamstime.com: Miramisska (tl/Milk). Science Photo Library: John Chumack (cra). 111 Alamy Stock Photo: Jackie Nix (bc/Cake); Roman Zaika (t). Depositphotos Inc: Ffolas (bc). Getty Images: 500px / Jorge Guerrero Aguilar (cl). 112 Alamy Stock Photo: UK Sports Pics Ltd (ca). Dreamstime.com: Verkoka (crb). 113 Alamy Stock Photo: Nik Taylor Sport (b); PA Images / Chandler Alan Chandler (cla). Dreamstime.com: Razihusin (tc). 114-115 Alamy Stock Photo: Artsiom Petrushenka. 116 Dreamstime.com: Anton Ignatenco (tl). Michael Lovemore: (tr). NASA: JSC (cl). Shutterstock.com: Merlin74 (crb). 117 Alamy Stock Photo: John Gollop (cla). Dreamstime.com: Kim Christensen (cr); Moviephotoo (tc). Getty Images / iStock: E+ / Cokada (b). 118 123RF.com: 2nix / Panithan Fakseemuang (cr). Getty Images / iStock: E+ / Mh-Fotos (tl). Shutterstock.com: Thanan (crb). 119 Alamy Stock Photo: Photopophb (tl). Dreamstime.com: Lianna Art (t); Steve Mann (cl). Science Photo Library: NASA (cr). 120 Dreamstime.com: Ruslan Minakryn (ca). Getty Images / iStock: Bespalyi (tl). Illuminated Apparel: (tr). Courtesy of Speedo/ Brandnation: (b). 121 Alamy Stock Photo: Bdstockphoto (b); Interfoto / History (tr). Dreamstime.com: Verastuchelova (tl). 122 Alamy Stock Photo: Action Plus Sports Images (l). Dreamstime.com: Vladimir Grigorev (bc). Getty Images / iStock: Romolo Tavani (cb). 123 123RF.com: Tomasz Trybus / Irontrybex (br). Dorling Kindersley: RGB Research Limited / Ruth Jenkinson (crb). Dreamstime.com: Zoom-zoom (tr). Getty Images / iStock: Dgiovann (c). 124 Alamy Stock Photo: Allen Creative / Steve Allen (tr). Caters News Agency: (cl). Dreamstime.com: Tebnad (bc). 125 Alamy Stock Photo: Riddypix (br). Dreamstime.com: Chernetskaya (tc). ESO: L. Calçada (bl). 126 Dreamstime.com: T.w. Van Urk (Background). 127 Alamy Stock Photo: Abaca Press (cla). Getty Images / iStock:

Bet_Noire (cra). 128-129 Alamy Stock Photo: Shaun Cunningham (c). 129 Alamy Stock Photo: EThamPhoto (tl). Dreamstime.com: Dashark (br); Nightman1965 (tr). Shutterstock.com: D'Action Images (bl). 130 Dreamstime.com: Pytyczech (br); Denys Zazimko (clb). Science Photo Library: Chongqing Tumi Technology Ltd (ca); Giphotostock (tr). 131 123RF.com: Iurii Kovalenko (ca). Alamy Stock Photo: Blickwinkel / D. U. M. Sheldon (bl). Dreamstime.com: Ekaterina Mikhailova (tl). Science Photo Library: Edward Kinsman (br). 132 Dorling Kindersley: Science Museum, London / Dave King (cra). NASA: Ben Smegelsky (c). 133 Alamy Stock Photo: Justin Kase zsixz (cr); ZUMA Press, Inc. (ca). Dorling Kindersley: The Science Museum / Dave King (cl). 134 Dreamstime.com: Seamartini (bl). Shutterstock.com: SurfsUp (br). 134-135 Getty Images: Matt Cardy / Stringer. 136 Getty Images / iStock: Diy13 (r). Getty Images: Ullstein Bild (tl). 137 Alamy Stock Photo: Associated Press / Christian Hartmann (t); qaphotos.com (cb); imageBROKER.com GmbH & Co. KG / Michael Szönyi (bl); PA Images / Gaetan Bally (br). 138 Alamy Stock Photo: Mariusz Burcz (tl); Mark Clemas Classics and Motorsport (cl). Shutterstock.com: Fotopanorama360 (b). 138-139 Alamy Stock Photo: Jouni Niskakoski. 139 Dreamstime.com: Haiyin (tr). 140 Getty Images / iStock: E+ / Janiecbros (b). Science Photo Library: Cern (tr). Shutterstock.com: Zapp2Photo (c). 141 NASA: (clb); NASA Ames Research Center (crb). 142 Alamy Stock Photo: Associated Press / Noriaki Sasaki (tr); Science Photo Library / Tek Image (clb). Dorling Kindersley: Andy Crawford / Bob Gathany (crb); The Science Museum / Clive Streeter (t). Dreamstime.com: Ifeelstock (clb). Science Photo Library: Gustoimages (clb/Laptop). 143 Dreamstime.com: Baloncici (clb); Aleksey Popov (tr); Staurora72 (cl). Science Photo Library: Gorodenkoff Productions (bl). Shutterstock.com: Lena_Hunt (crb). 144-145 Getty Images / iStock: E+ / AnnettVauteck. 146 Science Photo Library: © Gonville & Caius College / A. Barrington Brown (tl). 147 Alamy Stock Photo: Stu Gray (cra). Dreamstime.com: Francesco Sgura (bc). Getty Images / iStock: Simarik (br). Science Photo Library: Alfred Pasieka (cr). 148 Alamy Stock Photo: Science Photo Library. / Steve Gschmeissner (tl). Science Photo Library: Mauro Fermariello (bl); Steve Gschmeissner (tr). 149 Alamy Stock Photo: Tina Manley (tr). 150 123RF.com: Nrey (cl). Dreamstime.com: Tatya Luschyk (tc). Getty Images / iStock: E+ / FatCamera (tr). Shutterstock.com: Cunaplus (br). 151 Dreamstime.com: Zoom-Zoom (Background). Getty Images / iStock: E+ / Gawrav (cra). Science Photo Library: Steve Gschmeissner (ca). 152 Science Photo Library: (clb). 152-153 Shutterstock.com: Martan (c). 153 Alamy Stock Photo: Oksana Fedorchuk (c). 154 Getty Images: View Stock (tr). Science Photo Library: Martin Dohrn (bc). 155 Dreamstime.com: Viorelkurnosov (tl). Getty Images / iStock: Photodisc / Image Source (cb). 158 Getty Images / iStock: E+ / Fly View Productions (cra); MediaProduction (tl). 159 Science Photo Library: Steve Gschmeissner (cb). Shutterstock.com: siam.pukkato (crb). 160 Alamy Stock Photo: Science Photo Library (br). Science Photo Library: (tc/empty bladder, tc). 161 Dreamstime.com: Aaron Amat (bc); Sebastian Kaulitzki (cla). 162 Dreamstime.com: Caeri Hiraman (crb); Anton Vierietin (cla). Getty Images / iStock: Mihtiander (cl). 163 Alamy Stock Photo: Science History Images / Photo Researchers (c). Dorling Kindersley: Natural History Museum, London / Harry Taylor (bc). 164 Dreamstime.com: Weerapat Wattanapichayakul (bl). Getty Images: Moment / Huizeng Hu (crb). Shutterstock.com: sruilk (cl). 165 Alamy Stock Photo: Rudmer Zwerver (br). 166 Science Photo